C

D1453539

BETWEEN PAST AND PRESENT

BETWEEN PAST AND PRESENT

AN ESSAY ON HISTORY

by NATHAN ROTENSTREICH

with a foreword by Martin Buber

KENNIKAT PRESS
Port Washington, N. Y./London

BETWEEN PAST AND PRESENT

Copyright © 1958 by Yale University Press
Reprinted 1973 by Kennikat Press in an unaltered
and unabridged edition with permission
Library of Congress Catalog Card No.: 72-85291
ISBN 0-8046-1728-7

Manufactured by Taylor Publishing Company   Dallas, Texas

IN 1725 Vico sketched out his *Scientia nuova*. He thought of it as a history and a philosophy of mankind. But he did not pose the question as to what kind of knowledge this science was to be built upon. Nor did he consider this problem even later. When in 1781 Kant analyzed the principles of human knowledge, he did not attack the problem of a specific historical knowledge, its special presuppositions and particular methods. One might with justice think that the roots of this fact are to be found in Kant's scant interest in historical phenomena, since here as well as in several other points he belongs to the tradition of the philosophy of the Enlightenment. But even such a historically minded thinker as Hegel, in spite of the fact that he drew a precise demarcation line between *historia rerum gestarum* and *res gestae*, did not consider how res gestae become historia rerum gestarum. As a consequence his statement that "we must take history as it is" remained unexplained. To be sure, he knew that the historian brings his categories with him and that he sees reality through them, but we do not learn from Hegel anything about the nature of those categories or of the essence of this particular "seeing." Ranke, because of his serious concern with the nature of history, called history "the living memory of the human race." He failed, however, to raise the question as to how that memory comes out of individual memory and how it replaces it.

Only when we come to the end of the 19th century do we find historical knowledge subject to a process of self-reflection, and this only insofar as our century considers itself a "historical" one. Philosophers and historians tried to understand the nature of historical knowledge and thus to ascertain its influence on man. Only then did such important presuppositions as "the distinctive traits of the a priori through which we interpret and organize the historical facts" (Simmel, 1892) become the subject matter of analysis. But even now, after half a century of serious thought in this field between the theory of knowledge and the philosophy of history, a "Critique of Historical Reason" which Dilthey in 1908 considered one of the main tasks of the thought of our generation is still unwritten. Even the first of the main modern questions, "How do we get a historical picture of a past society?" (Huizinga, 1934), is not really answered. Nevertheless, several valuable monographs have been written in the last few decades which make real contributions toward a comprehensive epistemology of historical knowledge. Among those I count the present book.

This volume grew out of a philosophical spirit originating and flourishing in Jerusalem. The Jerusalem circle, under the leadership of my friend Hugo Bergmann, has been engaged since 1941 in a common effort of philosophical thinking, in the fields both of mind and of nature. Its work is characterized by thoroughness, ardor, and exactness. Not attached to any particular school of thought, it strives only to attain philosophical knowledge. This spirit enabled the small society, working in this time and in that city, to merge the open-minded experience of living history with a reflective perspective on past history. This essay too is to be understood from this vantage point.

MARTIN BUBER

THIS is a systematic study which attempts to combine a dialectical inquiry into some basic problems in history with a critical evaluation of some current views. Though the book attempts to offer a positive approach and a constructive analysis of the problems, it develops its argument by criticisms of some modern theories. These critical parts of the book are in turn arranged according to what seems to the author to be a systematic principle. Such cross-fertilization of the critical and the systematic approaches makes the reading of at least some of the parts not very easy. This is true mainly of the first two parts of Chapter 4. The reader may be well advised to skip these and to turn to the explicitly positive sections of the analysis. The Analytical Table of Contents may sometimes be of service, with its emphasis on the essential course of the argument.

With the good advice and patient guidance of my friend Paul Weiss the first draft of the book was considerably changed. I am very grateful to him for all he has done to improve the work and to help me to avoid many blunders, though I am afraid that there are still some left. Professor S. H. Bergman prompted me to expand and to clarify various parts of the book. His judgment offered continual challenge and guidance. Joseph Gruenfeld was good enough to read the entire text and to suggest various changes and improvements, and I am obliged to Meir Mindlin for his help in improving the style of the manuscript.

I would like to thank the Rabinowitz Foundation, the Littauer Foundation in New York, and Professor Moshe

Davis for aid, granted toward the cost of publication.

My sincere gratitude goes to Eugene Davidson and Miss Roberta Yerkes of the Yale University Press for the trouble they took in dealing with the book and corresponding across the ocean on matters related to it. I owe a profound debt to Mrs. Jane H. Carroll whose meticulous work made the book more readable.

NATHAN ROTENSTREICH

Jerusalem, 1957
The Hebrew University

CONTENTS

Chapter 1. Res Gestae and Their Narration

1. Three main theories as to the nature of history have been put forth in modern philosophy:

a. the theory expounded by Hegel which considers history to be a manifestation of Spirit

b. the theory taken for granted by many authors defining history from the angle of the subject matter history is concerned with, viz. man

c. the theory represented by Rickert and his many followers which considers the individual character of historical concepts and their relation to values. Hints toward a different approach are to be found in Vico, where the starting point is the identity of subject and object in history.

2. The present discussion lies in the field of the relationship between subject and object, but is concerned with elaborating the various aspects of the gulf existing between the subject and object in history. The first difference between the poles of subject and object lies in the fact that there is on the one hand an objective course of action called "history" and on the other a story of this course called "narration."

3. The main difference between the two connotations of the term history is the fact that the course of events is extended toward the future while narration reflects on the past. What is called "a historical development" is established from the point of view of the present looking back at the past. The present establishes itself as the focus and center of the process.

4. Historical reflection embodied in narration deals with data which are given in the present. The occurrence in the past is reached through the medium of the data. The change in the directions of time is ipso facto a change in the modal levels: data versus occurrences. The meaning of the datum depends upon the past occurrence.

5. In history time is not only the object of knowledge, it is also an element of knowledge itself. Time is the background of historical knowledge, a knowledge which starts with the present. But time is also an instrument of historical knowledge, for it serves to explain the datum encountered in the present. The occurrences at which historical knowledge terminates are not given but constructed. The relationship between the past and the present creates a kind of circle: The meaning of the datum in the present depends on the past, while the datum in the present guides us in selecting the past we need in order to explain the datum in the present.

6. Each datum is explicable in various ways, since it can be looked at from different points of view. Though the occurrences form a unity they are to be explained in terms of a plurality of factors. Historical knowledge isolates events from their real context and deals only with certain specific events. It is concerned with those events which mark a real change or with events which originate a course of historical succession. Historical knowledge is by nature open to the discovery of new links in the past and thus to the recognition in the future of new meanings of past events.

7. The difference between historical knowledge and historical occurrences, that between *res gestae* and their narration, can be shown in terms of the direction of time, the nature of the starting point in the two realms, and their respective meanings. The bridge between the two realms is to be found in the fact that creations of the historical proc-

ess, namely objectivations, are turned by historical reflection into data for it.

8–9. Hence historical reflection is based on tradition, if the term is understood rightly. In historical reflection we encounter a two-way determination: The present is determined by the past while the past is determined by the present. There is an ontological gap between the past and the present which historical knowledge tries to overcome by methodical means. Historical knowledge is directed toward the *meaning* of the past; to reach the past in its ontological nature is beyond its capacity. Hence we may point to the decisive feature of history: In spite of the identity between the knower of history and the object of his knowledge, there is no identity between them insofar as knowledge is concerned. Consciousness and the stream of events are parts of one unity, but still different and even alienated.

Chapter 2. Objectivity

1. The nature of objectivity is described in accordance with the main Kantian line, as validity of knowledge based
   a) on the application of concepts to sensible data, and
   b) on the integration of any statement within the scope of "the possibility of experience."
Hence in objective statements we find a synthesis of concepts and data on the one hand and the integration of the syntheses within the broad scope of experience on the other. There is a genuine problem in objectivity because of the very synthesis between the two heterogeneous factors: concepts and data. This problem has been solved in critical philosophy through the assumption that concepts refer intrinsically to data. Concepts give stability to data, though concepts are only *one* factor in the synthesis.

2. Within the scope of historical knowledge one en-

counters a difference between this branch of knowledge and the other branches, mainly between it and the natural sciences which served as the basis for the analysis performed in critical philosophy. The historical process is not a sheer datum, the meaning of which depends upon concepts imposed on it. It has a meaning of its own, that of shaping the future. Furthermore, there is in history the correlation between the process and reflection. Can it be assumed that reflection makes the process stable, that is to say that reflection performs the function which concepts are supposed to perform according to the assumptions of critical philosophy?

3. The difficulty characteristic of historical knowledge is that historical research as an embodiment of concepts cannot stabilize the datum, because historical research itself turns out to be a datum if looked at from the point of view of new, subsequent research. Hence it ceases to be, on a later view, an embodiment of concepts. While the theories of the natural sciences do not belong to the field of nature, historical theory is not only a correlate of the process but also a part of it. Hence in history we do not find the presupposition for an assumption of objectivity, that is to say the clear-cut distinction between the concepts and the data.

4. Here again the alleged identity between subject and object in history is not a factor promoting knowledge; rather it blocks knowledge. Ultimately historical knowledge becomes integrated in the historical process, and not vice versa. In history the object absorbs the knowledge of it. Hence knowledge lacks genuine sovereignty, as pointed out in the critical theory of objectivity.

5. Historical knowledge is not just knowledge rooted in a perspective, since there is actually no branch of knowledge which is not rooted in a perspective. Its main feature

is that its characteristic perspective is one of time. But a perspective of time is immanently ephemeric, because the present always becomes the past. Hence there is in history no minimum ground for objectivity, as there is no differentiation between the knower and the known facts.

6. Still there are several criteria for evaluating a piece of historical research: *a*) The "transcendental" presuppositions of any knowledge, like causality and substance, can be employed. *b*) History must be explained by itself; there is no way to reduce history and put it on a quasi more fundamental denominator, since only in history do we find this changing shift from occurrences to reflections and from reflections to occurrences. *c*) There is a comprehensiveness of research in terms both of the extent and of the inner density of the presentation, even when the research is concerned only with a historical fragment.

7. History is on the threshold of philosophy, because it is a problem for itself and hence is not only reflection but a beginning of reflection of reflection.

Chapter 3. Historical Time

A. A *Priori* Time

1. Historical time is one of the concrete manifestations of time in general. Time in general is understood here as form. Time as form is the form of succession, which is the starting point for the analysis of the generic meaning of time. In addition, we find the related terms which are the point of departure for the introduction of the concept of duration. Hence time as form comprises both the aspect of succession and the aspect of duration.

2. The two aspects lead to a further pair of aspects, continuity and discontinuity. The development of these two

aspects leads to the assumption that duration can be applied to succession, thus serving as the logical precondition for measuring time.

3. The idea of the form of time can be restated with reference to a critical evaluation of Bergson's theory of *durée*, which does not consider the distinction between time as form and time as content.

4. Furthermore, the idea can be restated through an analysis of Whitehead's concept of time, where dimensions of time—past, present, and future—are considered to be, though in a partially disguised way, aspects of the very notion of time. Time as form connotes only succession and duration and not dimensions of time. In the ladder of specifications of time, time as measured time, that is to say physical time, precedes time as split into dimensions, both in psychology and history.

5. The distinction between the form of time and its specifications can solve some of the puzzles implied in the position of time. Time as form is the form of flow which itself does not flow, since time as form is not a reality and hence the character of reality as flow cannot be applied to it. On the other hand, there is no need to assume that the correlate of time is eternity. It suffices to show that there is an epistemological correlation between time as content and time as form and that there is no need to assume the hasty correlation between time and eternity.

6. Irreversibility of time is again a feature of the very form of time because it is implied in the nature of succession. What appeared after something cannot then be before something. Yet the question is open whether this formal feature of time is complemented by the content of events taking place in time; whether the events in terms of their content are recurrences or not, in spite of the fact that in terms of succession they come one after another. This

problem leads beyond the scope of time as form and is a problem for an analysis of concrete time, and hence possibly a problem for historical time.

7. The elucidation of the status of time as form leads to the assumption that time is both form and datum and that time is to be differentiated according to the various domains of experience.

8. Three attempts to base time on something allegedly more fundamental are criticized: *a*) Solomon Maimon's attempt to base time on distinctions in terms of content; *b*) Hegel's attempt to base time on Spirit; *c*) the existentialist attempt to base time on the finitude of man. All these attempts fail because they actually presuppose time. Time is irreducible.

B. *An Example of Material Time*

1. Material time is concrete time, keeping abreast of the various domains of experience. Hence there is some talk of biological, religious time, etc.

2. Psychological time can be a starting point for an analysis of the nature of historical time because psychological time has a dimensional structure. A systematic summary of modern discussions of psychological time as presented by Richard Hoenigswald and William Stern shows some clear features: *a*) the relation of experience to the present; *b*) the integration of the present moment in time as such; *c*) the status of time in terms of its connection with the relationship of the experiencing subject to his world; *d*) the specific rhythm of psychological time as connected with growth and not only with flow; *e*) the psychic present as a plane and not a point; *f*) the aspect of meeting and distance between the dimensions; and ultimately *g*) the notion of personal time as transcending the sheer experimental field of the psychic subject.

C. *Material Transsubjective Time*

1. Historical time is time split into dimensions. The problem is how a transsubjective and hence transpsychic time can be split into dimensions, for dimensions presuppose an experiencing subject who divides the line of time into what was before him (past), what is with him (present), and what will be after this moment of experience (future).

2. The characteristic feature of historical time is the combination of meaning and temporality. It is a meaning which renders time the feature of transsubjectivity.

3. This combination is to be applied both to the aspect of succession and to the aspect of duration. Any historical event or period is characterized by the aspect of temporality on the one hand and of meaning inherent in it on the other. Delimitations of historical periods are but attempts to point out meaningful durations within the successive process.

4. The combination of the aspect of meaning and the aspect of temporality brings to the fore the dialectic characteristic of historical time: On the part of meanings there is no continuity in historical time while on the part of temporality continuity is upheld. Historical time cannot be regarded as durée in Bergson's sense because in historical time we find that heterogeneity is due to meanings while continuity is due to temporality.

5–6. A further feature of historical time as against the background of the synthesis of temporality and meanings is the split into dimensions. From this point of view there is an affinity between historical time and time in the sphere of psychology. The difficulty is that in history there is no clearly defined subject experiencing the world who, because of his act of experience, dwells in the dimension of the present. The present itself is defined by certain qualitative events. Hence different segments of historical time can be considered to be the historical present, as for instance the French Revolution, the events up to World War I, the Cold War, etc.

7. Historical time is constructed time. The only stable feature in the present is that it is what has to be explained and not what does explain. Hence the main feature is one in terms of position.

8. The historical present is thus the dimension of the explicable data and at the same time the dimension of acts of decisions and of plans for the future. There are links between the two meanings of the present, which in turn manifest the two meanings of history: The present as the dimension of data is understood in terms of historical knowledge, while the present as the dimension of acts is seen in terms of the historical process.

9. The relationship between the present and the past is constructed as well. The past appears for historical knowledge insofar as it has a meaning with reference to the present. Yet while searching for the past of the present we reach the present of the past.

10. The fact that past is constructed in history becomes clear in that feature of historical research which is bound to start with what is later, viz. the present, and reach what was earlier, that is to say the past.

11. The notion of historical progress presupposes that historical process has a center where all paths converge. This center is supposed to be a higher stage than that which preceded it. But an analysis of the relationship between past and present shows only that the relationship is one of correlation; it is not runged like a ladder. Every present is richer than any past but is not therefore superior to it.

12. The dimension of future is introduced into the scope of historical time in relation to the notion of occurrences

in the present. The present reaches the past through knowledge while it reaches the future as an occurrence. Thus the relationship of the present to each of the other dimensions reflects the twofold nature of history. In the future we find an aspect which is established, though it has not occurred as yet, for instance the fact that there will be a winter. What is not established is the bearing of the established fact on the historical events proper, for instance on the military operation which will take place during the winter. We in the present have a threefold attitude toward the future: We take account of it, know the possibilities inherent in it, and plan it.

13. Historical consciousness, though dealing with the past and not with the future, presupposes the future in some ways. The future is the dimension where new historical data are to be discovered. It is a new present and as such may throw light on the past.

14. The nature of the construction characteristic of historical time has to be re-emphasized: *a*) The notion of earlier and later is tied up with historical consciousness and is not given. *b*) The construction of the sequence from earlier to later is accomplished from the point of view of the later. *c*) Historical research assumes a sequence of events which does not exhaust the full extent of the events as they really occurred.

Chapter 4. History and Social Science

A. *The Implicit Relationship*

1. Though there have been attempts to deduce the common life of men (which is the proper subject matter of sociology) from an a priori source within consciousness, it is in fact necessary to assume that common life is historical and hence an empirical datum. There is therefore a neces-

sary relationship between history and social science which
has to be systematically elaborated.

2. There is a further assumption that there is a common
core to both history and social science: human action. This
common core points to the ontological identity between the
data of sociology on the one hand and of history on the
other. This assumption as to the data of sociology being
identical with the data of history must be criticized in
view of the preceding analysis which has shown that the
data of historical knowledge are not an action but a document.

3. Many sociologists have tried to define the subject
matter of sociology more precisely. Their theories tacitly
presupposed the historical character of the social facts,
without elucidating the nature of the shift from the historical aspect to the sociological.

4. Formal sociology as represented by Georg Simmel
is a systematic attempt to draw the line of distinction
between history proper and sociology proper. Sociology is
assumed to deal with forms only and not with the material
manifestations of social relations, the latter being the
subject matter of history. Yet this theory, though marking a
systematic advance, does not point to the functional relationship between form and matter in social existence and
thus to the functional two-way relationship between social
science and history.

5. From the point of view of the actual subject matter
"sociography," the description of the present social situation, is related to history by the very fact that it is concerned
with a specific part of historical time, precisely that of the
present. Yet the question remains open why it is that sociology has to deal with the present, since a branch of history,
contemporary history, deals with it too. Any systematic elucidation of the nature of sociology must account for the fact

that sociology deals both with the present and with institutions such as societies, states, etc. Hence it is bound to clarify the conceptual relationship between a fragment of time, i.e. present, and the nature of the social institutions (understood in terms of meanings and not in terms of position in time).

B. The Explicit Relationship

1. The implicit connection between history and social science as taken for granted in the theories hinted at before is supplemented by various attempts to lay bare the explicit connection between these two branches. This explicit connection is manifest in the fact that sociology as such grew out of some of the problems delineated by the philosophy of history.

2. A new outlook is brought to the fore by the sociology of culture as outlined by Alfred Weber and previously sketched by Jacob Burckhardt. The main feature of this outlook is the very concern with history as a structure and not as a process. Within this structure the various strata or potences are detected. Yet this outlook takes into account only the pattern of the process and not the pattern of the institutions. Furthermore, it leaves us uncertain as to whether the ongoing process may or may not change the already established pattern.

3. It is assumed that history needs a systematic science, the "science of culture," to serve as its foundation. However, we are left in the dark as to the relations of the systematic concept of culture to the process of history, because culture as such has a historical meaning.

4–5. The main step toward a systematic elucidation of the relation between history and social science was made in

Max Weber's theory of the Ideal Type. The origin of the Ideal Type is historical but its nature is sociological. The Ideal Type is supposed to perform a function in historical knowledge enabling us to see the individual historical events as deviations from the Type. The Ideal Type is an explicitly methodological device and hence different from an event in history, for history is a domain of realities. Weber is aware of this difference; hence he stresses the tension between the particular events and the Type. The Ideal Type is a meaning only, while historical events are both meanings and facts. The main shortcoming of the entire theory is to be found in the fact that it overstressed the aspect of action and neglected the aspect of institutions in social existence, thus failing to distinguish the social sciences adequately from history.

6. A different approach to the determination of the relation between the two branches has its roots in Comte and was elaborated further by Gottl. They stressed the difference between statics and dynamics, or between permanence and innovation. History, they held, deals with the growth of nations, for instance, while sociology is concerned with the being of nations. This approach leaves some questions unsolved, mainly as to the material concepts employed in investigating the quasi-static situations.

7. A somewhat equivalent distinction is suggested by the difference between the vertical and the horizontal approach to human existence. History is supposed to offer a horizontal approach while sociology represents a vertical one.

8. Lastly, there is the conception which assumes that society, which is the subject matter of sociology, is the ultimate subject of history. Yet precisely this view raises again the question of the justification of converting the subject matter into subject.

C. The Concatenation

1. The essential characteristic of a social institution is the interaction of a psychic act and its embodiment in a particular historical position. There is no way of reducing social institutions to psychic acts, just as there is no way of reducing language to sheer sounds. The social institution is relatively stable in spite of its immanent historicity. Hence the social institution can be looked at as a framework for historical occurrences. Yet what is on one level a framework may be considered to be a historical occurrence on another level. Thus the Greek *polis* is a framework for man acting in it and is an occurrence in the framework of the concept of statehood in general.

2. The concept of framework is analyzed in the light of some suggestions made by Paul Tillich and Herman Heller. We have a threefold composition of a social framework, namely the act, the meaning, and the framework proper.

3. The concept of framework can be considered as a permanent element in the historical process. We may conceive of one framework as included in another as the polis is included in state, but then the question arises whether or not there is an ultimate all-embracing framework. Mankind, for instance, can be considered to be both a framework and a content. Historical trends strive to establish themselves as institutions, and thus to cease to be entirely dependent on psychic acts as aims of struggle or strife. This shift from trends to frameworks may be considered a social progress. The notion of progress is necessarily confined only to those aspects of human existence where the very turn toward institutions is conceivable.

4. The connection between the notion of the framework as the main sociological category and the notion of the present as the subject matter of social science can be

established. The present itself as a segment of time is considered to be a framework for human action, similar to such frameworks as a state, associations, etc. The present is also a framework of frameworks, since all the frameworks in terms of content are contained in the framework of present in terms of time. Here lies the root of the temptation to project our own present and to look at it as the pattern for all presents. This is what historical materialism does; it makes the present of our own industrial society a pattern for all societies. Yet this step abolishes the autonomy of every particular present. The difference between the historical and the sociological approach to time comes to the fore here. History looks at time as open, while sociology encloses time in circles.

5. Because of the circular nature of the sociological institutions, there is no way to show that society or any stratum of it is ultimate, as historical materialism maintains. All the factors composing a social situation exist together, and there is no room for the distinction between what is fundamental and what is only derivative.

6. Reciprocity is the main feature of the structure of a social unit. The decision taking place in the present is a part of the social situation and as such points to a situation beyond the given present. The overstepping of the given situation introduces the dimension of the future into the horizon of social science.

7. The relationship between history and sociology turns out to be connected with a difference of outlook. A set of relations and functions in history is a subject for sociology just as a set of relations and functions in biology is a subject in history. Sociological investigation is based on history as its *ratio essendi*; on its side sociology provides history with concepts of general interest and hence relieves historical research of the need to take refuge in concepts of

values as the principle of selection. Sociological investigation, presupposing history, is ultimately more historical than historical investigation proper. History and sociology meet in terms both of historical reflection and of historical occurrence, though they are different in terms of the respective meanings bestowed upon their data.

Chapter 5. Causality and Laws

A. *De Facto Application*

1. The analysis of the historical object shows that the presupposition of historical knowledge is the category of casuality determining the relationship between events in a single direction. Every historical datum is an effect of a cause.

2–3. There are several actual forms of relation between a datum in the present and an event in the past: *a*) a relation of a symbolical representation; *b*) a relation of identity in content; and *c*) a relation of a work created in the past but still existing in the present. Yet in terms of structure all these relations can be reduced to a relation between effects and causes. Historical knowledge is essentially a conditioning-genetic knowledge, tied up with and rooted in the category of causality.

4. The cause, as considered in history, is bound to be in the past. But this does not imply that the effect is bound to be only in the present. The effect can be placed in the past as well. The decisive feature is not the position of the cause or of the effect but the relation between them. In historical knowledge we presuppose that the cause is always in the past, but we do not claim to know what this cause is in its factuality.

5–8. The factual employment of the category of causality in historical knowledge is re-emphasized through a critical examination of some theories which try to undermine the connection of historical knowledge with causality. The theory of "insight," the integration of the phenomenon in systems as against its integration in causal chains, the theory that the historical object is one rooted in acts of will, and ultimately the theory that it is an individual object—all are seen to be inadequate.

B. The Principle de Iure

1. The principle of causality in its purity connotes only the interdependence of phenomena. In the different fields of knowledge and experience this generic meaning can be interpreted according to the requirements of the fields.

2. There is the question in physics whether the difference between cause and effect is the basis for the distinction between what precedes and what follows or vice versa. In historical knowledge there can be no room for this question, because in history there is the presupposition that the cause is necessarily in the past. The historical material itself guides the application of the principle of causality.

3. Though historical knowledge presupposes that the cause is in the past, the principle of causality helps it to detect the specific past which is the cause of the present. The ontological distinction between the past and the present is given from the outset, but the methodological distinction is established only by means of historical knowledge proper.

4. The further function of causality in physics is suppose to be that of prediction. A closer examination of the idea of prediction as applied to historical knowledge shows that there is no room for prediction in history. Again, prediction dismissed from the scope of historical knowledge cannot be introduced into the scope of historical occurrence. The

attitude of the present toward the future within the realm of historical occurrence is one not of prediction but of projection.

5. The practical manifestation of the absence of prediction in historical knowledge is to be found in the fact that it is a knowledge of observation and not of experimentation. This again is an indication of the essence of the domain of history in general. Though there is an ontological identity between subject and object there is still the methodological chasm between them. The principle of causality is one of the main devices for stretching a bridge over the methodological chasm.

6. The principle of causality in history is not confined to establishing relations between events contiguous in time and space. The various phenomena of a historical revival exhibit this sort of action through distance. The further function of the principle of causality in historical knowledge is to construct a chain of continuity in terms of the material relations between events, even where there is no continuity in terms of the actual given sequence between events.

C. From the Principle of Causality to the Laws

1. The question which has to be raised next is whether there are in the realm of historical knowledge material laws dependent on transcendental principles but different from them, as is the case with the law of gravitation in physics, for example.

2. The idea of material laws is bound up with the possibility of disregarding, in conformity with Maxwell's maxim, the position of the events in terms of time and space. Such disregard is precluded in historical knowledge; hence there is no room for material laws in it. Historical knowledge directly employs the principle of causality on

data, without the advantage of a mediating link of material laws.

3. This leads to the conclusion that there is no room for induction in history. Historical knowledge, though empirical, is not inductive knowledge.

4. What is constant in history is not the relations between the elements but the elements themselves. Historical situations are different combinations of elements belonging to one and the same sphere, as for instance the elements composing the nature of statehood, or else different combinations of elements of different spheres, e.g. the sphere of state and church. This analysis leads to a criticism of historical materialism which assumes that there are permanent historical relations.

5–6. The discussion of the concept of evolution shows that this concept cannot be applied to history. Nor is there room in historical knowledge for "principles," which are different on the one hand from categories and on the other from material laws. The outcome of the discussion is a new evaluation of the causal aspect of historical knowledge.

CHAPTER 1

RES GESTAE AND THEIR NARRATION

PROBLEMS OF PHILOSOPHY OF HISTORY have occupied a central position in philosophical discussions for a generation. This is due to the logic of philosophical development itself and its interest in human activity and to the impact of humanity—which is supposed to be a historical reality totally or essentially—on philosophical thought. The systematic exposition of some of the problems related to history ought to be preceded by a short typology of positions which are held in the field of philosophy of history.

1. When we survey the various theories of the nature of history which have arisen in the course of the development of modern philosophy, three main types emerge:

a. The *metaphysical* theory. This theory explains the nature of history by placing it within the general scope and development of Spirit or Mind. The great exponent of this theory is Hegel. Its chief shortcoming lies in its attempt to deduce time from elements of meaning which are, according to Hegel, timeless. This theory also assumes that history exists only up to the point where Mind (Spirit) reaches the stage of the absolute. According to this theory, therefore, time itself is only temporal and transitional. Thus this view oscillates between time and eternity.

b. The theory of the *historical object or content*. This defines the nature of the historical domain in terms of its subject matter, i.e. man in his works. Historical knowledge is defined as knowledge concerned with this specific subject matter. This is the common description of history taken for granted in educational discussions of the idea of history as "teacher of life," sometimes elevated to the level of a metaphysical consideration, as, for instance, by Collingwood. The principal fault of this theory is its failure to distinguish between history proper and the various other branches of knowledge also concerned with man, such as psychology and sociology. This failure leads to an attempt to substitute history, for example, for psychology, as Collingwood suggests, and it is not made clear whether psychiatry as a branch of psychology proper should be replaced by history too. The theory also assumes fallaciously that the nature of an object accounts for and exhaustively defines the nature of a branch of knowledge concerned with it.

c. The theory of *individual concepts*. This emphasizes the nature of the concepts that are employed in historical knowledge. It defines history as that particular branch of knowledge which employs individual concepts. This theory has three main flaws: First, it recognizes only dichotomic classifications as, for example, science on the one hand and history or *Kulturwissenschaften* on the other. Second, it cannot explain the transition from the historical process to historical knowledge; that is, it cannot say precisely how and why history should be conceived in individual concepts which are tools of historical knowledge. And third, it cannot establish a necessary bridge between values and the historical process on the one hand and the individual concepts on the other. That is to say, it fails to show why the historical process is to be necessarily understood in terms of value concepts and why, in turn, these concepts should be individual concepts. It is faced, as it were, by both a metaphysical and a logical problem: a metaphysical one in terms of the immanent relation between process and value, and a logical one in terms of the immanent relation between values and individual concepts.

Indications of a theory going beyond these three are to be found in Vico, and more recently in Croce and Collingwood. The main feature of this fourth type of theory is that it does not place the problem either in metaphysics or in the content, the instruments, or the methods of knowledge. It puts forward the problem of the relation between subject and object as characteristic of history, taking the relation between them to be one of identity. On the basis of this relation of identity, the problem of historical knowledge is put in terms of Vico's maxim: "Verum et factum conventuntur." This theory makes the too hasty assumption that a genuine primary *relation* between subject and object in history is necessarily an *identity*.

In a way this fourth type is not an independent and fully developed line of thought. Various elements of it have been absorbed by various schools of thought on the nature of history. The problem of subject and object is intrinsic for the Hegelian line; the idea of history as a superior branch of knowledge, which is put forth in this school, is present in the theory of history as related to individual concepts; and generally the idea that there is a branch of knowledge which lies in between philosophy and history underlies the idea that history is the study of man. Hence the Viconian line is, historically speaking, more a reservoir of motifs than a school which can be put side by side with the other schools.[1]

Yet for the purpose of a new discussion of the problems of history it is both proper and fruitful to place the analysis

1. On the different types of approach to history see the analysis of Richard Peter McKeon in *Freedom and History* (New York, Noonday Press, 1952). For an earlier analysis see Fritz Kaufmann, *Geschichtsphilosophie der Gegenwart*, Berlin, Junker und Dünnhaupt Verlag, 1931.

in the domain of the relationship between subject and object. And for this one fundamental reason: The main feature of history is that knowledge and the known subject matter have to be dealt with jointly, and there is no way to distinguish with regard to history between the ontological and the epistemological points of view. For this concatenation the conception of the relationship between subject and object may serve as a starting point for discussion. Our main purpose will be to analyze the tension between the correlative poles of subject and object, to study the problems involved therein, and to draw some of the conclusions relevant for the nature of historical knowledge and of history in general in the human universe.

2. The starting point of this discussion will be Hegel's observation: "In our language the term *History* unites the objective with the subjective side, and denotes quite as much the *historia rerum gestarum* as the *res gestae* themselves: on the other hand it comprehends not less what has *happened* than the *narration* of what happened. This union of the two meanings we must regard as of a higher order than mere outward accident." [2] We are merely told in this statement of the connection between the two aspects of the term history; the problems and antinomies involved in this connection are not elucidated. Yet we must consider whether this connection is an identity of the meaning of the two aspects and of the categories implicitly used, or whether there is a very peculiar structure prevailing with respect to the inner tension of history.

3. Our point of departure is the notion that every occurrence *qua* occurrence has a temporal extension directed toward the future. Were there no such extension inherent

2. *Vorlesungen über die Philosophie der Weltgeschichte*, ed. by Georg Lasson (Leipzig, Meiner, 1919–20), 1, 144; English trans. by J. Sibree, *The Philosophy of History* (New York, Collier, 1900), p. 63.

in every event there would be no reason for assuming that it had a temporal character. We know from our everyday experience that there is an intentionality toward the future, as in its planning and anticipation, inherent in every deed or act of ours. As opposed to this, the narration of occurrences is fundamentally directed toward and refers to the past. Historical research, as manifested in historical narration, is research into the past, necessarily reversing the direction of time. As Kierkegaard observed, we live forward and we think backward.

The first distinction, between the objective and subjective sides of the term "history," advances the principal assumption that both occurrences and their narration are bound up with time. Time is the medium of both. We find ourselves inside time, and inside it we distinguish between the two sides of the term "history." The two sides maintain their different relations to time in terms of its direction, forward or backward.

A similar reversal of the direction of time is characteristic of historical research. 1) Reflection on, and scientific analysis of, the forms of human life generally proceed in a direction opposite to that which it actually followed. 2) It starts *post factum* and therefore with completed results. So-called historical development is generally based on the assumption that the latest form looks at the earlier ones as stages leading toward it and establishing it. In addition to the concern with a time direction opposite to that of the actual course of events in time, historical reflection takes the present form or situation as a center and assumes that various lines of development converge in it. Reversing the direction of time historical reflection thus splits time into two parts. It establishes itself as the center and assumes that the place it occupies *is* the center. Historical narration therefore sees past occurrences as having been *completed*,

so to speak, and ignores the essential fact that every occurrence, since it is directed toward the future, is necessarily incomplete. Historical reflection dissects the occurrences but does not complete them.

4. It is no mere accident that historical reflection elevates
the present to the position of a center. Only by so doing
is historical reflection at all possible. Reflection, as it were,
invades time and splits it into dimensions. Historical reflection is empirical because it deals with a datum. Its
starting point is a given document, physical or archaeological remains, manners, customs, laws, etc. All these are
given in the present, for a datum can exist only in the present. Historical knowledge as empirical must refer to what
is given in the present. It is knowledge which makes process a
datum because only through the assumption of the datum
does knowledge take place, and it is knowledge which makes
this assumption.

Historical knowledge, being empirical, cannot deal with
occurrences which took place before the present. These
occurrences are not data for historical knowledge. They
appear in knowledge as means for the explanation and the
understanding of present data. Thus historical research
explains a given document by considering it as an effect
or outcome of an occurrence in the past. It reaches the past
occurrence only through the medium of the data, the data
being understood to be a partial crystallization of that occurrence. Thus there is no direct face-to-face meeting of
research and occurrence. Historical research not only re-
verses the direction of time but also connects the two dimensions of time (present and past) with which it deals
by setting them on different *modal* levels: It treats the
present as a dimension of *data* and the past as a dimension
of *occurrence*. The occurrence dealt with in historical reflection is, of course, not the actual occurrence which is

directed toward the future. It is a *constructed occurrence*, a past, which ends in the present and manifests itself in the document existing in the present. Though history in its objective aspect proceeds from event to event, history in its subjective or reflective aspect starts from the document and endeavors to relate it to an event or series of events which is thought to express itself in it.

Any reflective consideration of a document is always of a critical nature. It first probes the structure of the datum. In this procedure it usually finds at least two strata, a material one (the stone, the paper of a document, outer behavior) and a meaningful one, expressed in the material. The question of the connection of these two sides of the datum approaches one of the central concepts of historical knowledge, i.e. objective Spirit or Mind.

The datum is understood by historical knowledge to be a product of a process, a crystallization of it. Historical knowledge by its very essence crystallizes the process, establishing the datum and then explaining it by the process. It conceives its datum to exist in the sphere of crystalization, the sphere which Hegel calls Objective Spirit, being, as he says, Spirit in the form of Reality.[3] Historical knowledge explains what is called Objective Spirit by placing in the past the occurrences which created the forms of existence in the sphere of factuality and reality, and considering the givenness of the forms as being in the present and occupying a position in it. Though in this discussion we do not refer to the forms of Spirit in Hegel's sense, we take advantage of the concept to indicate the objectified occurrences as encountered in the present, that is to say as data.

It is in this context that historical knowledge faces the

3. G. W. F. Hegel, *Encyclopädie der philosophischen Wissenschaften im Grundrisse*, sec. 385.

problem of the relationship existing between what it encounters and what created the datum. The question is
whence does the datum obtain its meaning. Is the meaning
ascribed by the very fact that historical knowledge conceives it to be a datum, or does its meaning depend upon
the occurrence which was crystallized in the datum? It is
obvious that without historical knowledge there would be
no datum at all, because without it we would remain within
a process directed toward the future. The meaning of the
datum cannot therefore be severed from historical knowledge. But on the other hand historical knowledge must
assume that the meaning of its data depends upon a past
process. Without historical knowledge no question will arise
concerning the fact that, for instance, the governor of
India bore the French title viceroy. Only historical knowledge—and it does not matter whether it appears as a result
of methodical research or as a vague reflection—raises this
question; it here abstracts the title from the problems of
the government of India, from the policy of the actual
viceroy, and examines the question of the name only; in
brief it turns it into a datum. Historical knowledge explains
the meaning of the datum through the history of England,
the past connection between England and France, and
the language of France. It builds up the datum by making
itself a focus of the rays converging in the datum. These
rays are not its own. They are rays from the actual process
in the past.

Historical knowledge is always compelled to make such a
transition from the datum to the process, even where it
explains the datum by ideas. Where the datum is understood to be a crystallization of ideas, a transition exists from
the datum to a certain actuality in past time. Historical
knowledge is in principle based only on the *necessity* of a
transition from one domain to another. It need not neces-

sarily deal with any particular *content*, with political, economic, or ideological events, etc. From the nature of historical knowledge we can derive only a *connection* between datum and process; in no case can we derive a specific *content* of the process leading to the datum. In sum, the nature of historical knowledge lies in a regression from the present to the past; it is a regression from data to occurrences.

5. By maintaining that historical knowledge determines its own place as the center and focus of the process, we assume that historical knowledge qua *knowledge* interweaves with history qua *occurrence*. Knowledge possesses a definite position in time—it is placed in a present. At this point there is a difference in terms of principles between historical and scientific knowledge. In history time not only constitutes the object of knowledge or is a coordinate of it but is a constitutive element of knowledge itself. The historical object is an object within time—this is clear. But even historical knowledge—not only as a psychological act of the individual historian but also as a domain of meaning—is constituted by time through its immanent relation to the present. We are in a position to consider the meaning of a historical object only if we look at it as a meaning which was assigned by knowledge; we must explain it through occurrences in time. Knowledge placed in the present is placed in a dimension of actual occurrences, a dimension of works, deeds, and desires. Historical knowledge explains this present by means of conceptual methods, i.e. by constructing an occurrence in the past. Historical knowledge is therefore related to time in a twofold way: It is connected with the stream of time as knowledge grounded in a segment of time, i.e. in the present, and it employs time as a means for understanding what is given in the present. To put it differently, time is

the basis of historical knowledge on the one hand and its instrument on the other. The dialectic considered above in connection with the problem of the meaning of the historical datum arises here again. Knowledge as a focus is knowledge within time, but for that focus to concentrate its rays within itself, historical knowledge must *build* its object as an object in time. There is a circular movement inherent in the very nature of historical knowledge. August Boekh's observation on philology holds true for history, too; to explain or to comment upon a document we need history, yet the document itself is a product of history. The document throws light both on itself and on the historical occurrence which produced it and expresses itself in it. This circle of historical knowledge is connected with the regression from documents to occurrences which was commented on above. The document is made understandable by the occurrence, that is to say the product is conceivable through the process, while the process is conceivable through the product. The two are different but not separable.

Historical knowledge thus necessarily correlates the datum and the explanation. This correlation holds good notwithstanding the modal difference between the correlates. The datum lies in the domain of what has been formed and shaped in the course of time—what may be termed *objectivations,* because processes are here turned into objects expressing and crystallizing them. In contrast, the occurrence, as a process, exists in the domain of *reality* proper. This correlation is possible only through the fact that the process in the domain of reality is *constructed* from the perspective of the datum existing in the domain of objectivations.

To sum up, historical knowledge is by no means immediately connected with an *actual occurrence;* the occurrence appears as a methodical instrument of explanation only. The correlation is not between the datum as an objectivation and the occurrence as reality; it is between the objectivations and a post factum *construction* of the actual occurrence for the sake of the objectivations and in order to explain them. Reality is constructed in order to gain knowledge of the historical datum.

This problem of correlation between the meaningful datum and the actual occurrences does not arise with respect to the actual, living process in which we take part as living and acting beings. In the actual occurrence there is no separation of process from meaning. This separation arises and exists only from the viewpoint of knowledge. Historical knowledge changes the nature of historical process not only by diverting consideration from the future to the past but also by dismembering the historical reality. The occurrence assigns meaning to the datum through the medium of knowledge. Thus the occurrence as a domain of reality becomes a causative factor, since the meaning of the datum depends upon the occurrence qua cause. Conversely the datum in the present determines which sections of the past we must seek in order to explain the present. The datum holds a meaningful position with respect to the past; the past in explaining the present holds a meaningful position with respect to the datum.

Historical knowledge is inherently synthetic. Its object is to establish a unity of occurrence and meaning, a juncture between an element of existence and an element of essence. Yet in order to arrive at such a synthesis historical knowledge needs both analysis and hypothesis. It starts from an analysis, first by dissolving the datum into its material and meaningful facets, as the stone and the inscription on it, and second by dissolving the immediate synthesis of the process into the elements of the datum on the one hand (present) and the constructed occurrence on the other (past). But by the very construction of the occurrence in the past historical knowledge becomes hypothetical, because the past, which is built up in order to explain the present, is never certain. We cannot be sure that we have arrived at the real cause of the datum in the present nor can we be sure that we have understood it properly or at any rate exhaustively. No regression from an effect to its cause is ever certain. To this extent we must agree with Schlegel that history is prophecy in reverse.

To sum up, there are three steps involved in historical knowledge: synthesis (the objective of historical knowledge), which involves analysis, which in turn involves hypothesis. The synthesis thus becomes hypothetical, though in the immediate process the synthetic unity of an action is a given fact. Historical knowledge is reconstructive —and not only do we stress the *re* as expressing the fact that the starting point of historical knowledge lies in the present, but the "construction" is also implied.[4]

6. Historical knowledge shows a further characteristic feature in dealing with a datum. Its aim, as has been said, is to understand the datum by regarding it as a crystallization of a process. It therefore necessarily presupposes that a plurality of meanings is ascribed to the datum. The datum can be explained in various ways, since it can be connected with various occurrences, and/or can yield various meanings which can still be connected with one and the same occurrence. The ruins of a city, for instance, might be connected with a series of events whose meaning is expressed in the succession of styles of building. They might also be connected with a different series of events, for instance political or military happenings, etc. The same datum

4. Concerning this problem see F. H. Bradley, "The Presuppositions of Critical History," *Collected Essays* (Oxford, Clarendon Press, 1935), 1, 1 ff.

can be explained in various ways. The difference of meanings need not necessarily rest on a difference of processes or series of occurrences, i.e. on the fact that the one process had crystallized archaeologically or architecturally while the other had crystallized politically or militarily. Each process may explain the various meanings involved in itself. Thus we again face the gulf between the two sides of the term "history": The occurrence, whole in itself, appears through the medium of historical knowledge to be complex and many-sided. Historical knowledge dissolves the process and sometimes concentrates on one meaning involved in the process at the expense of another, since it is the cause of the datum which contains its main explanation. Such a dissolution implies the methodological justification of a study of the history of art, for instance, as distinct from the political or religious background of the works of art. The unity of the occurrence stands over against the plurality of explanations, actual or possible.

Moreover, historical knowledge and its concrete and practical expression, historical research, isolate events from their actual context. They choose from the domain of occurrence *some* events and then contract the process into a fragment or composition of fragments. From the tapestry of life, as Georg Simmel has so well put it, a few threads are chosen. Therefore this knowledge faces the problem of choice, i.e. how and what to take from the actual occurrence. This problem, too, is connected with the nature of historical knowledge. The first contraction which takes place in the domain of history is the crystallization of the occurrence by making it convergent in the present and stopping, as it were, the continuing stream of occurrences. Each particular choice in considering this or that fragment involves a further contraction.

We choose those events which are apt to explain the

datum in the present. The starting point of historical research does not lie in the tapestry but in the isolated threads, for the tapestry has to be rewoven from the threads. In other words, at its starting point historical knowledge does not face the complexity and the unity of the process. Because the starting point lies in the datum we start with a contraction as it is encountered, and proceed by expansion and extrapolation. Historical knowledge contracts the process by the very establishment of a focus in the present. But after contracting the process it tries again to explain this contraction by means of an extended series of occurrences. The extension is not given; it is not the extension of the actual process as a broad stream of occurrences but a hypothesis of knowledge. There is no self-evident identity between the extension of an actual occurrence and that supposed in knowledge and constituted by it for the sake of explanation. The difference between the plain extension of the occurrence as it is in history and that constructed in historical narration is the difference between what is simply there and what has to be justified; this difference has to be retained even when we assume that historical narration is adequate to the historical process. This is in the last resort a difference between the immediate and mediated, and only a dialectical optimism (Hegel) considers the two to be identical.

Historical research contracts the process of the past, limiting its own interest to those events and matters which are apt to explain the present. It deals with *qualified* events only. It thus destroys the integrity of the sequence of time, since research deals with those events which constitute a *change* in the course of time, in contrast to what preceded them, and those which effect subsequent *changes,* and not with "gray" events and deeds which are "nameless" processes and no more, processes in themselves but not dealt with historically. The events are chosen from the point of view of the change effected by them. The presupposition is that those events in the past which possess the power of becoming causes are causes of what occurs after them. This attitude or, to put it differently, this bias in historical knowledge appears *in concreto* in the fact that historical research looks for the *origin* of the events, i.e. for their first appearance. These questions of origin are in their essence questions as to where and through what medium the gray and neutral (from the point of view of the datum at stake) process has been broken up and has become a historical process proper, a cause and an explanation of the datum which served as the starting point. Historical knowledge leads the process to a convergence in the present, but then by its own means erects a new process, different from the actual one, that is to say a process of selected links only. The expansion which is characteristic of historical knowledge in its second step—after the contraction—does not go beyond the limits of an *epistemological* correlation between the datum and the process. Historical knowledge does not and cannot reach the actual process. The difference between them is one not only between the immediate and the mediated but also between the process as it is in itself and that composed of selected links.

From what has hitherto been said the conclusion must be drawn that historical research is always *open,* and this because its starting point lies in the present, which is always changing. Today is the yesterday of tomorrow. The datum moves together with the process that a new datum will appear tomorrow. Besides, historical research is always capable of discovering new links in the process or new meanings which had not been considered before. The economic analysis of history, for example, created a new conception; it showed how various data could be understood in a new light by noting their connection with a specific meaning of the process. Historical *knowledge* is thus open in principle since it always has to cognize an emerged datum and the datum, having a plurality of meanings, may be understood in various ways. Historical knowledge is open because it directs its attention toward the past and because it tries to connect an objective crystallization with a process. Historical *process* is open because it expands toward the future, toward a dimension of time, the content of which does not yet exist. The openness of the process is inherent; the openness of research is characteristic of its methods.

We may conclude from this analysis that there can be no identity between historical knowledge and historical process. This result can be summed up in the following points:

a. The two have different time directions.

b. The two have different loci. The locus of the process is reality, the locus of knowledge is method. The method converts the process into a methodological means.

c. The process is open toward the future; historical knowledge is convergent in the present and open toward new interrelations in the past. Knowledge is open toward the past, which is ontologically closed.

d. The process is broad. Research contracts it and then constructs a quasi process not identical with the actual. There is both a difference in time and locus and an interaction of content between res gestae and their narration.

7. This description of both the tension and the interaction between both sides of the term "history" is to be stressed and supplemented from another point of view by an analysis of the architectonic structure of the two sides of history.

In each we may distinguish three strata: *a*) *data; b*) *function* or the activity in its specific nature, and *c*) *meaning* or the chief content of that aspect. To apply this distinction to historical knowledge we may say that the datum of historical knowledge is the *document*. Its function is the *apparatus* of *concepts* employed (for instance, time, the principles of causality, reciprocity—in sum, the concepts which an epistemological analysis lays down as the presuppositions and tools of historical knowledge). The meaning is what historical consciousness discovers to be the meeting between past and present. Historical knowledge explains the datum by using the functional apparatus in order to find out how the present is determined by the past. The guide in the search for the meeting of the past and the present is truth, whatever its definition, as the highest principle of knowledge, including historical knowledge.

On the other hand we find in the structure of historical occurrences the following strata: *a*) the *data*, such as deeds and acts of the historical agents, individual or social; *b*) the *function* or the activity which shapes the deeds, lending them their actual form as political, economic, etc., acts (what was previously called objectivations)—more specifically a war, a diplomatic action, the fact of unemployment, etc., and lastly, *c*) a *meaning* of the historical process which is always related to the end toward which the process directs itself, that is to say the end which makes the shaped activity instrumental in the process of realizing the *future* or creating a situation which for the process is always a future situation. Historical process thus builds the future by deeds which get their content from the interaction of the process and the situation which is the end to be achieved. The activity of shaping (objectivation) and attaching specific contents to acts is the bridge between the act as sheer act and the

eventual end. These features of the respective spheres of
history can perhaps be better exhibited in the form of a
chart.

Strata	*Knowledge*	*Process*
DATUM	Document	Deeds
FUNCTION	The apparatus of concepts	Objectivation
MEANING	The meeting between the past and the present	Intention toward the future

From this chart it is evident that

a. In the sphere of meaning there is no coincidence between knowledge and process. One faces the past, the other is projected into the future.

b. There is a coincidence between the datum of research and the function or activity of the process, because the shaping of the deed in the process turns the deed into the datum of knowledge. If the deed remained within the domain of mere subjectivity, i.e. if it did not shape itself into matter, laws, manners, war, etc., it would be altogether impossible to turn it into an object of research and to deal with it from the point of view of research. Historical reality would in this case be a reality of monads which understood—or perhaps would not understand—themselves and themselves only. Therefore we may say that the objectivations create the data, or alternatively that they *are* the data, of historical research. *From the point of view of research, objectivations cease to be functions (of the process) and become data (for knowledge).*

c. The deed, which is the datum in the sphere of process, does not appear in the sphere of knowledge. Historical knowledge supposes, as a methodological assumption based on the analogy drawn from introspective experience, that beyond the datum the deed exists as an actual event. But this actual event is only a *background* or reservoir of the datum; it is not inherent, let alone apparent, in the datum itself as a factor of the datum as such. By means of the apparatus of concepts we try to understand the datum as an objectivation resting ultimately on a deed. The deed as such, being the datum of a process, is not given as a datum for knowledge; it is a methodological assumption, such as would explain not the content of the datum but its very existence. It points to the fact that historical research is semi-self-sufficient. But beyond this realm lies the realm of the process which is not patent as it is but rather taken for granted because it provides the factum of the datum. To be sure, this presupposition is not made for the sake of understanding the nature of the datum as it stands. It is presupposed once we turn our eyes from the confined realm of research to the complementary aspect of the process.

Thus the bridge between historical research and historical process is stretched out only into that part in which objectivations become data, or rather are conceived as data, because to be a datum is a status assigned by historical conception and not one inherent in the process itself. But even here objectivation does not maintain its quality as an active shaping; it becomes a crystallized datum. The crystallizable becomes crystallized. Nevertheless the objectivation is still the meeting ground of the two spheres comprised by the term "history"; there is no other meeting ground between them. Therefore, as was pointed out above, historical knowledge cannot be adequate to the process. The spheres meet one another in one sector only. This partial meeting is decisive insofar as it establishes the two meanings of the concept "history" as two sides of one and the same coin. This meeting makes history conceivable and makes conception open to the process. Still, as against this narrow meeting, there is always a tension between the two sides of "history" and a semi-independence of each one of them.

8. By saying that historical research is an explanation of the document as a datum in the present, an explanation carried out by connecting the present with the past, stress is placed on another feature of historical knowledge. The meeting between the present and the past is actually a two-directional meeting. Assuming that the essence and the task of historical knowledge are to discover how the past determines the present and what this past is, we have also assumed that its essence is to discover how the past determines the present which is searching for the past—that is to say its own past. The present directs us to determine the nature of the past which determined it. The meeting between past and present involves a mutual determination.

From the point of view of its "narration," history is seen to have the shape of an ellipse with two focal points, one in the past, the other in the present. While the historical process has one direction only, i.e. toward the future, historical research, because of its enclosure in an ellipse, has two directions. History is immanently *tradition*, if the concept of tradition is understood in its basic meaning, though this meaning is not always clearly evident in everyday discourse and even in traditionalistic pronunciamentos. As a matter of fact tradition does not connote a simple and passive *determinability* and *determinateness* of the present by the past. This determination by the past needs, moreover presupposes, an active consciousness in the present, i.e. an acknowledgment by the present that it is in fact determined by the past, an acknowledgment which also admits on its own part the value of the past as the determining factor. Fundamentally the present is not only a passive object of influence but also a selective focus and acknowledging factor. Its activity is bound to reveal itself in the interplay characteristic of tradition—that between the past and the present. In tradition we realize the status of an activity as inherent in the position of the two inter-related factors of historical consciousness, both past and present.

This consciousness actually comprises two kinds of re-lationship between the present and the past: nearness and distance. The past determines and shapes the present, and from this angle the two are close together. But the present must also be independent of and in that respect distant from the past, for it is the present which chooses its own specific past and turns to it for understanding of itself and of the past as well. Since an ontological approximation between the past and the present is precluded because of the flow in time, historical knowledge tries to bridge the gap between the two dimensions of time by the only available, i.e. the methodological, device. Yet it is clear that the bridge erected over the gulf remains one within con-sciousness only. There is no way of getting outside the realm of consciousness to touch the past, as it were, immediately. Tradition maintains a relationship between the different and distant dimensions of time. It establishes this relation-ship in such a way that the past determines the present while the present in turn faces the past. It creates a back-ground of constructed simultaneity and inherence, though there is still a real gap of temporal succession, where the pres-ent succeeds the past and cannot in reality be simultaneous with it.

No other way is open to historical research than to assume a past which has determined and is actually in-volved in the present. This past is not the past in general and cannot be abstract. It is composed of *institutions and events* in the past which are encountered in the present or whose traces are discernible there. The inherence of the past in the present is not due to the flow of time as time but to the events occupying time. These are dealt with in historical research as being close to the present in spite of a position in time which makes them distant.

Practical historical research, resting on and guided, as it is, by historical consciousness, turns to the *meaning* of the past and not to its existence. But the meaning of the past cannot be found out without knowing the meaning of the present, that is to say without the turn of the present to the past in search of its meaning in its relation to the present. Thus we come back to the mutual determination of the dimensions of time. There is some analogy to aesthetics, where we have to assume "the aesthetic experience" as an integral component of the aesthetic domain. Not only must the reality of the objects or the status of aesthetic value be assumed but the reality of the subject directed toward the object must be presupposed as well. What is called aesthetic enjoyment is the product of a meeting of these two. The aesthetic resonance is the expression and the indication of the fact that the meeting of the two correlates took place. Similarly in history not only the past, as the object constituting the framework of the domain, but the present too, as the locus of the subject directed toward the object, is presupposed. There is a kind of historical resonance which is the expression of the meeting of the historical correlates.

This resonance is not an accidental and additional feature of the domain of history but an essential component of it. If this meeting between the past and the present took place in the sphere of actual occurrences there would be no room for a tension between the dimensions of time. In the sphere of occurrence there is a relationship in a single direction only, due to the irreversibility of time, from the past to the present. But since this meeting between the past and the present takes place in the sphere of consciousness, or a sphere established by it, the meeting becomes a meeting in two directions. Various definitions of the nature of history like, for example, Huizinga's: "History is the intellectual form in which a civilization renders account to itself on its past," [5] rest implicitly on this idea of the mutual determination of the past and the present, i.e. in the last resort on the idea of tradition.

The historical process is an everlasting stream. Here we find deeds based on decisions shaped by contents and projecting a future. Each single occurrence, because it rests on decision, is entitled to look at itself (as far as it reflects on itself) as a new start. If we consider this process from "within" we find ourselves in a domain which is not continuous; it is a domain of individuated decisions or events. Historical knowledge tries to overcome these interruptions. It tries to discover continuity by determining the causes of the decisions. It can do this because it *constructs* the continuity by its own means. The tension between res gestae and their narration thereby becomes eventually a tension between the unceasing stream and tradition, between nonrecurrent decisions and the mutual determination of aspects of time, between the individuated deeds and the embracing context of meaning. This tension can never be neutralized, let alone abolished.

9. The domain of history, since it involves tension between process and consciousness, has meaning only as a domain related to man qua being possessing consciousness. There is, strictly speaking, no history of nature, for nature is not conscious of itself and does not integrate subject and object in one and the same domain. The objectivations of nature do not and cannot become data of a historical

5. "A Definition of the Concept of History," included in *Philosophy and History, Essays Presented to Ernst Cassirer*, ed. by R. Klibansky and H. J. Paton, Oxford, Clarendon Press, 1936.

consciousness of nature itself. The objectivations, if we are to use this term at all, are carried out by nature, but they are contemplated by man who as a thinking being stands vis-à-vis nature and is not a sheer fact of nature. Consciousness reflecting on nature is the consciousness of an intelligent being and hence, at least partially, a detached being. In contrast to this the consciousness investigating history is a consciousness of history itself, because the intelligent being produces history by deeds and considers and contemplates it by reason and reflection. In spite of the fact that consciousness is placed in the historical process it is still consciousness and as such is not entirely of the process. Consciousness stands vis-à-vis nature but it stands also vis-à-vis history. Nature is given, and from the human point of view history is given too. Consciousness is never totally submerged in what is given, even when the given domain is a human one, history, and even when it entails consciousness in itself precisely because it is human. This is one of the weaknesses of the historicist interpretation of history, for it considers consciousness and reason as being wholly a part of the process to which consciousness refers.[6]

To deal with history one must assume initial identity between subject and object. It is the human present (subject) which turns to the human past (object) to decipher it and to understand it. The individual historian acts in the human present and his task is to know the human past. Yet history is a paradoxical domain, because in spite of there being the initial and fundamental ontological identity between subject and object there is still a gap between the two. The fundamental identity does not automatically safeguard the understanding of the object by the subject and the success of the task performed by the subject. The

6. For the problem of historicism see Leo Strauss, *Natural Right and History*, Chicago, 1953.

gap in terms of knowledge exists in spite of the ontological identity. The ontological identity even makes the feeling of the gap sharper, precisely because the knowing subject is aware of the fact that the object is his own and that he is related to it. The identity is a background but not an immanent component of the meeting in the domain of knowledge. The identity poses the problem which is by no means the solution. Furthermore, consciousness will never catch up with the stream of the process because the stream is not part of the horizon of consciousness. And conversely, the stream will never submerge consciousness, because consciousness always retains its sovereignty. This is so in spite of the fact that both process and consciousness are two aspects of one single unit—history.

CHAPTER 2

OBJECTIVITY

1. THE TENSION between the two aspects of history poses the problem of the objectivity of historical knowledge. Since the two aspects are semi-independent and the meeting between them can never be total in the sense that they become necessarily mutually dependent, the question as to the meaning of objective historical knowledge must arise.

Let us begin our analysis of this problem with a short summary of the idea of objectivity as it has been formulated within critical philosophy, because this idea can guide us in our investigations in the field of history. The approach of critical philosophy is pertinent to the discussion of the objectivity of historical knowledge for one main reason: Critical philosophy places objectivity between the knower and the known. Since, as shown in Chapter 1, history is essentially linked with the question of the relation between the knower and the known, the critical approach to objectivity is a natural starting point for the discussion of history.

From the criticist point of view we may distinguish between two aspects of our problem:

a. The problem of objectivity as the problem of validity of knowledge, resting on the reference and application of a concept to material supplied by sensibility or intuition. "Nothing is really given us save perception and the em-

pirical advance from this to other possible perceptions." [1]
The first question to be asked is, How can knowledge be
valid if it rests on the relation between concepts and perceptions and on an advance from perception to perception,
while perceptions as such are neither valid nor invalid?

b. The second aspect of the problem of objectivity
is connected with "the possibility of experience" in its two
connotations: When Kant speaks of experience he implies
both an individual experience of this or that particular
individual, and also things or occurrences possible in experience in general. Knowledge is objective if experience
qua contact with the datum verifies it. But verification
at once releases any single item of knowledge of one
particular individual from its isolation and integrates it
in the context of possible experience, "being mere representations, which as perceptions can mark out a real object
only in so far as the perception connects with all others
according to the rules of the unity of experience." [2] The
idea of objectivity is thus linked with the idea of the
relationship between the concept and the material given
by perception, and the problem involved in this idea is
implied in the problematic nature of this very relationship.
It is also linked with the question whether and to what extent an embracing unity of concepts and percepts forming
the whole of possible experience in terms of objective
knowledge is possible altogether. There are thus two steps
in providing objectivity according to this view: the step
from concept to percept, and the step from the synthesis of
concepts and percepts in an individual case to the whole
of knowledge which embraces the individual case and yet

1. Kant, *Kritik der reinen Vernunft* (2d. ed. Riga, 1787), p. 521; English
trans. by Kemp Smith, *Critique of Pure Reason* (London, Macmillan,
1933), p. 441.
2. *Ibid.*, p. 523; English trans., p. 442.

transcends it and establishes the nonindividual realm of experience qua knowledge proper as "objective knowledge."

In terms of Kant's approach the *idea* of objectivity is at once the *problem* of objectivity. We have to analyze the way Kant suggests solving the problem in its aspect of the reference of concepts to percepts and in its aspect of integration in possible experience. It seems that the suggested solution can be summed up as follows:

a. Critical philosophy assumes the fundamental intentionality of the concept toward the material given by perception; it takes concept and percept to be heterogeneous, final, and irreducible elements. The possibility of a common source of the two elements is only reluctantly envisaged by Kant and does not help solve the actual problem of knowledge. This possibility of a hidden unity does not explain the actual relationship encountered in knowledge proper between the distinguished and heterogeneous factors as such. The assumption of the contact of the elements is the starting point of the epistemological analysis. It is of the nature of concepts to be capable of dealing with the percepts. This nature is in a way inexplicable or at least taken for granted. As such it provides the basis of the contact between the elements. This conception points to what may be considered as a limited superiority of the conceptional elements in the total synthesis.

b. The validity of knowledge qua synthesis rests on supposedly valid concepts. The contribution of the concepts to the synthesis lies in their validity, as the contribution of perception lies in providing the datum. Knowledge as a synthesis derives its validity from the validity of the concepts, although knowledge contains both concepts and percepts. Knowledge is more than concepts yet concepts make it valid knowledge.

To put it differently, the problematic nature of the validity of empirical knowledge is inherent in the fact that concepts render validity to a knowledge which is a synthesis of both concepts and percepts. The problematic nature of empirical knowledge lies therefore in the very fact that it is an *empirical* knowledge. It lies in the nature of the contact of the elements and in the impossibility of deducing one of the elements from the other, or of justifying the contact of them through some third element outside both. The problematic nature of this kind of knowledge lies in the fact that this knowledge which *demands validity* is based on a contact which in itself is *not validated*. Here the difference between mathematical and empirical knowledge becomes apparent. In mathematical knowledge the very fact that the object is constructed by thought guarantees the validity of that object, since validity is a feature of thought as such; in empirical knowledge it is thought which extends validity to a synthesis of both thought and percept.

Critical philosophy is based on the assumption that although the material or the percept is an indispensable element of valid knowledge, it is not *this* element which makes knowledge valid. The validity of knowledge is provided by the concept, as an element of stability and unity. The superiority of the conceptual elements stems *a*) from its intrinsic ability to deal with what is not conceptual and *b*) from its being the element of stability and one-meaning-ness. As such it provides the stability of knowledge, that is to say transforms the unstable datum into a stable item in the possible experience. The main point is to retain the difference of the elements and still unite them through the means provided by the element of concepts. Empirical knowledge is a synthesis but not a shifting process of inter-changeability between the elements composing this synthesis. Both the permanence of the distinction and the relation established between the distinct elements are essential.

The element of stability must be inherent in any objective statement. The only question which can be raised is whether this element is due to the datum *referred to* in the statement or else due to the concept *referring* in the statement. This question as far as history is concerned has been decided beforehand by the very nature of history. In history the conceptual element inherent in the statement of the historian deals with the past and ties up the datum with the past; only through the conceptual element does the past appear on the horizon. The superiority of the conceptual element is established by its dynamic-active-selective-interpreting position. The datum itself cannot provide stability because the datum needs interpretation and needs the establishment of the relationship with its explaining past. To put it differently, precisely because the datum is in the present and the past is hypothetically constructed for its sake, the datum cannot guarantee the meaningfulness of the statement referring to it. Since an objective statement is necessarily a meaningful one, and since meaningfulness of historical knowledge is due to concepts, objective statements can obtain their objective character only from concepts.

The question is whether concepts involved in historical knowledge provide stability besides providing meaningfulness.

2. The attempt to apply the concept of objectivity and its basis to historical knowledge, as proposed by critical philosophy, raises some complicated questions. The concept does not here validate knowledge, nor does it guarantee that a synthesis will be stable and united. The historical process has a meaning of its own; it is a projection into the future.

Historical knowledge, which is concerned with historical processes and which produces a construction of concepts, therefore deals with a content which is meaningful in itself and thus is only quasi, i.e. not fully, material. It does not make a statue from a shapeless stone, but rather converts, as it were, one statue into another. The very nature of history depends on a specific correlation between historical process and historical consciousness. We cannot go outside the boundaries of this correlation. To cross these boundaries is to pass beyond the "universe of discourse" of historical knowledge altogether.

Two questions arise.

a. Objective knowledge becomes objective through its relation to a given material; it becomes valid through a concept providing unity and stability for the material. Can the concept which appears in historical knowledge also be regarded as providing the element of validity, in the sense of stability and unity, to the extent that the statement has one meaning only and can be regarded as valid without taking into consideration the time perspective of its emergence; or is historical knowledge, as a knowledge of a datum possessing a meaning of it own, a pendulum moving between concept and datum?

b. The quasi material (the process) of historical knowledge has a meaning of its own because of its fundamental feature of being directed toward the future and thus realizing an end. What happens to this meaning at the moment when the process ceases to be a process projecting into the future and becomes the material of a historical-conceptual analysis? There is a connection between these two questions which will be elaborated further.

3. An analysis of the status of the concept vis-à-vis the historical material and a consideration of the nature of the synthesis constituting historical knowledge leads us to

a distinction between three types, or levels, of concepts.

a. *Categories.* For instance, substance, causality—found in historical knowledge qua knowledge in general, without the qualification of its being historical. These categories are inherent in knowledge as such, and they hold good in history because they are fundamental in any branch of knowledge. Yet we may ask the question as to the relation between these various categories and the specific nature of historical knowledge. In spite of the question as to their specific application, the general assumption is that historical knowledge qua knowledge rests upon formal and transcendental principles.

b. *Laws.* There is in various branches of knowledge a level of material laws, like the law of gravitation in physics. We have to deal with the question of whether laws of this sort also exist in history. The two problems, that of categories and laws, are related but not identical and will be expounded in detail in the last chapter of this book.

c. *Applied concepts.* The content of any work of historical research is a product of categories, used explicitly or not, and of a concrete description of a fragment in terms of time and meaning. As such, any piece of historical research describes these fragments of the process not only by taking advantage of categories like causality, and of laws if any, but also by employing concepts like state, revolution, class, industry, occurrences, personality, drives, etc. It is the unity of all these aspects which shapes the character of the particular historical work. This unity, because it is a unity, can be analyzed and the elements of which it is composed can be shown to be of different levels, starting from the level of categories to that of the concepts, sociological, psychological, biographical, etc., pointing to the various features of the historical item under consideration or describing the act of an individual historical agent. In a historical analysis of an event, for example the Civil War, we find these various and different levels of concepts united and constituting the historical description of that event. This composition of concepts at their various levels is the work of the individual historian and partakes of the nature of his intellectual and imaginative grasp. It is certainly one (at least one) of the reasonable criteria of an evaluation of a piece of historical research whether or not these different levels of concepts have actually merged or whether there is rather a discrepancy, let us say, between the assumption of causality and a lack of psychological understanding of the historical agents. The balanced employment of the different levels of concepts, the simultaneous use of them, accounts for the success or failure of the research. Hence where we find an overstress of one of the levels, as for example in Marxist literature, where the causative factor or structure is emphasized over against the different factors involved in the process, there is a lack of an organic unity of the concepts. The organic unity has then to find its concrete embodiment in the particular piece of historical research. Where there is no unity of that kind, historical research—as again in Marxist literature—becomes a repetition of categories or pseudo categories, or (as in impressionistic writings about history, common in essays on historical personalities) it involves an employment of biographical data without a grounding in the fundamental concepts represented by categories. The consideration of the objective character of the historical work is imperative because for all practical purposes of an epistemological analysis the work of research represents knowledge as it appears in concreto. The problem of objectivity is not solved by a validition of principles and categories. The establishment of that validity is at most the first—to be sure, fundamental—step. Objectivity has to be assigned to a concrete statement. It is here where the question is asked and where the scrutiny takes place. This is the case in physics and in biology where objectivity is assigned or denied to a concrete statement about velocity or a family of flowers. The objectivity of the concrete historical statement, that created by the synthesis of the concepts in their various levels and their reference to a datum—this objectivity has to be examined. The assumption of validity of causality in history, for instance, does not solve the problem of whether World War I was caused by imperialism or not. Validity of principles and categories may be a condition for assigning objectivity to historical statements but is not a fulfillment of objectivity.

Yet what happens in the last analysis is that historical research, representing and embodying this unity of concepts, shifts or is shifted by definition from the domain of concepts to the domain of process and thus loses its genuine character as an activity of concepts. We may formulate our problem in other words as well: The theories of physics and chemistry do not belong to the material domain of physics or chemistry. In contradistinction to this, historical research itself becomes a part or an element of historical process, becoming eventually a historical document, in spite of the fact that it was a conceptual reflection on documents in the first place. The works of Thucydides and Flavius, Tacitus and Gibbon, Ranke and Graetz, which, viewed from their own positions, are expressions of historical consciousness, have themselves become historical documents. Their works have ceased to be *correlative* factors of the process and have become *parts* of the process itself. It is not only that we consider the historical works from the point of view of the history of historiography (here no difference exists between history and physics because we are entitled to consider the theories of physics from the point of view of the history of science), but we treat historical works of research as data for subsequent historical research. They become virtually related to the individual historian and are related to his position within the domain of the historical process. This is an important feature of historical research insofar as this kind of research preserves the individual character of the historian. But precisely because the individual historian counts he and his work become part of the process dealt with in his research. As an individual he withdraws from the process to write history, but an individual and his work are considered to be part of the process he attempted to withdraw from. He has withdrawn by the very fact that he has written a piece of historical research. Yet his work ultimately creates a plane *in* the process though it attempted to be and was for a while a plane reflecting *on* process. In history concepts thus become data, i.e. the research itself becomes a datum and hence a datum for further research. Thucydides is part of Greek history though he is also—and from his own point of view was—a historian. The subsequent author integrates historical research with the historical subject matter, though the distinction between the two is retained insofar as they are differences within the totality of the process. Process was understood and reflected in research but research then submerges in its subject matter.

This is not an accidental movement, since it results from the very structure of historical consciousness. "Practice," the dynamics of the deeds which produces the historical process and expresses itself in the various objectivations, continues to exist. Therefore every theoretical reflection when understood from a more advanced aspect, which in the historical context means only from a *later* one, is considered as an objectivation of practice and not only as an expression of reflection. The theoretical reflection itself is understood,

from a later point of view, as a deed, and qua deed it belongs
to the process in spite of its being a cognitive deed. Here we
encounter the dialectical structure of history: Historio-
graphical work is theoretical-reflective work. From its own
position it is understood as such; viewed from its own position it constitutes a correlate of the process. But the reflection of historical consciousness at a later stage looks
at the previous reflection not as at a reflection placed in
opposition to the process but as a reflection *emerging* from
the process and integrated in it. Consciousness in its later
stage conceives consciousness in its previous stage not as a
correlate of the process but as a part of the whole process.
Historical reflection becomes a datum because the process
continues to exist and in its existence carries with itself the
former historical reflection and incorporates it in the process. But this shift of the reflection to the domain of datum
is again an act of consciousness. Historical reflection becomes a datum itself due to the work of historical reflection
which continues to work and to accomplish the very act of
reflection, i.e. the turning of the process into a datum. This
continuous regrouping serves as further evidence of the
problematic character of the historical sphere. As a matter
of principle the characteristic feature of this domain lies
in the correlation between the process and consciousness. But
in actual fact there is no possibility of maintaining this distinction in concreto, or at least as a stable and clear-cut
distinction. From the point of view of principle this distinction holds good, since there is a fundamental difference
between past and future or between practice building
up the future and theory reflecting on it. But from the
concrete point of view this distinction is not stable or fixed,
since the boundaries between the past and the future, and
hence between practice and theory, are constantly changing.
These boundaries are determined from time to time by

changing perspectives. The distinction between consciousness and process does not become an actual distinction save in the act of living cognition. But at the moment when consciousness expresses itself in an objectivation of content, i.e. in a description in terms of a historical work instead of remaining only a reflection, it makes itself into a datum, or at least is capable of being a datum. Reflection tries to reach the process but unfortunately becomes submerged in it. This submersion is recognized again by reflection at a later stage. There always remains a surplus on both sides. The process perpetually absorbs consciousness in itself, but consciousness in turn recognizes and acknowledges this absorption.

Now to sum up this part of our discussion of the problem of objectivity in the domain of history. The standard of objective knowledge is as suggested by critical philosophy, based on a clear-cut distinction between the conceptual and the perceptual. The latter is part of the data. The conceptual element which stands vis-à-vis this perceptual element, being for the perceptual an element coming from the outside or from above, provides for the stability of that element. But in historical knowledge there is no permanent distinction between the element of concept qua cognition of a process and the element of process as a datum for cognition. The piece of historical research, though it is intrinsically a piece of knowledge referring to the process, turns out to be a part of the very process. History itself compels us to integrate the embodiment of knowledge in the historical process. The distinction between the poles becomes an ephemeral one; there is therefore no point in stressing the objectivity of knowledge when the very knowledge itself becomes a datum. As a datum it stands for a further, i.e. later, act of knowledge. In a sense we may say that it is the power of a historical cognition that it ceases to be re-

flection only and becomes a part of the process. This is a
one-way movement; process as such does not become
reflection, but reflection is both reflection and process. This
movement explains the often stressed ideological fact that
historical consciousness in itself is a historical factor. Reflection is not only a deed in a metaphorical sense; it is a
deed in a real ontological sense. Yet historical knowledge
pays a forfeit for its nature as a deed: It loses its character
as an independent domain. It becomes a historical factor
as knowledge but not as objective knowledge, that is to say
as knowledge which retains its position vis-à-vis the known
subject matter.

4. Husserl describes the method of psychologism in the
following statement: "The organization itself is an object,
a part of this development; therefore if we want to explain
and to determine the fundamentals of the world, we presuppose it in the idea of our own organization . . . Thus
we are playing a curious game; from the world man develops;
from man the world; God creates man and man creates
God." [3] Following Husserl's description we may say that
historical knowledge develops from the process and returns
to it, and in doing so ceases to be knowledge, at least knowledge alone. This oscillation of historical knowledge, if
considered from the point of view of the general theory of
objectivity, can be described as a *psychologism* transferred
to the plane of history. The usual psychologism converts
facts into concepts by turning psychic acts into categories
or by making categories into psychic facts. In the domain
of history one finds concepts turned into facts. Here we
envisage the paradox inherent in the problem of the objectivity of historical knowledge: Vico and those who continued along his line of thought, including Hegel, Marx,

3. E. Husserl, *Logische Untersuchungen* (Halle, M. Niemeyer, 1913),
1, 121.

Croce, and Collingwood, have tried to base the very possibility of historical knowledge on the identity of subject and object. But two obstacles prevent this identity from serving as the basis for the objectivity of historical knowledge.

a. There is no identity between subject and object from the point of view of methods, because reflection and process are distinct.

b. An identity of reflection and process actually exists for the object but not for the subject. Reflection eventually becomes process, and only through this change are the correlates included in one and the same region. Thus insofar as an identity *exists* between subject and object there is no *knowledge* of an object. The objectivity of historical knowledge, insofar as it depends upon concepts, is always attacked by the object invading the sphere of the historical subject and hence the sphere of the concepts. In history the power of the historical object, which inundates knowledge, shakes the possibility of objectivity in the sense that knowledge has to be considered as dealing with the object in a defined way and not as making itself its own object of study. Herein lies the power of the historical process, in that it invades knowledge and levels knowledge to the plane of the object, i.e. to its being part of the process. A historical description which knows from the outset that it will be part of the process must be cautious and humble in its pretension to be objective, adequate, stable, and an accepted expression of knowledge. Yet it is knowledge in general, or reflection, which knows this fundamental limitation of historical knowledge. There is a kind of superiority in historical knowledge as it becomes a historical deed. But there is a greater superiority of knowledge, i.e. reason and reflection, which transcends both historical process and historical knowledge, confining the latter to the domain of history and preventing it from pretending to be identical with knowledge in general. Historical knowledge carries in itself the recognition of its fundamental limitation and not, as it is now fashionable to say, the imperative to surpass history or to make whatever is, and is known, into history. A critique of historical consciousness means here the delimitation of the boundaries of this consciousness.

To put it differently, the objectivity of knowledge, as pointed out before, depends on the transcendence of the concepts beyond mere reference to the given perceptions as data, and on the integration of a single item of knowledge into the whole of knowledge. As against this we have to emphasize that the objectivity of historical knowledge is shaken, because the concepts used by it not only go beyond the limits of the concepts and are directed to the data but are eventually submerged in the data. The totality into which the single work of knowledge is integrated is the totality of objects and not the totality of knowledge, though there is a totality of historical knowledge as the sum total of the factual and possible historical research and information. Yet this sum total, being on the one hand correlative to the totality of the historical objects, becomes on the other hand a part of those very objects, because a later historical understanding of a former expression of historical understanding, as formulated in a piece of research, becomes part of the understood process. Objectivity is meaningful only when a concept points to something different from itself and establishes through its contact with the different element a heterogeneous synthesis. The overcoming of the distinction between concepts and data undermines the very basis of the objectivity of knowledge. Objectivity is meaningful within a knowledge where the elements are related though different. But in historical knowledge there is an identity of the elements in the realm of the object. Objective knowledge erects a bridge from the end of knowledge itself; in history the object *absorbs* the concepts whose function it was to conceive that object.

5. The common criticism against the objectivity of historical knowledge, a criticism appearing in a number of variations, is that this knowledge conceives its object from a partial and determined angle, which is not and cannot be absolute or at least all-embracing. The underlying principles of this alleged perspectivism are usually not elucidated. An elucidation of the dialectic inherent in historical knowledge is first needed, and it may throw some light on the idea of historical perspective and its precise meaning.

F. Medicus rightly remarked [4] that all knowledge, including that of natural science, is knowledge from a specific perspective. Chemistry understands the organism from the viewpoint of its material structure, biology understands the organism from that of its anatomic and physiological structure, while physics conceives of it from the viewpoint of the dynamics of its material elements, etc. Each branch of knowledge is then connected with a specific meaning and this meaning establishes its specific perspective. In other words, this meaning defines the essence of the branch of knowledge and determines the direction of the research work conducted in it. The question therefore arises as to the characteristic feature of the historical perspective proper, if perspective connotes the confinement of the cognitive concern to a particular angle and interest. What are the specific differences between this perspective and

4. "Definition of History" in the above-mentioned volume, *Philosophy and History*. Cf. the discussion of "the perspective theory" in W. H. Walsh, *An Introduction to Philosophy of History* (London, 1951), p. 112. We are not dealing here with Nietzsche's theory of perspectives.

those of other branches of knowledge? I shall try to answer this question from two points of view and thus elaborate the main idea expounded hitherto.

a. The perspective of historical knowledge is determined by the *time* in which the concrete historical knowledge takes place, or by the time of the emergence of the content through which we consider the process. It is not linked up with elements of content only—i.e. it is not merely restricted to the points of view of political, economic, religious history—nor even with the fact that the time in which the research takes place determines which of the various perspectives chosen is most relevant. The chief point lies in the fact that historical knowledge is linked up with a perspective in terms of a *dimension* of time, a dimension which is directed toward the past. Historical knowledge, as clarified above, makes the present its focus. Thus historical knowledge imposes on itself the provisionality of its perspective, because the perspective of this knowledge is not and cannot be stable and well-defined forever; today is tomorrow's yesterday. The perspective of historical knowledge is one of a *moment* and therefore not a stable perspective at all. This provisionality is a result of splitting up the process and making it convergent, a convergence which is constructed and imposed. Historical knowledge is linked up with a momentary, nonpermanent perspective and is therefore not immunized against the everlasting process which deletes, as it were, a given perspective and makes it a part of itself. Historical perspective is due to the invasion of the background or main coordinate of historical knowledge, i.e. time, into the body of historical knowledge itself. In a way we may say that the perspective of historical knowledge is more fundamental than any of the perspectives in terms of material content characteristic of the different branches of knowledge. It is a perspective rooted in the principal plane of human existence, i.e. time. Since we are in time we have a historical interest, the establishment of the relationship between past and present, and we are driven to our interest in this relationship precisely because every present moment is turned into past and becomes a riddle for us in both dimension and meaning. But historical knowledge pays a price for its fundamental perspective, the price of not retaining the clear-cut distinction between itself and what is known by and in it. Since historical perspective is rooted in historical interest, which is in turn rooted in the nature of time, historical perspective itself stands for historical knowledge. Historical knowledge expresses itself in partial works of knowledge and these become part of the historical past. Historical knowledge emerging in its own present becomes a part of the past and its time position is fundamental to it. This leads to the second point.

b. In historical knowledge one dimension of time reviews the previous one. Time contemplates itself; the process reflects upon itself. The perspective becomes part of the process and here, as stressed above, we encounter the difference between historical knowledge and the knowledge of natural sciences.

Here we have to come back to our starting point: The objectivity of historical knowledge lacks a foundation not because it is a fragmentary knowledge but because it lacks a *minimum* of objectivity, i.e. a stable differentiation between knower and known. Historical knowledge cannot be objective because its assertions are not stable and do not remain in the plane of assertions only, but ultimately become part of the plane of the asserted facts.

This does not mean that historical knowledge does not face the question of objectivity—as far as it is knowledge it faces the standard of knowledge, that of adequately referring to its subject matter. The characteristic feature is not the lack of the standard or a disregard for it but the impossibility of reaching it. It is important to stress this because the gap between the standard and its attainment precludes the relativistic self-complacency of historical knowledge and historians. The historian who knows that it is the fate of his work to become history cannot treat his work from the perspective of what is ontologically about to happen to his work. The standpoint of his work is that of knowledge and not that of its fate. In his work he must be guided by cognitive criteria and strive for objectivity. Precisely because of the fact that the absence of objectivity is not due to any defect in content, he has to treat his work in terms of content as if objectivity were realizable, i.e. without the view of the historical future of his work. The position in the present gives rise to knowledge, and as there is no way of avoiding the present there is no way of avoiding the imperative inherent in knowledge of the present.

6. Hence it is fallacious to conclude from this analysis that the lack of objectivity in historical knowledge suggests that this knowledge is chaotic and arbitrary. On the contrary, there is room for immanent criticism and preferences within the field of historical knowledge based on well-determined criteria.

a. We can see, in the first place, whether or not the concrete historical research rests on transcendental presuppositions such as causality, reciprocity, etc. or whether the alleged research is only intuitive or artistic. In our age many attempts have been made to write history from a "pneumatic," suprarational point of view, for instance from an exclusively psychological point of view. These attempts are to be criticized in terms of the conceptual foundations of any knowledge as such, historic as well as scientific. Historical knowledge is conceptual and as such rests on conceptual presuppositions, both formal and transcendental. It has been said before that these conceptual presuppositions do not suffice for guaranteeing objectivity of historical knowledge, but they cannot be disregarded.

b. All attempts to place the domain of history in a different ontological domain must be rejected. For example, the attempt to reduce history and its meaningful process to biological or psychological elements must be rejected not only because it annihilates the complexity of meaning of the process but also because it abolishes the very essence of history. This essence requires the interconnection of process and consciousness, the emerging of consciousness from the process and its return to the process. That interconnection is not only the basis for the elucidation of the nature of historical knowledge, it also determines the boundary of the entire field of history by providing guidance in concrete research. Historical knowledge cannot search for explanations beyond the domain of history. It necessarily explains history by history. Biological or physical factors active in history are not active as such, but only if adopted by man in his response to them. They cease to be factors of nature beyond or apart from man and become factors of meaning, because they are shaped and absorbed by man. What really matters here is not the ontological *origin* of the factors but their actual *positions* and effects within the human-historical realm. From the point of view of its actual effect on human life even a landscape becomes a part of history. A reduction of history, therefore, to any quasi-primary domain is not feasible. It is important to stress this precisely because history is a narrower domain than nature and nature is chronologically prior to history. In spite of that history is a semiclosed domain. This aspect of its nature is expressed in the oscillation between process and knowledge, and this oscillation in turn solidly establishes the fact that history is a semiclosed domain.

History is an autonomous domain creating itself. Marx rightly stressed this feature of history. There is no need though to accept his view of the content and nature of the factors acting on the creation of history itself. A historical conception which attributes, for example, a biological rhythm to the historical process is unable to explain the specific structure of the historical domain as a semiclosed domain of interconnection between process and consciousness. Such an interconnection is not to be found either in geography or in biology. It is characteristic of history only, and therefore it can and must be used as a criterion of any concrete historical view. A work of historical research has to be estimated according to its attainment of the immanent explanation of the historical process and according to the density of motives understood as active in the process. The confinement of the immanent motivations provides room for a pluralistic explanation of the process by various driving forces and not always by the same forces. The semiclosed domain of history is an intricate domain.

c. The above two criteria are contained in the presuppositions of historical knowledge. In dealing with concrete pieces of historical research another question arises, that of giving preference to one work over another. A criterion based on principles can be laid down for this task too. The work of concrete research is to be evaluated in terms of the scope of events and facts with which it deals. The standard of research is proportionate to its scope, i.e. to its synoptic view of various branches of activity or, in the case of research done in one field, the comprehensiveness of the picture it provides. If a work deals with the Middle Ages it should give a unified picture of its manifold reality, or if it deals with an individual it should reveal the many complex aspects of his life. Even where the object of the research is limited from a quantitative point of view, the criterion of comprehensiveness is applicable.

Where may we place the justification of this criterion if we take the essence of historical knowledge into account? As a matter of fact, this quasi-technical criterion has its basis in a principle. Historical knowledge is immanently fragmentary. It chooses some qualified events from the process and splits up time by making it convergent in the present. This feature of historical knowledge is essential and necessitates a permanent effort to find a possible counterbalance for it. Just because historical knowledge is essentially limited it must strive toward an ever increasing extension.[5] Just because historical knowledge constructs a series of events and establishes relationships of causes and effects, it must try to make this series as *dense* as possible and the relationships of causes and effects as *continuous* as possible. Historical knowledge is necessarily inadequate and therefore ought to impose on itself the permanent task of striving toward adequacy, in spite of the fact that this adequacy will never be attained. Adequacy is not the ideal of historical knowledge, if by "ideal" we understand an end commensurate with relevant endeavors. But adequacy is the "bad conscience" of historical knowledge. History must always be aware of its necessary limitations as an impetus toward further discoveries of events and their causes. What has been said before about objectivity can be applied *mutatis mutandis* to the idea of adequacy.

In spite of the fact that the strict demands which result from the idea of objectivity cannot be applied to historical knowledge (as they could be applied to the natural

5. On this point cf. R. G. Collingwood, *Speculum Mentis* (Oxford, 1924), p. 231.

sciences), other demands resulting from the very essence
of this knowledge can and must be put forward. Historical
knowledge is subject to the principle of truth. It is a *knowledge*; its assertions are to be measured by a theoretical
standard. The subjection to the principle of truth is the
imperative of the historian because he is engaged in knowledge and not in the envisaging of the fate of his work, as
stated before. He is a historian and not a historian of
himself. Hence though he is subject to the idea of truth as
the guiding idea of knowledge, as that which justifies the
very procedure of knowledge, he is not subject to the
apparatus of objectivity proper set up in the natural sciences
to ascertain truth; the function of this apparatus is to give
phenomena a single meaning and thus to give the propo-
sitions dealing with them a single meaning too. Historical
phenomena cannot have one meaning only, for they are
always in motion and looked at from ever moving perspectives of the respective presents. Historical knowledge must
be measured by the standard of comprehensiveness and
depth—not by the standard of a fixed or unitary meaning.
In terms of the principle of truth this can be stated as follows:
A historical statement has to be true, though it cannot be
totally true. Total truth would be obtained only from the perspective of a present which never ceases to be a present, i.e.
from the end of history. There is this fundamental difference
between a statement which is true though only partially so
and that which is untrue and suggests for its justification the
fact that it is bound to be tied up with the perspective.
Within this perspective of time it has to be true and must
be subject to the very criterion of truth. In the process
of the changing perspectives of the continually disappearing
presents the principle of truth is *the* principle delimiting the
very horizon of any attempt to know things historically.

7. This shortcoming of historical knowledge compared

with scientific knowledge is balanced by an advantage. The historian will perhaps not be consoled by such a balance, but philosophy must bring it to light, at least for its own sake and its own interest. Like philosophy history is different from other branches of knowledge in that it constitutes a problem for itself. It has to determine its own nature. History is necessarily a problem for itself, since its essence lies in the interrelation between the practice directed toward the future and theory directed toward the past, and in the perpetual movement between these interrelated poles. Since historical knowledge is concerned, among other things, with former historical knowledge and considers it as a datum and not as knowledge alone, historical knowledge always mirrors itself. In history there is not only a reflection but also a reflection of reflection. It is irrelevant whether or not this reflection is present in the living consciousness of the historian. This does not mean that we must identify history and philosophy, a view held by Croce and his followers. They arrived at that idea by confining historical knowledge to the content presented in cognition, while ignoring the process of time. It has been shown above that it is precisely for knowledge that the time perspective is essential. But since historical knowledge implies an immanent relation to a moving object and rests on everlasting reflection, it is a knowledge which lies on the threshold of philosophy. History stands between practice and theory. Theory emerges from practice and returns to it, whereupon it is replaced by another theory. There is a history of the process and a history of the knowledge of the process, but there is also a historical relationship between the process and its knowledge. History in its interrelation between practice and theory can be likened to a landscape including both a river and mountains, on the summits of which observation points are located.

Here again an observation with regard to the historicist pretension might be called for. The turning of historical research into a historical datum by no means
implies that reflection or reason in general is only historical,
that is to say determined by the historical situation which
gives rise to the specific historical work. In the first place
we do not stress the fact that the historical reflection is determined by the historical *situation*. We stress the fact that
because it emerges in a present it is bound to submerge
in the ongoing process, as any present must. Thus we stress
the determination of the historical reflection not by historical *content* but by historical *time* in its fundamental,
ontological nature. And in the second place the historicist's
assumption is that there is only historical reflection, that
is to say that reason is historical and hence partial only.
But this analysis attempts to show that research may be
historical in the sense that it becomes integrated post
factum in the process, but neither research nor any particular outlook exhausts reflection and reason. Reason and reflection embody themselves partially in historical research
and get involved in time, but it is a partial embodiment
only. Only reason which can be a datum, that is a particular
historical work, can be looked at as a part of the process
though not determined by it. But reason itself is more than
its expression qua datum.

It has been shown that the background of this interrelation between history and historical research involves
time. Time therefore must be the next subject for analysis.

CHAPTER 3

HISTORICAL TIME

A. A *Priori Time*

THE ELUCIDATION of the nature of historical time ought to be preceded by an analysis of some problems involved in the meaning of the concept of time in general, and in an understanding of its status in knowledge. Since historical time is but a specific concretization of time in general, it is first necessary to clarify the idea of time in general.

1. Time is a *form* of the relation of succession. Form is understood here as the minimum of the meaning inherent in a concept and as a condition of any more specific and hence fuller meaning. As such time as form does not furnish any indication as to just what specific nature this relation of succession has. When referring to a time relation we do not therefore say anything about the nature or manner of succession. It is because time indicates only a relation of succession that it can first be only a *form* of the relation of succession.

Further determinations of time presuppose this general form of succession; each determination of time is arrived at inside the form of succession. Cassirer showed that the theory of relativity (in its starting point and in its conclusions concerning the nature of time) does not change the essence of the notion "time" as a form of succession, nor does it shake its status and validity as a condition of knowledge.[1] The determination of time as, for example, the fourth dimension is possible only through the presupposition of pure time, i.e. time as form. It is a specific understanding of time as such. This amounts to the statement that each qualification of time, i.e. each concrete assertion of time relations, depends upon time as form; it relates to empirical time, empirical being understood here as more particular and as related to a narrow field of application like the field of physics, biology, history, etc. This distinction between specific-empirical and general-formal time will lead us to some relevant conclusions with reference to the problem of historical time. But let us first continue to point out some features of the form of time.

Succession includes two aspects whose union is required if time is to be a concept with a definite content. We must distinguish between the fact of following as such and between the elements which follow one on the other, i.e. between the *relation* of following and between the *terms* which follow. We do not yet say anything about the content and ontological position of the terms in relation, as to whether they are material or spiritual particles, events or ideas, historical institutions or psychic acts, etc. A relation of succession implies related terms. It is impossible to reverse this assertion: From the givenness of some related terms we are unable to arrive at the assumption that they are successive. The related terms can be related in more ways than that of succession. Hence the procedure is in a single direction only; from the givenness of succession we arrive, by explaining the meaning of succession, at the assumption of related terms and not vice versa.

1. E. Cassirer, *Zur Einstein'schen Relativitätstheorie* (Berlin, B. Cassirer, 1921), pp. 75 ff.; English trans. by W. C. and M. C. Swabey in *Substance and Function* (Chicago and London, Open Court Pub. Co., 1923), pp. 409 ff.

By acknowledging the related terms we lay down quasi points (of space, as it were) in the sequence of time. From the point of view of the immanent content of the concept of time we may say only that the very relation of succession necessarily leads to the consideration of a notion of duration, duration meaning a span of time or as Kant says a "magnitude." Duration is involved in succession. Were succession to exhaust the meaning of time there would be no difference between succession and a sequence, say, of natural numbers. Only because there is duration in succession does the character of the time series come to the fore as against any other shape of sequence. We may now assume that time is the form of a relation *between* as well as the form of the occurrence *of* an event and what occurs in that event. The possible separation of events amounts to the idea that not only the series as such but also each of the terms involved in it has a time character. Time is not only collective but distributive as well. Hence we may say that there is succession, that the succession has duration, and that there is duration in each of the succeeding terms.

2. These two aspects of the term "time," i.e. sequence and duration, imply two other aspects as well. Sequence is connected with continuity, duration is connected with discontinuity. The assertion of continuity rests on a prior assertion that there is a transition from one term to another. If, however, we consider not the relationship of sequence but the terms in themselves from the point of view of their duration, we detach them from their continuous succession and make them into discrete points or lines against a background of continuity.[2] To be sure, we do not maintain that discontinuity is a product of a limitation of continuity. We use the distinction in order to throw light on the two

2. See Eduard von Hartmann, *Kategorienlehre* (Leipzig, Hermann Haacke, 1896), p. 73.

sides of the term. We start with continuity as manifested
in succession, and from there we arrive at discontinuity, i.e.
duration, just as we started with the relation and obtained
the related terms from it.

The notion of duration can be applied not only to the
terms in relation but, as already hinted, to succession as
well. It then serves as a principle for measuring time.
The reason for this transition from the terms in relation to
the relation as such is clear. To determine the character
of duration it is necessary to draw lines within which something continues to exist. This drawing of lines can be transferred to the sphere of succession, provided that we think
of a succession between at least two terms. For instance,
the time elapsed between the moment a kettle of water is
put on the fire and the moment it boils is a measure of
the duration of time between the two terms. Each act of
measuring detaches the terms from the whole of time and
puts a certain continuity within boundaries marked by the
two terms, for example the putting of the water on the fire
and the boiling. From this point of view detaching a fragment which is a continuous occurrence in itself, the event in
question, is analogous to the act of detaching a term from the
totality of relations. The very possibility of measuring time
lies in the relation existing between its two aspects, i.e.
between succession and duration. Measurement is the act
of combining duration with succession, or of applying duration to succession.

Duration is thus a precondition for the measurement of
time within a succession between two terms. But it is also
the condition for measuring time within the limits of a
single term as such. Since the term has duration, a basis is
provided for the possibility of measuring it. It is duration
and not succession which offers the epistemological condition and basis for measuring time. Succession as such

can be understood only as a qualitative phenomenon; duration implies a quantitative aspect, or at least can offer a vantage point for a quantitative aspect. This can be put differently: Because duration is a magnitude, a span of time, it has extension and as such lends itself to measurement. The aspect of succession where only the relation is stressed does not lend itself to measurement simply because relation implies a way or a mode of being together and not an extension or span. Only if the togetherness of relation is assumed may we look at the related terms from the point of view of their occupying a position in time, i.e. of the magnitude of time their existence covers.

3. This brief explanation of the meaning and status of duration contains an implicit criticism of Bergson's well-known concept of *durée*. The concept refers to the specific nature of the transition from event to event. As Bergson says, "Duration is the continuous progress of the past which grows into the future and which swells as it advances." [3] And differently, "Prolongation of the past into present." [4] The idea of duration as explained by Bergson stresses the kind of relation composing the succession in time, i.e. the nature of the process in time. It is because of this stress laid on the nature of the process of time qua duration that Bergson identifies duration with "creation of form, the continual elaboration of the absolutely new." [5]

But Bergson actually makes a hasty identification of time with succession and of succession with duration in his sense. He takes the aspect of succession for granted and does not see that, in order to assume that succession is actually manifested in the specific nature of duration, succession

3. Henri Bergson, *Creative Evolution*, authorized trans. by Arthur Mitchell (London, Macmillan, 1911), p. 5.
4. *Ibid.*, p. 17.
5. *Ibid.*, p. 11.

as a formal aspect of time has first to be presupposed.
Because Bergson proceeds to duration overhastily he disregards the priority and the independence of succession.
Only this disregard enables him to present his theory of
time as being a comprehensive one. Actually his theory
is about one of the possible representations of manifestations of time qua succession, where succession acquires
in a specific frame of reference the character of durée. In
his view time appears only as a continuous transition between heterogeneous contents; but precisely such a view as
to the *nature* of transition presupposes the *notion* of succession, that is to say that aspect of time where the aspect
of transition from event to event is implied in its formal
character.

Furthermore, Bergson overstresses the opposition existing between durée and measurement and is oblivious of
the relation of dependence existing between them.[6] Duration involving a span of time involves an aspect of magnitude; hence measurement of time is made possible by the
fundamental nature of time and is preconditioned by it.
It is by no means an opposition to the nature of time, let
alone a deterioration of it. As an operation, measurement
is justified by duration—itself an essential feature of time as
a form. The fact that Bergson fails to distinguish between
formal and material time is responsible for the confusion
characteristic of his view of time. Thus Bergson indirectly
introduces into the conception of time as a form a specific
content that.*may* be in time but is by no means *necessarily*
identical with it. Each specific content must rest on time as
a formal principle and must be conditioned by it. It cannot
serve as a substitute for the form of time. This distinction
will be made clearer from an analysis of some features of
Whitehead's theory of time.

6.·*Ibid.*, pp. 355 ff.

4. Whitehead, who enjoined us "to take time seriously," distinguishes three fundamental categories of time: *a*) supersession, *b*) prehension, *c*) incompleteness.[7] Of these three fundamental categories one, namely supersession, can be regarded as close to the concept of succession clarified above. But there is a difference between succession and supersession. Supersession in Whitehead's view involves the coming to be of one event *in place* of the other; it does not refer to a mere sequence and succession. From the outset Whitehead thus shifts the analysis of the meaning of the concept of time from the domain of form to the domain of content, i.e. the actual process taking place in time. He therefore imposes on time not only the form of succession but the content of a particular succession, that of replacing. The formal analysis had to lead him to imply that a change in content takes place against a background of succession, i.e. that one event supersedes another. Thus supersession involves a qualified determination of the nature of transition in time; here we state what actually happens in the course of this transition. Again there is no epistemological justification for the assumption of an "instead" (supersession), just as there was no justification in Bergson's theory for assuming durée without the presupposition of the form of succession. "After" is the formal minimum, and as such it can—but need not—be understood in particular circumstances as an "instead." But Whitehead erroneously elevates the "instead" to the level of a fundamental category.

The other two fundamental categories pointed out by Whitehead, namely prehension and incompleteness, serve Whitehead in making a most interesting attempt at giving the dimensions of time (past, present, and future) the

7. "Time," in *Proceedings of the Sixth International Congress of Philosophy*, ed. by E. S. Brightman (New York, Longmans, Green, 1927), p. 60.

status of categories, without an explicit description of their character as dimensions of time in their proper sense. Whitehead remarks that "Each occasion is temporal because it is incomplete. . . . Thus the category of incompleteness means that every occasion holds in itself its own future." [8] Incompleteness for him implies continuation, and continuation implies what is about to be. Similarly he takes the past to be prehended in the present and the present to prehend the past. The three aspects inherent in the three fundamental categories are combined. Supersession does not for him annihilate the connection between superseding occasions.

It is clear that the trend of this attempt is to divest the dimensions of time of their possible subjective character, or at least of their being connected with the subjective points of view of the spectators involved, those who determine what is past, present, and future respectively. Whitehead in fact tries to give the dimensions of time a status in terms of categories. But this attempt is possible only through a confusion of form with content, the confusion we found in Bergson too. Whitehead elevates a specific content, which may—but need not—be connected with time, to the level of a category by a procedure which might be called a "filtration" of the dimensions, and thereby gives them nontemporal or objective-ontological features. He deals with prehension and not explicitly with the past, just as he deals with incompleteness and not explicitly with the future. But the form relates to time at its *minimum;* it refers only to succession and duration. Such a minimum does not contain any specific determination either of the relation between relata or of their ontological level. Form as such does not involve either an assertion of constancy or a reference

8. *Ibid.,* p. 61; cf. his *Adventures of Ideas* (New York, Macmillan, 1933), *passim.*

to a tendency of occasions toward a completeness located outside their present, i.e. in the future.

From the point of view of principles we may henceforth assume that time primarily provides a basis for measurement but not for a distinction of the dimensions of past, present, and future. The dimensions of time presuppose the existence of a *fundamentum relationis* while measure rests on relation only. The measurement of time is epistemologically prior to the distinction among dimensions of time, for it presupposes less about time than does the distinction among dimensions. This has to be stressed because Bergson's biological model or Whitehead's cosmic concern lead to an overhasty ontological interpretation of time. The fact that we care more for actual time than for an epistemological analysis cannot count as a philosophical basis for the establishment of a theory of time. The fact that we discovered as it were "inner time" should not lead us to be oblivious of the philosophical presupposition of that inner time. The fact that we are concerned with historical time and even consider cosmic time as historical time cannot justify us in assuming that time as time is identical with the process in time.

In the ladder of specifications of time physical time logically precedes psychic or historical time, since physical time is time only as measured while psychic or historical time possesses *qualitative* dimensions as well. The determination of dimensions possessing directions (past, future) presupposes the measurement of time, just as the measurement presupposes succession. One should stress, though, that these are *logical* and not *genetic* relations. We must not assume that, from the point of view of what is present in our actual consciousness, physical time as measured time factually precedes psychic time. What is meant here is that an objective determination of the status and nature of psychic time is impossible without a preceding assumption—be it even implicit—of physical time, while an assumption of physical time inevitably rests on the presupposition of the form of time. Bergson, we may point out again, did not recognize the distinction between the genetic approach to our consciousness of time and the epistemological elucidation of the concept of time. Therefore he saw time as made up of antitheses; the actual relationship is rather one of strata or rungs in a ladder.

To sum up this part of the discussion: Time in its formal nature connotes the form both of succession and of duration. In succession we point to the transition; through the aspect of duration we proceed to the determination of the rate of both the span of transition from one event to the other and the magnitude of endurance of a single event in itself.

5. On the basis of what has been said before regarding the essence of time from the aspect of form, we can undertake to clarify some of the antinomies advanced as involved in time and thus further clarify the above analysis. It is usual to ask whether time flows or whether the events occurring in time flow, whether time depends on events or events depend upon time.[9] This antinomy can be solved by making a distinction between pure time and the events or occasions for which time serves as a form. Pure time does not flow, for the simple reason that it is not a reality but rather a form used for the cognition of the reality. We conceive the dynamic flow of reality by means of time because flowing, in its formal aspect, connotes that one event comes after the other, i.e. amounts to succession. "Flowing" does of course add some qualitative features to the formal

9. See V. F. Lenzen, *The Schema of Time,* University of California Publications in Philosophy (Berkeley, University of California Press, 1935), 18, 23.

aspect of time, whether those stressed by Whitehead, those stressed by Bergson, or those put forth in the theory of evolution, etc. Time as a form is neutral in relation to these assumptions as to the content and specific quality of events. These need the form of time; it does not need them. The relationship between time as a form and what occurs in it is from this point of view a one-way relationship.

Let us, with Cassirer, distinguish between pure time and empirical time. Pure time means the form of succession and duration (Cassirer considered only the aspect of succession); empirical time means this form plus a configuration of relations considered, such as the physical configuration with its "at the same time," the psychological configuration with its relation between the past and the present, the biological configuration with the growth directed toward the future, etc. In all these configurations the specific structure of time is set over against the background of its formal nature. Time is the form of flow free from flow,[10] because it is both form and content, form and datum. In knowledge it is a form becoming a content, although qua content it is no longer pure. As a form it is a *conditio sine qua non* for every datum. Yet as a content it is split up according to the various configurations and sets of contents contained in these configurations. As soon as time is considered in the sphere of content it necessarily loses its purity and formal universality.

Heinrich Barth takes the correlation of time as form and time as content to be actually a correlation between eternity and time,[11] for he identifies form with eternity from the outset. But if we insist on retaining the meaning of the terms used we must oppose this attempt, if only because

10. Jonas Cohn, *Theorie der Dialektik* (Leipzig, F. Meiner, 1923), p. 75.
11. Heinrich Barth, *Das Sein in der Zeit* (Tübingen, J. C. B. Mohr, 1933), pp. 26–30

of the leap which it involves. Barth seems to think that time
relations can be assumed only against a background which
is timeless; he does not realize that because time as a
form does not belong to reality at all it is nontemporal
though not eternal. Barth views time relations against a
timeless background and identifies this background with
eternity. He assumes, implicitly, and this without any epistemological justification, that all relations must have an
ontological basis. But why may not relations in time be
treated as categories released from reality altogether, and
thus released also from the process of time? Barth seems
to have been prompted to leap up to eternity—and he
represents a quite common tendency—by faith. Just
as a demonstration may try to derive a necessary existence from the contingency of world, Barth tries to attain
eternity by a regression from temporality. From temporality, however, we can of course only progress to a *form*
of temporality, for in order to assume temporality as a
datum we must presuppose time as a form. But we cannot accomplish a regression from temporality to eternity,
that is to say from—as it were—a lower to a higher level
of existence. We can only proceed from content as an
existence to form as an existence, or be indifferent to the
distinction between existence and nonexistence. Form is
an assumption, an *ens rationis* only. The distinction between
principle and the content dependent upon it is not one
between two levels of existence.[12]

6. The epistemological position of time as pure form
and as datum split into various realms of experience will
be brought into relief by an analysis of the notion of the
direction of time. By saying that time has a direction,
and a single direction only, we intend in fact to say that

12. A similar shift from time to eternity is to be encountered in Collingwood's *Speculum Mentis*, p. 301.

the series of *succession* has one, and only one, direction.
It is usual to say that the direction is from past to future.
But within the scope of pure form there is no justification
for dealing with time dimensions; it is therefore impossible
to assume from the outset an identity between the direction
of time and the stream which flows from the past to the
future. The direction of time qua form is essential to pure
time; it must therefore be implied in the features of time
as such, i.e. either in succession or in duration.

It is clear that duration cannot serve as the foundation
for direction, because duration is connected with a term or
with events, while direction applies to a *series* of terms
and their position within a series. Therefore only one alternative is open, i.e. to connect the direction of time with
succession. Indeed, direction as an aspect of pure time
connotes that time is a form of "following." What appeared
after something cannot at the same time be *before* something. Hence the notion of succession itself implies direction. But from the formal point of view this direction
cannot be understood as a progress toward an end, that
is to say toward a limit of the succession. As long as we
are concerned with form, direction follows from the "topological" nature of succession. It lies in the very aspect of
one *after* another which is the main, or at least the first,
aspect of time, first in the sense that it provides the very
basis of an analysis of the nature of time.

But the concept of direction is not limited to this formal or a priori aspect and cannot be limited to it once we
enter the sphere of experience. Direction in its concrete appearance in biology, physics, or perhaps in history does not
convey only the meaning of succession. An aspect of content is always involved when time is empirical: Direction
becomes irreversibility of time in its material meaning, that
is to say as this or that process in time. The pure direction

of succession becomes connected, for instance, with the
direction of the process of nature or of the growth of an
organism. In the case of the process of nature the direction is connected with the law of entropy, for example,
which concerns not time as form but the nature of physical
processes which occur against the generic background of
succession, the latter being the minimum formal aspect
only. Or the direction becomes connected with the growth
of an organism, according to the biogenetic law which
governs the direction of the growth of the organism on
the basis of a relation between phylogenesis and ontogenesis.
In the existential sphere the direction of time can be interpreted—as it actually is—as linked with the progress toward death. In all these cases we find the pure form of time
implying both succession and direction serving as an explication of succession and as a qualified material configuration, or, from the other end, an actual material process
combined with the formal aspect. It is impossible to say
whether the process is a result of the formal structure of
time or whether it is a necessary feature of the material
process as such. They seem to be interconnected.[13] In any
case the formal aspect of time as succession, precisely
because of its position as a form, is involved in any process
occurring in time. The formal aspect of direction is realized,
as it were, in the material nature of the process; it gets
its particular meaning which is both particular and concrete.

Since direction implied in succession has the minimum
meaning as a form and the more concrete meaning as
related to this or that field of experience, the relationship
between the minimum aspect of it and the concrete realization must not be assumed to be a relationship of harmony.
At least it cannot be taken for granted that the two aspects
coincide, because it cannot be taken for granted that pure

13. Cf. Paul Weiss, *Reality* (New York, 1949), pp. 228 ff.

time as form singly turns out to be a specific configuration within time. Pure form is only a *condition* for any more concrete statement about the direction of the process in time. But the process in time is not simply a continuation of the formal meaning of direction as implied in succession. Let us recall that in history we find an attempt to explain the process as being reversible or circular. In this conception—Vico's *corsi* and *ricorsi*, for example—we must try to assume the character of time as a form of succession. And yet against this background the tendency in circular theories is to assign to the events in time not irreversibility but, on the contrary, a direction of both progression and regression. Although the pure form of time characterized by irreversibility is implied in the succession of the events, the direction of time is not identical with the specific direction of the events as such, which are reversible. A distinction must therefore be made between a mere chronological order (succession) and the order in terms of content and meaning embedded in that chronological order.

To put it differently, irreversibility is an essential feature of time as time, that is to say of formal time. Yet it may happen that this feature (as in the concept of corsi and ricorsi as well as Nietzsche's doctrine of eternal recurrence) does not find its complementary expression in the material order of time. In this case the formal feature of time does not actualize in experience, as it were, and there is a gap between the irreversible nature of time as time and the reversible order of things, looked at from the material and not formal point of view. Similarly, when the rhythm of history is considered to be a rhythm of generations, here too there is a tension between the actual process as encompassed in the irreversible and linear course of time as form and the historical rhythm in concreto. Opposed to the difference between formal time and its material realization in the historical rhythm is the liberal idea of progress. This idea, considered from the point of view of its principal trend, suggests an attempt to assume a harmony, or at least coincidence, between the single direction of formal time and the single direction of the material-meaningful historical process within time. Progress is supposed to be the material expression and equivalent of the irreversible nature of linear time. Yet once we move from the formal to the material point of view the formal feature of irreversibility acquires in the actual historical process a material connotation in terms of an ascension, improvement, perfection, etc.—in brief, progress. What is formally related to succession as succession becomes at once a materially meaningful course of events. Thus in the liberal idea of progress there is supposed or expressed this coincidence between the formal and the material aspect of time. Yet this coincidence does not blur the fact that there are two different points of view, one formal and the other material-historical. Harmony between the aspects does not mean identity of the different planes where the harmonious aspects are placed.

7. Two further conclusions regarding the epistemological position of time are to be drawn.

a. Time is both form and datum. It is a priori insofar as it is a form only; but being both form and datum it becomes a content in itself. It occupies a characteristic status, an intermediary one, between an a priori or formal domain and a domain of datum and material. This conception of the status of time is in a sense related to Kant's conception of time as a form of intuition. For Kant time is a medium for concepts. Here, however, we are not concerned with the distinction between concepts and intuition but only with the fact that intuition is always nearer to the domain of data than the concept is. Applying this idea to the status of time as suggested in the foregoing discussions we may say that time is close to the datum because in a way time itself is both a form and a datum, though as a datum it gets features in addition to those inherent in it as a form.

b. Since in time there are these two levels, form and datum, no specification of its relation to an empirical datum can be detached from the pure form. Time as form is a whole of which time as content is a part. Yet within the correlative structure of time as form and datum also lies the basis of a differentiation of time according to the various domains of experience. This differentiation can take place within the total scope of time qua form and is not identical with but included in it.

8. What has to be introduced as historical time proper is time of a defined configuration, a fragmentary time. 1) Historical time presupposes time as a pure form; it is material, that is to say "regional," time related to a specific configuration of experience. 2) Historical time is *historical* and by definition empirical. 3) Hence it must represent the specific essence of the historical experience qua experience of a particular region of content. It is in history and not in any other domain beyond or outside it that we must try to detect the specific quality which converts time as such and as form into historical time. But historical time is *time,* and its character as time cannot be deprived from the domain of history as a domain of specific contents. Temporality as such is an a priori supposition and therefore a form of all the various material domains. Yet there are quite a few prominent attempts in the history of philosophy which do try to derive the specific essence of historical time as time from specific contents, assuming one specific level of contents to embrace not only *historical quality* proper but even *time as such.* No status is attributed in theories of this sort to formal time as presup-

position or condition for some of its specifications. Time as such, i.e. as form, becomes based primarily on something outside it, be it material, ontological, or existential. Let us briefly examine some attempts to derive the specific essence of time from different kinds of content. This critical examination may throw some light on the problem of historical time, for the point of view of its material essence must still require us to retain the fundamental distinction between the principle aspect of time and any of its secondary qua empirical aspects.

a. Though Solomon Maimon's doctrine has no explicit link with the problem of history, it still gives expression to a conception which considers time as a secondary phenomenon resting ultimately on meanings and logic. For him a temporal difference between two events or occasions must, in the last analysis, be conceptual. The temporal difference in his view is only an expression or a reflection of the difference in intrinsic features, which are determinable through conceptual factors. In his doctrine things are different in time (and in space) because they differ in their intrinsic natures. This nature of theirs is to be determined through concepts. Hence what is different in time indicates a difference in nature as well; the difference in time being only an expression is secondary and has an independent status. Maimon expresses this conception of the relation existing between the conceptual nature of phenomena and their position in time by saying that the faculty of imagination copies reason and that it imagines A and B to be different in time and space because reason thinks of them as being different from one another.[14] The object of this doctrine is clear: It aims toward an annihilation of irrationality by transforming given temporal differ-

14. Salomon Maimon, *Versuch über die Transcendentalphilosophie* (Berlin, 1790), p. 134.

ences into conceptual differences to be discerned by reason and not by the faculty of imagination. Yet what actually happens is that Maimon imposes on succession, which is only a *minimum* of difference (let us call it a "topological" difference), a maximum of conceptual difference. There is certainly less content expressed when we say that B follows A in time than when we say A and B are different, perhaps big and small, or sun and moon. In other words Maimon introduces a content, in terms of a difference between two phenomena, into a difference which is in a way prior to the difference in content and in a way independent of it. He has to introduce the faculty of imagination as responsible for this shift to the plane of time. As the faculty of imagination is lower than the faculty of reason so the assertion of differences in time is lower than that of differences in content. The question must be raised how it is that the faculty of imagination copies reason by shifting reason to a different realm. Why is the copy not photographic but involving cognition or perception in a domain (time) which is not real in the true sense? In fact, time must be presupposed, because in order to copy reason in time—assuming that this is the relationship—time has to be taken for granted. Time is at the most the plane where the copying impresses itself, but copying does not create the very plane of time.

Yet there is one main thing to learn from Maimon's doctrine. When we talk of material time, and of historical time especially, the differences in contents or meanings between the events in time are most relevant. Precisely where we are concerned with material time we are concerned with contents embodied in time. Hence here in the domain of content differences in content legitimately arise and have to be accounted for. We have to object to Maimon's idea of basing time as such on something beyond time and prior to it. But we have to retain the very relationship between contents and time where this relationship really appears.

b. In spite of the difference between Spinoza and Kant, Hegel accepted both their views on time. He treated time as a form of imagination (Spinoza) and of intuition (Kant). As a form of imagination it does not belong to the system of dialectic of thought and reality but is only a manifestation of Spirit on its way from opaque reality to consciousness, from an immediate to a meditated reality, on the way between consciousness and self-consciousness.[15] For a progressing and self-developing Spirit, time is fundamental and hence a category of history, history being a manifestation of Spirit which has not yet reached its end. Hence Hegel assumed time to lie in the field of history; he linked it with the dynamics of reality or with a dynamic potency, i.e. with Spirit. In this attempt to base time on something which is not time itself, to look at time not as a form or independent component of knowledge and reality but as an intermediate between the two atemporal points, consciousness and self-consciousness, and thus as a provisional phenomenon which will cease to exist with the attainment of the complete self-manifestation of Spirit—in all this Hegel approaches Maimon. Hegel assumed time to exist within the scope of the philosophy of history (and of nature) but he did not include it within the field of logic, though logic is clearly in his sense not merely formal. He therefore ignored the structure of time as form

15. "Spirit necessarily appears in time, and it appears in time so long as it does not grasp its pure notion, i.e. so long as it does not annul time . . . When this notion grasps itself it supersedes its time character . . . Time therefore appears as spirit's destiny and necessity, where spirit is not yet complete within itself." *Phänomenologie des Geistes*, ed. by Georg Lasson (Leipzig, F. Meiner, 1921), p. 515; Eng. trans. by J. B. Baillie, *The Phenomenology of Mind* (London, 1931), p. 800.

and set time in the realm of the Spirit, that which goes through a process in order to reach its ideal self-conscious stage. Time is for him essentially a process and not a form which has to be presupposed in order to deal with the process. As a process it applies to what is in process, i.e. the development of Spirit.

But in fact Hegel could not avoid employing, at least implicitly, a formal concept of time when he dealt with problems of history, since the very entrance of Spirit into the sphere of history involves transition into the sphere of time. Time can by no means be a product of this transfer; it is a presupposition of it. In order to draw a systematic conclusion with regard to history as a manifestation of Spirit, Hegel must first specify the features of history and then connect the substance of history with Spirit, that is to say he must know that history is in time in the first place and then assume a *tertium comparationis* between history and Spirit. In the movement of Spirit from logic to history, from the dialectic of concepts to the dialectic of powers and institutions, Hegel implicitly uses a form of succession and of duration. This form is explained or understood by him as a process of Spirit in its manifestations. Hegel's Absolute Spirit does not create time by converting itself into a World Spirit of history. But in order for the Absolute Spirit to convert itself into the World Spirit it is necessary to presuppose time as an a priori form. For history to be a revelation of Spirit it must presuppose the notion of time and not create this notion out of itself. It must, in short, try to create time out of what is above time.

c. In explaining the essence of time Hegel emphasizes the fact of passage and transition. But passage is one specific *material* embodiment of succession. Heidegger, on the other hand, and existentialist philosophy along with him, emphasizes the *finitude* of time, or more exactly they consider temporality, which in their view is identical with historicity, to be the manifestation of the finitude of man's existence.

From an epistemological point of view this assumption is unfounded unless we assume that existentialism implicitly bases the finitude of time on one of the aspects of pure time as form, namely on duration, and that it presupposes this aspect. Finitude, which is the central idea of existentialist theory, is only a specific determination or limitation of duration, or it is a quantitative and qualitative assertion regarding the extension of time. This theory assumes that temporality is based on an existential datum, namely finitude. But in order to be able to assume this datum it is compelled to presuppose the formal feature of pure time, namely the aspect of duration. This example serves to show how right Julius Guttmann was in his objection to existentialism when he observed that without ideal presuppositions it is not possible to define existence.[16] To take advantage of this contention in the field under discussion we say that without a supposition of time qua *form*, the assumption of an existential time qua *fate* would be meaningless.

Because it is assumed that the finitude of time is at the root of historicity, existentialism is unable to solve some of the most important problems of historical reality, and of course also—and most paradoxically—the problem of historical time. How can historical ties exist within the scope of time? How can the historical process exist within time, and how are we conscious of it? Duration serves as the foundation for the continuity of time. The con-

16. J. Guttmann, "Existence and Idea," in the Hebrew volume, *Haggut*, presented to S. H. Bergman, ed. by M. Buber and N. Rotenstreich, Jerusalem, The Philosophical Society, 1944.

traction of the horizon of time into finitude wrongly contracts the very essence of time. This essence lies in a dialectical interplay between continuity and distinction. But without continuity there is no room for historical reality, let alone for historical consciousness which transcends the given portion of time and reaches in reflection what is beyond it. Several of existentialism's radical consequences are based on its denial of continuity. Nihilism, for instance, is possible only on the basis of the destruction of continuity; conversely, continuity is a presupposition for grasping a "meaning" in history. To assume an understanding of a meaning connotes that the occurrence has an extension beyond its instantaneous emergence. Grasping a meaning depends on a resonance which the occurrence evokes in the subject conceiving it. Once it is assumed that the occurrence is given only in its own boundaries it is but a short step to the consideration of it as only ephemeral. To go from ephemerism to nihilism is merely to make explicit what is already implicit.

Indeed, the existentialist theory of historical time is the result of an attempt to transfer existential time of the confined personal sphere to the sphere of history. Historical time might perhaps be considered as the totality of the existential times, but it is by no means possible to identify it simply with existential time. This fallacy of existentialism is most illustrative from the methodological point of view. Historical time is a material time, conditioned and logically preceded by formal time. This conditionality means, among other things, that it is neither necessary nor possible to derive the rhythm of time from the content of time. This rhythm is a part of the very temporality of the phenomena in regard to which the form of succession and duration is applicable.

The realm of material time comprises various types of

experiences, all of them temporal but not all of them historical; we must therefore distinguish between historical
time and other types of material time and see how those
other types are similar to and different from historical time.

B. An Example of Material Time

1. Material time may be identified with empirical time.
What is present in experience is material not formal time.
Pure formal time is a *condition* of experience; it is not an
experience itself and does not appear as a material component of it.

Material time is a regional time qua empirical, or present in experience, and does not have a single meaning
only. We shall deal briefly with some of the attempts to
clarify the various types of empirical time which are
parallel to and embedded in various regions of experience.

a. Let us start with an observation on physiological or
biological time. Le Comte de Noüy wanted to give prominence to the specific essence of physiological time. He
said that it is a time which changes in accordance with
individual circumstances and that its nature is "granular,"
i.e. encompasses distinct occasions and therefore differs
from continuous, integral, and universal time. On this basis
he distinguished between man's calendar age and his physiological age. The older the person physiologically, the longer
the time necessary for the cicatrization of his wounds. Physiological age is therefore to be regarded as a material specification of universal calendar time.[1]

This suggested elucidation of physiological time seems to
be quite vague and turns upon one point only: generality
against individuality. Yet it is obvious that the personal
experience of every man—and not only the process in terms

1. See a summary of this discussion in Pitirim A. Sorokin, *Sociocultural
Causality, Space, Time* (Durham, N.C., 1943), p. 163.

of physiological or organic development—bears an individual character. Since every experience is a process in time an individuation of time takes place in experience. Experience in this sense is essentially individual. This means that there is a distinction to be made between the time of a limited sphere, such as that of physiological events, and the more universal sphere such as the time of our daily life. The latter has a specific quality of its own apart from merely succession, a quality appearing in acceleration, in the relation of earlier and later, etc. Moreover, as Richard Hoenigswald remarked, the rhythm of organic growth is structured according to the three dimensions: past, present, and future. The organism can be understood only in the light of both its past and future, and the joined aspect of past and future refers again to the aspect of "at the same time." The organism exists within time, on the one hand, and temporality enters into the organism's existence on the other. The organism *has* a history and *is* a history of itself.[2] This observation is relevant in this context because it goes beyond a vague description of a relationship between biological and nonbiological time—and even pure time—as merely one between the universal and the individual. Here an attempt is made to discover the particular structure of a specific part of time. The particular is not only a *limitation* of the universal, it is also a *correlate* of it. Time as such is, on the one hand, the background for the description of the features of the material time of the organism and, on the other hand, the content of organic rhythm. To be sure, this observation is also a generic one; it connects biological time with dimensions and with a relationship both of likeness and of difference between these dimensions, a relationship which can be

2. R. Hoenigswald, *Die Grundlagen der Denkpsychologie* (2d ed. Leipzig, 1925), pp. 283, 293.

applied to psychology and history as well. But this observation points in the right direction.

b. Mention ought also to be made of the role of time in art, for example in music and poetry. In music we encounter a complexity of various time series which converge in the whole of a melody. Here more clearly and evidently are to be found the various modes of time of daily life, such as slowness and acceleration. It is in music that these modes appear in their purity, free from any mixture with material events, and the time rhythm is presented as being of the essence of time and not of the essence of the events. Yet a closer analysis will show that the rhythm is not of the essence of time as such but of the essence of material time. The step accomplished in music is that it releases *material* time from material *events* and establishes what sounds like a paradox: material time without events. This observation serves only to indicate that various approaches to material time are possible.

c. Mention should also be made of magic or religious time. Characteristic features attributed to it are: 1) The parts of time are not homogeneous, because qualitative events occur in them. 2) Against the background of the continuity of time, critical dates stand out, such as holidays, seasons for ceremonies, etc.[3] These two features cannot, however, be taken to be peculiar features of what is called religious time, for they do not depend on the particular meaning of religion either as faith or, broadly, as a relation between man and the transcendent. They have nothing of the specific nature of religion. The lack of homogeneity, for instance, pointed out as a mark of religious time proper is in fact a mark of every material succession. Bergson considered such a lack to be the main feature of durée as immanent time, even without any relation to religion. Again, the

3. See Sorokin, p. 183.

occurrence of critical days—holidays, celebrations—is a trait of historical time too, and cannot be a specific mark of religious time qua religious. From the religious point of view what is important is not the dates but their contents, i.e. their manifesting a significant religious meaning. Religious time as it is presented in the usual discussions is actually history considered from a religious point of view. Hence in this view the emphasis is placed on critical events, because the historical interest even religiously colored is an interest in events. The question is not what is history when viewed religiously, but what is the essence and position of time in religion.

In view of the special position and essence of religion, emphasis must be laid instead on the past moment in which time itself was created, for instance, or on the peculiar tension involved between the concreteness of time and the tendency toward annihilation of that concreteness in a mystical act. Or it might be possible to show the future as a dimension of redemption in general or as a *restitutio in integrum*, which involves an identity between the future and the past. Franz Rosenzweig's doctrine about Judaism being outside the scope of time and Christianity being a religion in time would also be a case in point. A different distinction relevant for the domain of religion might be that between the time of creation and the time of revelation, thus giving rise to the problems involved in the relationship between the two aspects.

What is relevant from the methodological point of view is that the characteristic features of religious time must reflect the material domain of religion. This observation holds good with reference not only to religious time and the domain connected with it but also to any other material region of experience. Generally speaking, material time is time of the material region of experience. The materiality of time must express the special material essence of the realm of experience.

2. The above brief observations must be considered only as illustrations serving to indicate the fact, or the possibility, of a variety of material times. Now we ought to consider at some length the problems involved in time within the psychological region, chiefly for two reasons. First, this problem has been subjected to a profound analysis in modern philosophical literature, and second—more important still—because there is much regarding historical time to be learned from psychology. Let us survey for this purpose the conclusions of both Richard Hoenigswald's and William Stern's theories in order to obtain the systematic outlook relevant to our analysis.

Psychic time is subjective,[4] since it is inherent in what is the axis of psychic events and as such the central term of psychology, namely *experience* (in the German meaning of *Erlebnis*). Experience is the very datum of psychology. It serves as the bridge between an experiencing subject and what is given outside him. Experience is the contact of the subject with his world. Thus psychic time is subjective, because it is related to a concrete subject and hence is experimental time. But experience is essentially connected with "now," i.e. with a peculiar moment within time. It takes place in a particular moment of time. Experience is a datum and like every datum is present. Experience is present as something given in relation to a subject, and it is present as a datum occurring in time. Thus we arrive at a conclusion which has bearing upon our further discussion.

4. I do not use in this description the notion of "specious present" as it is accepted in the literature, since as far as I can see this notion has not been elaborated philosophically to the extent that the notion "immanent time" has been and cannot serve as a basis for conclusions to be drawn with reference to historical time.

In the domain of psychology, experience as the datum itself has a meaning in terms of time, or, to put it differently, temporality is an immanent feature of the datum, not only as its locus but also as an immanent factor in its meaning. The time factor is a component of experience and not its background only.

Through its location in the domain of time the experiential datum ceases to be merely subjective. This is certainly a dialectical feature of experience. Because of its relation to the subject it is related to time, and from this point of view has a subjective nature. But the very fact that it occurs in time places experience in what is at least potentially beyond the confined subjective field. It ceases to exist in its self-containedness and absoluteness and gets integrated in time, structured in dimensions. In the actual experience a combination is to be discovered of the isolated content and the absolute or discrete "now" which is an extension in or a span of time. Volkelt was right in observing that a position within time can be *determined* by relative means only, while the *position itself* is absolute. We can add to this observation a further one to the effect that the absoluteness of the position runs parallel to the absoluteness of every act of experience. Thus there is in psychic time an essential link between the temporal-given position of experience as an act in itself and its integration in the continuity of time. By saying that the particular psychic time is the present we have already integrated the "now" in a system or in a whole of time.

There are a number of features which are worth remarking about the present and its structure as psychic time.

a. The present offers a meeting place for man and his world.[5] The present is an occurrence, an act of meeting,

5. William Stern, "Raum und Zeit als personale Dimensionen," *Acta Psychologica*, Vol. 1 (1935).

and the moment when the meeting takes place. It is a temporal bridge between two poles which are not exclusively temporal. It mediates between or reconciles two realities disconnected in space and distant from one another— man and world. But just because the present is the moment of their meeting it is a dimension of experience, for experience is grounded in the actual contact man makes with his world. The present is the time of the datum, because the datum expresses an influx of the world into man or, conversely, the departure of man toward the world.

b. The present, being the *moment* (in terms of time) between man and the world and therefore the *bridge* (in terms of space) between them, ceases to be purely subjective and becomes an integral part of an objective world and its objective time. This feature of psychic time has been analyzed by Hoenigswald in his works on the psychology of thinking. We may put this idea differently in order to stress a point which is relevant for the analysis of historical time: Time of experience is related to or even inherent in the act of experiencing. But since no act is a sheer act but has at least the additional dimension of relating the experiencing subject with what it experiences, the act places the subject in the realm of material time which is not merely subjective.

Our discussion started by stressing both the subjective character and the position of experience and its time. But it becomes clear that subjective experience lies in the objective world and the latter finds its expression in objective time. We may formulate this idea in a quite paradoxical way: The *subjective* experience considered from the *objective* point of view occurs within *objective* time. Hoenigswald rightly argued that "the time of the present," as the dimension of psychic occurrence, is only another manifestation of the peculiar form of unity characteristic of experience in general. When we consider a psychological object we assume a relationship existing between immanent time and the order of time beyond the actual experience, called "transeunt time" by Hoenigswald. Experience, being in the present, is linked with transeunt time, although from the inner aspect, from the aspect of the experiencing subject itself, it is determined within and by immanent time. Indeed, when we consider the connection between the two orders of time (the immanent and transcendent—in Hoenigswald's own terminology, transeunt) we do not intend to say that this connection is always one of harmony or adequacy. In psychopathological phenomena, for instance, the lack of harmony between the orders is evident; experience, in psychopathic cases, is unable to integrate itself in the objective process of the world order and its events. But even that lack of harmony or adequacy is envisaged by taking account of the two coordinates of experience, "inside" and "outside" time.[6]

c. The connection between the two orders of time cannot change the difference in the nature of their respective time rhythms. Objective time qua framework *flows and passes*, while subjective time steadily *progresses and grows* along with the process of the biological and psychological growth of man. This difference is not an objective or formal feature of time as such; it is a difference in a relationship of events to time. Insofar as there exists a psychological, historical, social, or moral possibility of the experiencing subject's identification with the objective world order and absorption of it into part of the personality, the world order becomes an immanent part of the personality and grows

6. R. Hoenigswald, pp. 84–5. With reference to this issue cf. Kurt Goldstein, *Human Nature in the Light of Psychopathology*, Cambridge, Mass., 1940.

along with the personality. But, as in many cases where discrepancy exists between the two orders, the world order —being outside the individual order—is conceived of as an indifferent external framework only. The changes in the world order are understood against a background of flowing and passing, while the changes of the inside order are understood to be personal and therefore growing along with the personality. Again it has to be stressed that these different features are not features of time as such but rather features of experience within time, or features of time qua a component or factor of experience.

d. The psychic present is not identical with the "at the same time." It is not confined to the tension between the inside and the outside sphere. There is also a tension within the inside sphere itself. Attention was drawn to this by William Stern in one of his first works, and Hoenigswald raised it to the level of the central idea of his theory of time in psychology. Stern showed that the psychic occurrence that takes place within a span of time can be conceived of as a single act of consciousness, in spite of the fact that various parts of this occurrence do not occur at the same time, for the psychic present is not a point but a line and even a plane. As an example of this Stern refers to the perception of the tones of a melody. These are perceived as being present at the same time although they appear in fact one after another. The objective succession of the tones does not affect their experiential position within the sphere of the present.[7] Hoenigswald formulated this in the observation that the psychic "at the same time" is not identical with the physical "at the same time." From the psychological point of view the "at the same time" is

7. William Stern discussed this problem in one of his early papers, "Psychische Praesenszeit," *Zeitschrift für Psychologie* (1897). This is the point where the concept of specious present comes in.

actually a complexity of elements. Moreover, the very essence of present time lies in experiencing something as simultaneous, although from the point of view of objective time this experienced something is successive. What exists in the tension between earlier and later, i.e. what exists at a distance, appears in one and the same scope of experience.[8] Here in the domain of experience the order of succession appears as one of simultaneity or inherence.[9]

The concrete embodiment of this complexity is to be found in the continuity of the self, for a phenomenon is psychic just insofar as it is rooted in the continuity of the self. But this continuity is in time, and from this point of view time is an ingredient of the self. It is not only a possible background for this existence but a part of this existence. But precisely this inherence of time in the self makes the inner structure of psychic time apparent. The continuity of the self is there because past and future, although disconnected from the objective point of view (i.e. existing in a process of succession), do meet in present experience and compose the present jointly. This continuity exists, and it becomes conscious because we give the past and future an explicit presence within the present, an implicit presence being a part of the present by the very definition of the self. The psychic present is at once past and future, because the continuity of experience and the continuity of content are to be found in it.[10]

This point can be summed up as follows: The psychic present is a meeting ground for the phases of time that do not meet objectively. The present is therefore not only the moment of a meeting of man and the world but also

8. R. Hoenigswald, p. 87.

9. *Ibid.*, pp. 257–8.

10. This is a free formulation of Hoenigswald's description, *ibid.*, p. 294.

a meeting ground of the self with itself. It is both the mani-festation and the guarantee of the continuity of the con-scious self and therefore ceases to be an absolute "now." Essentially integrated in a system of transeunt and im-manent time, the present also contains the past and the future of this very self.

e. This idea can be put differently in anticipation of what might be significant for the description of the nature of historical time. The past and the future seem to exist both inside and outside the present. Psychic time is both the time of the *meeting* of the dimensions and a *dis-tance* between them. It is both rest and flow.

f. Stern aptly formulated the idea that the psychic present is not a point but a plane by terming it a sphere.[11] The present has its own extension and structure since it is not pure time but material time.[12] It has a breadth and a density of its own, for it is not an empty moment in empty time but is essentially charged with the past and the future. It is a link in the continuity of the self. This continuity is a *conditio sine qua non* for the localization of an ex-perience in the domain of the subject. But continuity in-volves by definition a passing beyond the moment, since any moment, as a moment in continuity, becomes part of a set of one self, while this set appears, as it were, contracted or condensed in the single moment. The single moment is meaningful only due to its inherence in the continuity of the self, and yet this continuity does not exist *in ab-stracto*, detached from its manifestations in the plurality of the single moments.

The psychological manifestation of this continuity is memory, of which, as Stern observed, there are two kinds,

11. William Stern, *Studien zur Personenwissenschaft* (Leipzig, 1930), p. 116.

12. *Ibid.*, pp. 117–18.

memory in general and *remembrance.* Memory is the power by which what has passed continues to affect man's psychic life; remembrance is a conscious experience of the history of the personality. Memory thus is the background of a relationship between past and present within the scope of one person; remembrance is a dynamic or active relation of the present of a person toward his past, occasioned by an experiential or actual return to the past, in which the past influences the present through the agency of the present's own force.

Within the scope of the self there thus exists a double relationship toward the past: an opaque relation which precedes actual consciousness and a conscious relation resulting from actual experience. The past and the present within the scope of the self provide a type of relation parallel to the two kinds of memory elucidated by William James. James distinguished between primary and secondary memory. In the primary memory "an object . . . is not thus brought back for it never was lost; its date was never cut off in consciousness from that of the immediately present moment. In fact it comes to us as belonging to the recurrent position of the present space of time, and not to the genuine past." As against this the phenomenon of "memory proper, or secondary memory as it might be styled, is the knowledge of a former state of mind after it has already once dropped from consciousness; or rather *it is the knowledge of an event, or fact,* of which meantime we have not been thinking, with the *additional consciousness that we have thought or experienced it before."* [13] This distinction is significant because one finds here an allusion to the ambivalent position of the past in the present of a man. The past exists there both potentially and actually,

13. William James, *The Principles of Psychology* (New York, Dover Publications, 1950), ch. 16, pp. 646, 648.

which is to say a man maintains a relationship of both closeness and distance toward his own past. So far as the past does not exist in actual consciousness and serves as a reservoir only, it is a potentiality, elastic or plastic, allowing various attitudes to be assumed toward it. The past is a reality, but being distant from the present it serves as a reservoir of nonactual impressions and thus lends itself to being understood and connected with the present in various ways. The future has various aspects because it can be shaped in various ways by actual *deeds;* the past had various aspects because it can be *understood* in various ways and differently remembered by consciousness.

Following James' distinction we may again say that the past as enclosed in the present—in the phenomenon of primary memory—does not need actual consciousness to serve as a bridge between the dimensions of time. Actual consciousness is needed once the past event has disappeared from the present state of mind. As a matter of fact consciousness is involved twice: the consciousness of the fact that we have thought or experienced the event before and the consciousness as the driving force and medium for going back to a former state of consciousness. The consciousness in the first sense is the background for the relationship existent in memory; consciousness in the second sense revives this relationship and makes it present again.

g. A further step forward has been made by Stern in his analysis of the "personal present" and the personal dimensions in general. His analysis is of special value for understanding historical time, because it makes an attempt to analyze the dimensions of time within the domain of individuality, called by Stern "personal." These dimensions are not purely subjective. Stern distinguishes two meanings of "now": 1) a *momentary* now, such as a momentary shock, and 2) a now as a *portion of life*, as in

Stern's remark, when lecturing to an audience in Copenhagen, that he was "now" a teacher at the University of Hamburg. "Now" passes in such a case beyond the duration of an individual moment to become an objective portion of time, over against the time of the person.[14] The present, we may sum up, is structured in concentric circles the smallest of which being momentary experience and the largest, objective time.

Stern also observed that the present is neutral in regard to the distinction of time and space and involves a determination of both time and space. The determination "here" belongs to the present, like the determination "now." The audience belongs to the present of the lecturer because it exists with the lecturer not only at that time but also within the space of his activity. Space enters into the present as a determination of time, for the present is not merely a point in time but has, so to speak, breadth and density as well. The breadth and density are connected not only with the continuity of the self but also with the framework of space in which the experience of the subject occurs.

After this summary survey of some of the qualities of psychic time, both in its experiential and personal aspects, we may proceed with the clarification of historical time. We shall start by examining both its similarity to and dissimilarity from psychic time as analyzed above.

C. *Material Transsubjective Time*

1. The analysis of the nature of psychic time brought into relief the subjective-experiential quality of time in psychology and its bearing upon an objective set of time. The dimensions of psychic time are connected with the continuity of the subject. Since we find all the dimensions

14. Stern, *Studien zur Personenwissenschaft*, pp. 118–19.

meeting within the present, the present must not be considered as a mere point but as a plane or sphere. In considering the time of the personal sphere, we went beyond the
boundaries of momentary experience but remained in the
sphere of personality.

We have no clue whatsoever in individual experience
regarding the nature of historical time. Historical time
lies clearly beyond experience (Erlebnis) and beyond the
individual subject altogether; at the most it can be understood as a composition of or a correlation between various
individual times. But this suggests that we look at the composition of historical time post factum, i.e. once it is there
we may analyze its individual components. But clearly the
question will always remain as to how the togetherness of
individual times creates historical time. To answer it we
must look into historical time as it is encountered in history.
Hence we may indicate the primary fact that historical time,
when compared with psychic time, is objective or at least
transsubjective. It has a dimensional structure similar to
that of psychic time, i.e. a past, present, and future; but
it does not offer any scope for the setting up of dimensions,
because unlike psychic time it is not connected with the
actual experience of any individual being. The problem of
historical time must, therefore, be discussed with respect
to both its similarity to and its difference from psychic time.[1]

In the psychic sphere we may perhaps speak of the purity
of psychic elements, although here too the problem of the
relationship between soul and body arises, a problem which
may obscure the purity of the elements unless the non-
psychic factors be removed. But in the domain of history
we find from the beginning a considerable complexity of

1. I refer to George Herbert Mead's philosophy of time, as presented
chiefly in *The Philosophy of the Present*, Chicago and London, 1932, and
The Philosophy of the Act, Chicago, 1938.

such elements as the geographical, geological, biological, psychic, social, etc. An example from one of the modern theories may throw light on this issue, namely the theory of generations. This theory undertakes to explain the specific rhythm of the historical process by demonstrating that within the time which passes and proceeds in the form of a line there enters a biological factor of generations. This factor brings with it psychological, intellectual, and spiritual differences between the various generations. An effort is thereby made to demonstrate how a qualitative element of changing generations enters into quantitative time. Concrete historical time is then conceived of as a unity of the quantitative and qualitative aspects. To be sure, this theory is also expressive of a tendency in various schools of thought to base the historicity of time on some qualitative rhythm which is not necessarily historical. Since we have already rejected any attempt to reduce the domain of history to something which is ahistorical, let alone nonhistorical, we cannot take this approach. Instead we are compelled to assume the complex nature of historical time and discover the nature of its peculiar features as being specifically *historical*. We have to assume that historical time is split up into the dimensions of past, present, and future. It is complex, as is the sphere of history. The problem before us is to analyze the peculiar traits of historical time with regard to the notion of its division into dimensions and with the awareness of its specific historicity.

2. Let us start with the question of how transsubjective material time is possible at all. Transsubjective nonmaterial time like the *t* of physics finds its justification in its quantitative nature. Since quantity is a nonexperiential, i.e. a constructed, determination, its transsubjectivity is guaranteed from the outset by definition. But in the case of *material* time, transsubjectivity rests necessarily on the nature of the

material which makes time material. Indeed, the material element of historical time does not lie in individual experiences but in objectivations, like political actions and institutions, economic processes and ideas, etc. Hence the material element of history can be determined only by a conceptual-meaningful approach. Since, as a matter of principle, the material element can at least be understood through a nonsubjective meaningful approach, the nonsubjective nature of the material accounts for the nonsubjective nature of historical time. Again this question as to the relevance of the factor accounting for the transsubjectivity of historical time points to the idea of time as form. Time as form only cannot be the basis of the nature of material time, in our case of historical time, because time as form lies beyond the differences in material. Hence the problem is to single out the material nonsubjective element in historical time. This must be the element of what happens in history and not what an individual experiences at random.

In historical time succession and duration on the one hand and meanings on the other are combined. Historical time is transsubjective time, thanks to the composition found in it of meaningful events and their temporality. We are able to write a history of meanings by extracting the meanings from their temporal environment, but only because it is our objective to find connections of succession, i.e. connections in time between the meanings themselves. The general scheme of time as the form of succession holds good in this case too, but is it not identical with the chronological solar or lunar fixed succession of dates. Temporality in its pure form as succession remains; it cannot be exhausted by any given time rhythm or time order. From the point of view of meaning, the Greek polis, in contrast with the modern liberal state, can offer us a starting point for a history of statehood as a decline from a climax. The "highest" point, from the angle of meaning, need not be the latest point in terms of time order. The connection of meanings existing between the phenomena accordingly need not be considered as corresponding to the chronological relation between them. It is possible, in principle and in fact, for the chronologically *later* stage to throw light on the chronologically *preceding* stage. But it is impossible to reverse this and say that if it is possible to construct a series of successions according to meanings, it is possible to build up a series of meanings according to the order of succession as such. Succession as such is not historical time, because it does not yet contain the elements of content and meaning and is of the nature of form only. It becomes historical time only at the moment when an element of meaning is added, for instance a causal relation between events. We identify the order of historical time with that of astronomical time only because we look at the order of succession as a basis for a causal explanation of relations existing within the order of succession. Without this causal explanation the series of succession would be historically meaningless or, to coin an expression, antemeaningful. Thus only the combination of meaning and temporality constitutes historical time. The astronomical succession becomes historical only from the point of view of meaning, while meaning can be considered historically only if we succeed in discovering a relation of meaningful succession between the events in time, such as progress or decline, development, influence, etc. Whatever the case, the very combination of the two elements must remain. We should not try to dissolve it by stressing either meaning or temporality. Spengler, for example, tried to show a connection between historical phenomena by emphasizing only their meaning. Such an attempt, although it may discover common features in the data from the point of view of content, actually annihilates historicity. In his effort to reduce temporality to meaningfulness Spengler tears temporality from the domain of history and disintegrates the specific composition which constitutes historical time.

3. The composition of meaning and temporality characteristic of historical succession is also characteristic of historical duration. In the domain of history a subject can be considered as a unit, although it is obviously composed of various temporal events which happened successively. For instance, we obviously presuppose that the period of the Renaissance is a composition of various elements from the historical point of view, i.e. various occurrences, struggles, individual acts, etc. Nevertheless, historical research conceives of these various events from the point of view not only of succession but also of duration and regards them as a single historical unit. Historical research tries in such a case to define or to describe the essence of that period against the background of duration, by means of various substantive elements such as the rise of individuality, the return to classic values, etc. To this composition temporality as such contributes the aspect of duration while meaning contributes certain common features making up a unit, features created out of items separated from each other in terms of time, i.e. distinct and succeeding one another in time. The period is historical, being composed of both temporality and meaning.

This very composition explains the actual historical procedure of delineating periods within the process. Every attempt to delimit periods of history is an attempt to lay down meanings which will serve as boundaries of duration, i.e. to create historical units against the background of succession or within it. Each delineation of periods is an endeavor to bring about a determination of *meaningful durations within succession.* Such an endeavor is to be examined from the point of view of its ability to discover meanings suitable to serve as concrete boundaries within the process. The usual division of periods (ancient times, Middle Ages, modern times) does not define specific *meanings* different from one another. This division points only to phases of succession as such. It is necessary that each delimitation of periods in history fulfill two requirements: meaningfulness and temporality. The delimitation of periods qua units of measure of historical time must fulfill the requirements inherent in the essence of this time. As against the conventional delimitation of periods the question here arises regarding the justification for converting topological marks (ancient, middle, etc.) into meanings; i.e. it becomes a question as to whether we have actually reached the level of meanings by pointing to what are sheer phases in succession or whether we assume that these phases coincide with what are actually distinct meanings. This scheme of delimitation of periods is applied to spheres, such as the history of Greece or China, which were not originally considered as falling into these periods. Classical Greek history belongs to the ancient period of comprehensive European history. Yet attempts have been made to divide Greek history itself into an ancient period, middle period, etc., without considering the fact that all of classical Greek history corresponds to the ancient period within European history. But if this procedure is adopted then the distinction between periods in terms of phases of the process becomes one based merely on units of time and not on units which embrace specific and delimiting meanings. Hence the historian is charged with the task of elevating the distinction in time to the level of content. Thus we may conclude that the delimitation of periods is to be examined from the point of view of presenting the composition essential for historical time, insofar as this

delineation is not merely a technical scheme to be applied
to every succession qua succession.

4. From this a necessary conclusion is to be drawn
regarding the structure of historical time. The very essence
of this type of time lies in a dialectic between the absence
of continuity on the part of meanings and the presence
of continuity on the part of the succession of time. The
aspect of meaning within historical time becomes prominent
in the contents of historical institutions or actions. Each
institution or action has a content of its own, being a
regime, a decision, a battle, or an economic crisis. The
actions and the institutions as historical events are the
material side of historical time and offer the aspect of
quality within historical time. Qualities and meanings are
discrete and come into relief against the background of
the continuity of time qua succession. The aspect of quality
determines every action and institution in both their positive and negative aspects; it defines their content and their
differences from other actions and institutions. Hence
through their qualities the respective actions and institutions become in a way disconnected from the neutral
background of time and from the meanings of all the other
actions and institutions, although all the meanings are
situated in the continuous succession of time. The aspect
of meaning implies a double step of separation: separation of actions and events from the totality of the flow
of time and separation of the different actions and institutions from other actions and institutions. To put
this differently, the aspect of meaning brings to the fore
the emphasis placed on the content of the historical successions. We cannot therefore accept the usual description
stating that the historical datum qua datum is a heterogeneous continuum, i.e. a continuum of given events which
differ from each other. We have to analyze the datum it-

self, and once this is accomplished we are bound to find that in historical time we encounter heterogeneity on the part of the aspect of meaning, and continuity on the part of the aspect of time as time; or else we are bound to find differences as related to meanings, and succession as related to the background of time. The differences themselves do not create succession but are rather to be conceived of as arising from the stream of succession. The composition of meaning and temporality as the characteristic feature of historical time proper appears now to be a dialectic between the discrete differences and the continuous succession. Historical research in practice therefore always faces the task of discovering relations of succession between meaningful phenomena which are different from each other in their contents. The continuity of time qua time cannot be a sufficient basis for the assumption of relations between events which are characterized in terms of meanings, though without the continuity of time there would be no basis for the search after the relations between the actions and the institutions. The conceptual difference, as pointed out before, which Solomon Maimon thought to be the constituting factor of time as *time* is actually the constituting factor of *historical* time, because in historical time the aspect of meaning which involves difference is one of the two components of the composed entity which is precisely called historical time.

Here again a close view will prevent a possible misunderstanding. It is wrong to assume that the differences in meanings create out of themselves or through the faculty of imagination differences in time, the latter appearing in successive events. The component of succession is not secondary in historical time—it is as primary as the component of meanings. The two primary components combine and create the meaningful succession or process which is in time because every process is there and is meaningful because of its historicity.

Historical time cannot be regarded as durée in Bergson's sense, since in durée both continuity and heterogeneity exist on one and the same level. In point of fact we have to regard these two features as existing in two *different* spheres, that of meaning and that of time proper, and meeting each other in historical time. Bergson unified these features because he did not take formal time as distinct from pure meanings into consideration and hence put forward a conception of different times in terms of an antithesis and not as a complementary structure. As a matter of fact one has to consider historical time as a meeting ground of meaning and temporality and therefore to assume, at least as a logical supposition, each of the components to be self-contained. A case in point would be the meaning of political events as they are embodied and expressed in actual events in the course of time, which we decipher as having a political meaning. The meeting between what is a meaning, considered in the abstract, and the process in time constitutes historical time, where what is historical proper is due to the meanings and what is time is due to the relation of history with formal time. The systematic position of historical time may now be stated: *Historical time is a specific material concretization of succession and duration which comes into existence by means of transsubjective meanings.*

5. Georg Simmel realized that this composition of meaning and time is characteristic of historical temporality. He also pointed out that a break in continuity is involved in this composition. Yet he did not develop his idea in a systematic manner and did not ground it in principles. Simmel argued that history tries to understand the phenomena of human behavior from the point of view of their content

and not their position in time. Yet it appears that there are phenomena that cannot be understood save in their temporal complexity. In this case time ceases to be an empty external framework and becomes a concrete situation, i.e. a part of the phenomenon itself. Thus the penetration of content into time or the penetration of time into content abolishes the formal indifferent position of time. Time is shifted from the sphere of mere form to that of content, i.e. the phenomenon. So far so good. But Simmel did not take into account that, parallel to the change which takes place in the position of time, another change takes place in the position of content as well. Temporality itself changes the content because it adds another meaning to the primary one. Consider St. Paul, for instance (Simmel's own example), in his characterological quality, from the point of view of the theory or the dogmas formulated by him of the changes he introduced in the original trend of Christianity. But when we consider St. Paul from a historical perspective we do not merely analyze the theoretical meaning of his dogmas; we try to understand them in the light of his Judaism on the one hand and of his encounter with the civilization of the pagan world on the other. We understand his dogmatic attitude historically not only by placing it in a particular order of succession but also by analyzing the very meaning of his doctrine. Thus temporality becomes an integral part of the phenomenon; it changes the abstract meaning and thus turns out to be a meaning in itself. Time becomes meaningful while the meaning becomes timeful.

We must therefore reject Simmel's idea that time appears in history as a relation between peculiar historical contents while history as a whole is timeless,[2] as if history as a whole could have a mode of existence different from that of the

2. Georg Simmel, *Problem der historischen Zeit* (Berlin, 1916), p. 10.

particular and actual historical phenomena. Simmel apparently advanced this idea because he did not take into consideration the fact that historical time is conditioned by the category of time in general and therefore did not consider historical time as a concretization of time in general. The fact that historical time is rooted in formal time ensures the presence of the time factor in any historical consideration. From this point of view there is no difference between the time character of particular events and the time character of the domain of history. But he was right in saying that the event becomes historical by a determination of its content's peculiar position in time. For instance, if we succeed in explaining St. Paul's attitude by analyzing its data of content, and succeed in showing how and why these specific data appear in that specific time, we rightly contend that they did not emerge at that particular time by mere accident, in other words that the time situation is not external to the content and essence of the event but truly a part of it. That the time situation is essential is the guiding idea of historical research and the key to an evaluation of a historical statement in terms of its success or failure to show that the occurrence is set in this or that particular time. We emphasize that temporality is already inherent in the theory under consideration, in our case St. Paul's doctrine. In other words, when we determine the historical position of a phenomenon we do not determine the sheer fact that it is situated in time or even in a specific time. We determine (or at least try to determine) the exact date. Thus the procedure is quite complicated. We analyze the meaning of a given phenomenon—such as St. Paul—from the various points of view. Then we see that this analysis of, for instance, the dogmatic, characterological traits, etc. does not exhaust the "polychromatic" essence of the phenomenon. Henceforth we add to these factors the explanation of the aspect of time, the historical situation. At the third step there appears the determination that this phenomenon occurred at a definite moment in time. This step is not a merely technical one, because it actually serves as a quantitative expression (the date) of the composition of meaning and time characteristic of the historical phenomenon. The determination of dates reminds us that we are not dealing with pure meanings but are concerned with meanings within time. Thus the addition of the date to the composition of time and meaning expresses the essence of the historical domain and hence also of historical time. The fact is that the problem of fixing the exact date in a historical statement is not due only to the essential connection between the historical meaning and the time situation. The limits of historical time are narrow, unlike time in geology or biological evolution, mainly because historical time is related to human reality. Human reality is narrow in the sense of the human species and certainly in the sense of the career of human individuals. Hence the exact determination of dates is the rule, or at least the goal, because it points to the fact that the meaning of the historical event is incorporated in the historical time which is human time proper.

6. A further shortcoming of Simmel's analysis lies in the fact that he did not complete it by an elucidation of the dimensions of historical time. Since historical time possesses dimensions it has a clear affinity with the structure of psychic time dealt with above. Indeed, in the center of historical time lies the dimension of the present, which is also the axis of psychic time. The reason for this position of the present in historical time lies in the fact that historical knowledge deals with data (in Kant's words, *cognito ex datis*) which are always in the present.

.The datum which is to be explained by historical knowledge must thus be present. But here again the peculiar trait of the historical present becomes prominent. Unlike the psychic present, the historical present is not a dimension of *experience*. In the domain of history we do not find a determined, well-defined *subject* of experience. The psychic present—as elucidated in the previous discussion —is subjective, and for two reasons: It is related to a subject, and it is conceived through a subjective medium, namely experience. In the historical present we do not find a subject in relation to which this present would be determined as a meeting point between the subject and the world. Who is the subject in history? Is it the individual connected with the world, the reality of this or that people, of the generation of fifty-year-olds or twenty-year-olds? Is it the reality of the peasant class or of the mineworkers, etc.? Again, the psychic present is the sphere in which the past and the future meet. By this meeting the present ceases to be a point and becomes a plane. There is a tension in it between the subjects' meeting with the world through the channel of their actual experiences and the relation of this point of meeting to what lies beyond it, i.e. objective time. In the domain of history, in contrast, there is no room for actual experience as related to the present, and the present as a consequence cannot be a point. The present there can have only the status of a plane or fragment defined by qualitative events which occupy a particular position within the continuity of time. Here again various possibilities are open to us, which again are to be explained in connection with the procedure of delimitation of historical periods. Those who see the beginning of the modern age in Europe in the French Revolution assume that the French Revolution belongs to the present. The term "modern age" in its totality is conceived as the present. Here considerations regarding the *meaning* are decisive, namely that even our near historical surroundings depend upon the meaning and trend of the French Revolution, the uprising of the masses, the gulf which became manifest between state and society, the introduction of a planned political order based on principles rather than tradition, etc. But it is possible and certainly helpful to contract the scope of the present and consider it as, say, a fragment between two world wars, since the vital problems of our age arose during that fragment of time, and this fragment considered as present can be even more contracted to the aftermath of World War II. In any case it is clear that the present, namely the dimension of the datum dealt with in historical knowledge, possesses more than one meaning. It is itself determinable from various points of view, and in it there exists at least a differentiation between the near and the distant present. This is an unstable differentiation, and in point of fact it is but another form of the differentiation between the past and the present. It too reveals the difficulty of defining clearly the limits of each of the dimensions of time, because of the fundamental fact that there is no clearly defined subject experiencing the present as there is in the personal realm where the subject is backed or guaranteed, as it were, through its being a psychophysical unit. Since there is such a subject in the personal or psychic present, this present is *not* totally constructed. Since there is no subject taken for granted in the historical realm, the historical present *is* totally constructed.

7. Historical time is *constructed* time. The main indication of its construction—and indeed the most expressive one—lies in the fact that *even* the present is a product of a construction. The present is not simply given; it is determined and established by historical knowledge itself. Like

every other construction it is made up of concepts and meanings (as mentioned above in connection with the concepts of mass society, society and state, etc. defining the "modern era"). Here we have the paradox of historical knowledge: The dimension of temporality understood as immediate is not immediate, since it is not given immediately; it is constructed. Time as time is taken for granted because it rests on the assumption of time as form. But which is the time in concreto—this has to be decided by a consideration of content. And this consideration leads to and even demands a construction.

The present is always the dimension of the datum, although the clear-cut determination of the datum is not inherent in temporality itself. The datum ceases to be shapeless because it is necessarily constructed, like the dimension of time in which it exists. Of the *given* datum only the architectonic quality remains, which may be styled a counterpart of the topological aspect of temporality: It is this which is to *be* explained; it does not *do* the explaining. We deal with it and it does not deal with anything itself. Thus the constructed present retains the epistemological status of passivity as an object for which historical knowledge seeks an explanation in the past. We cannot therefore accept the simple and common definition of historical knowledge as an endeavor to explain the present, because the present qua focus of that knowledge itself is not simply given; it needs an explanation, and this explanation in turn leads to a construction. Only by that means does it become a historical present at all. The conclusion drawn from this might be formulated in the following way: The absolute distinction between the dimensions of time does not hold good any more. Since the present is not the immediate datum there is no essential distinction between the present and the past. The difference between them depends on the status assigned to these dimensions from the point of view of historical knowledge itself, i.e. of what is to be explained and what explains. Hence the topological position of past and present respectively becomes related to the meaningful position of the explaining and explained factor respectively. The task of historical knowledge is to exchange the topological position for the meaningful one and to make the former only the support of the latter. But it will be shown that even this distinction does not remain absolute and rigid.

8. Yet the historical present has a further meaning too. It is not only the dimension of the datum of knowledge. It is the dimension of the decision and the actual act carried out as well. This aspect of the present has been described by Georg Lukacs in a fine passage: "The concrete 'now' and the 'here' . . . is . . . the moment of decision, the moment of the birth of the new. Insofar as man directs his interest . . . toward the past *or* the future these two are rigid and become strange. . . . Only when man is capable of conceiving the present as coming into being —by knowing those of its tendencies, from the dialectic opposition of which he is able to *create* the future— is the present as coming into being made into *his* present. Only one whose destiny it is and who has the will to realize the future is able to see the concrete truth of the present." [3] In this formulation Lukacs—in accordance with his general tendency to identify theory and practice—tries to place the present as the medium of decision above the present as the locus of the datum for historical or conceptual reflection, or at any rate he causes reflection to become inherent in decision. We have to reject his general presupposition because we maintain the fundamental distinction

3. Georg Lukacs, *Geschichte und Klassenbewusstsein* (Berlin, Malik, 1923), p. 223.

between the process and its knowledge. This prevents us from blurring the distinction between the present as the locus of the act—belonging to the process—and the present as the locus of the datum—belonging to historical knowledge. Nevertheless, one finds in Lukacs' formulation the second aspect of the present as that sphere in which occurs the deed projecting and producing the future. Here we envisage what is perhaps the most relevant quality of the historical present. The present as the sphere of acts is neither immediate nor experiential. It obtains its position not through the time character as such but through the meaning inherent in or rendered to it, viz. through the decision directed toward and establishing the future. It may be that we ought not to speak here of the present as a product of a conceptual construction, since a decision is not a pure conceptual act but involves moral and social action as well. Decision can be motivated by conceptual deliberation, but as a decision, that is to say as an act of giving momentum to a course of action, it transcends the conceptual framework. In spite of this difference between the conceptual construction related to reflection and the shaping of the future by the present through decision, there is a feature common to the two sides of the historical present. This feature results from the very essence of historical time, namely the correlation or combination of meaning and temporality. In the case of historical knowledge the meaning is purely conceptual; in the case of historical decision it is a meaning of an action. Thus the historical present must be considered in its two aspects: as the dimension of the datum of historical knowledge and as the dimension of the decision building the future or at least anticipating it. Here again the question arises as to whether the present as the dimension of the decision has an absolute meaning or whether it too, like the present as the dimension of the datum, depends upon a standpoint. Lukacs clearly holds that the present as the dimension of the decision of the "proletariat" (as the class representing the future society) occupies an absolute status, since it is the dimension of the struggle for a unified society materializing the categories of unity and totality. If so, then the absoluteness of the present cannot be inherent in the present as such; it must be inherent in the subject of decision carried out in it and related to the goal of the decision. Thus even in this case the present depends upon the *meaning* bestowed upon it, and beyond or without this meaning it would lose its determinate, let alone absolute, position. Therefore the feature common to the two concepts of the present—as the dimension of datum and of decision—remains in force, namely its relation to a meaning. In the one case the present as the locus of the *datum* is the dimension which is to be explained, while in the other as the locus of *decision* it is the dimension in which the change creating the further process of history takes place.

Two links can be forged between the two aspects of the present.

a. The present as the dimension of the actual occurrence can be converted into a datum of historical research. If we set, for instance, the struggle for national independence as the content of an actual decision we may, from the point of view of historical research, seek for an explanation of this occurrence in the past. The decision can be looked at historically, i.e. from the point of view of historical narration, and hence be turned into a datum. In this case it becomes the fact to be explained. This in turn leads us to determine the past of the present decision now considered as a datum. The procedure of historical construction is again set in motion, for example we ask for the explanation of the national struggle in the French Revolution or in the period following the Congress of Vienna. The link between the two concepts of the historical present enables us to turn the decision into a datum, and we know from the outset the datum which we seek to explain historically. In spite of this we have to stress that the status of decision belonging to the historical process and the status of datum related to historical knowledge are by no means identical. The turning of a decision into a datum is still a construction. We construct the fragment of time where our decision was located in the first place. We construct the time limits of that present we seek to explain. The moment of decision is stretched, as it were, by turning it into a datum. The moment may be a point but the locus of the datum is certainly a plane. Yet the link between the two sides of the historical present enables us in this case to be watched in action.

b. From the point of view of knowledge the present is the dimension of the datum, i.e. it is that which has to be explained. But the present of the historical decision or of the actual occurrence as understood historically can be taken as an explanation not only of itself but of the past as well. The past explains the given present, but in some cases the actual present explains the past or throws some light on it and thus indirectly explains itself. If a modern historian even unconsciously shifts the experience of the modern return to Zion to that of the Persian epoch, or if he generally builds his conception on facts existing and understandable in the present (since they belong to the horizon of his own sphere of experience), he attempts to throw light on the past from the present. By means of the past, understandable through the present, he tries to understand not only what actually exists in the present but also the past itself as the present experience throws light on it. He goes back from the present through the past to the present. But even here the distinction between what is to be explained and what explains has not been abolished, though it gets blurred in some cases.

We may thus sum up: The present is the dimension of historical knowledge on the one hand and of historical occurrence on the other. In both its aspects it is a composition of meaning and temporality. The present is the storehouse of the remnants of the past and thus the present for knowledge, and a reservoir of the potentialities of the future and thus a present of the ongoing historical process.

9. One of the distinctive traits of psychic time has been considered to be its continuity. Continuity depends upon the convergence in the present of various lines of experience in the past, and upon the awareness of the subject experiencing the fact in the present and the certainty that the past is his own. This convergence is possible only because of the consciousness of the self. Continuity of the self is established by the convergence of the past in the present; yet this self establishes this convergence itself. In the realm of historical time continuity is not established from the outset, because there is no clearly defined subject which carries continuity in itself and becomes conscious of it. Husserl observed that the unity of consciousness comprising the past is an ultimate phenomenological datum so far as there is a defined sphere in which this unity exists, for instance the sphere of the self. The psychic manifestation of this unity will be memory. But in the transsubjective domain of history we are not allowed to speak of memory, because there is no bearer of the memory, no one to engage in a psychological act of referring a present awareness to the past.[4] The relation of the present to the past is hence not a primary datum and cannot be a phenomenological datum

4. See Michael Oakeshott, *Experience and Its Modes* (Cambridge, Eng., 1933), p. 102.

in Husserl's sense. It is *constructed* by using the means at the disposal of historical knowledge.

The relation of the present to the past is constructed by historical knowledge in order to explain the datum in the present. Without this construction there would be altogether no justification for that relation. The past appears in regard to the present as an introduced means and not as a datum. Sometimes it is said that the past has an "ideal" existence in historical consciousness. This connotes that the past is an existence introduced through the means of historical knowledge and justified by the end it serves, i.e. explaining the actual datum in the present. Continuity in history will thus not be an established datum or one expressing itself immediately as is the case in the realm of the self. Since the awareness of the past is not immediate, continuity too is not immediate. Historical knowledge is striving to establish continuity and to convince itself of its factuality. The test of continuity lies in its task of throwing light on its datum. Continuity is to be attained through the discovery of the relations connecting the present and the past. If historical knowledge faces a datum, for example the political parties in the United States of America, and does not find it possible to formulate exactly the programs which divide them, it tries to explain the phenomenon historically. It searches in the past for the causes or reasons which are apt to explain the phenomenon in the present and creates the continuity between the past and the datum in the present. Here again we find that for historical consciousness the past exists not as what actually has been but as what explains the present. Once more we encounter the composition of temporality and meaning characteristic of historical time: The past exists insofar as it possesses a meaning with reference to the present; it exists insofar as it fulfills a function in knowledge.

But from this dependence upon the present a hasty conclusion has been drawn which has produced, from St. Augustine (who, to be sure, considered the nature of time in general and not of historical time especially) to Croce and Collingwood, a mistaken attitude and a general misconception regarding the nature of historical time. St. Augustine assumed that the past like the future has no existence of its own. The past, he thought, exists only as the past of the present, and the future exists only as the future of the present. "Past, which now are not, or the future which are not yet, who can measure? Unless a man shall presume to say, that can be measured which is not. . . . Wheresoever then is whatsoever is, it is only as present." [5] St. Augustine dealt with time in the theological context because he was interested in establishing the relationship between eternity and time and between occurrences in the past like creation and revelation and reality in the present. As has happened several times in the history of philosophy the theological connotation of the conception has been replaced by an immanent conception. There is no longer the problem of the relationship between eternity and time; the problem arises as to the relationship between dimensions of time itself without the background in eternity. This replacement of the theological conception by the immanent conception is to be found in modern theories, mainly in Croce and Collingwood. For these theories, by their confinement to time only, past exists only as it is present, and future exists insofar as there is present going out toward future. These theories do not consider the fact that, in spite of the existence of remnants of the past in the present, the time dimension of past does not become part of the present. Croce and Collingwood exhausted the

5. *The Confessions of St. Augustine,* The Guild Classics (Literary Guild of America), ch. 11, pp. 270–1.

meaning of St. Augustine's theory in their conclusion regarding the nature of the historical consciousness. Consciousness, they thought, receives the past not in its existence beyond the present but insofar as it is intermixed with the present and encapsulated in it. Croce and Collingwood did not make a distinction between two forms of intermixture with the present. The past is intermixed with the present since its remains are found in documents and even in living phenomena. But the past also exists as the background of the present and as such explains it. It is through the past that we disclose the meaning of "messages" stemming from it. A man finds pieces of pottery, the so-called Lachish documents, and investigates them historically; he regards them as messages from the past, testifying to actual events which took place in the past. He does not seek their meaning in themselves; he seeks in them the content assigned to them in the past, i.e. in the meaningful temporal situation of the past. The past is the past of the present. But this fact does not abolish the difference and the tension between the present and the past. The past which explains the present does so thanks to its distance from it and not to its proximity. The theory of St. Augustine points at only *one* distinctive feature in the essence of historical time—the proximity existing between the "far" dimensions of time (past and future) and that dimension which serves as an axis of time, namely the present. But it must be said that historical time comprises both nearness of and distance between the dimensions; the distance between dimensions cannot be passed over or skipped. Historical time is both concentrated and expanded. The concentration is expressed in relation to the datum in the present; the expansion is expressed in relation to the meaning resulting from the past. The fact that the past has a position of its own for historical research—in spite of its relatedness to the datum in the present—is due to the structure of time itself: Time is the form of succession and succession as such does not abolish time nor does it create it. The aspect of succession must be retained in historical time itself. Present succeeds past but does not make it cease to be real. The idea of succession prevents us from looking at the present as inheriting only the past and encapsulating it in itself. Succession itself has a historical meaning, and as such it provides for the distance between the dimensions in time. In terms of meaning there may be a proximity between the dimensions of time. But in terms of time itself there is distance inherent in the aspect of succession.

From here we may proceed to a further conclusion concerning the actual procedure and function of historical research. The past exists for the present and we discover it, or at least approach it, because it exists for the present. But once we have discovered it we proceed to understand the *present of the past* and do not stop with the *past of the present*. Indeed, the past is not primarily given; it is a product of the construction which establishes the connection between the datum in the present and what should explain it in the past. From this point of view the past is a secondary object of historical consciousness. Yet in spite of that it is an object that has a value in itself.

History thus cannot be defined simply as a science of the past. It is, *among other things*, a science dealing with the past because the past appears within the horizon of the historical consciousness which is directed toward the past from the present. To express this metaphorically, the past first appears to historical research as a point on a line leading to the present. Once this point appears it becomes, or may become, a plane, and hence we may endeavor to disclose occurrences within it, its structure and order. The past acquires a present of its own and thus acquires the quality of a plane which is a feature of every present.

St. Augustine, who stressed the connection and the nearness of the past and the present, spoke of the past of the present. Had he stressed also the distance between them he would have analyzed the present of the past too. The past of the present is the ground for the contact between the dimensions of historical time. The present of the past separates them. Historical time has in itself a tension between the two aspects and is not unilateral as the theories originated by St. Augustine presuppose.

We must therefore reject Collingwood's view that the future as such and the past as such have an ideal existence only.[6] Collingwood thought that the past exists only insofar as it lives in the present; it does not exist in itself. But if we distinguish between the past as possessing a relation to the present and the past as possessing a meaning of its own, we cannot accept this sharp distinction between real and ideal existences applied to the dimensions of time. The past qua explanation of the present exists ideally, but the past as having a present of its own appears as a self-contained domain, at a distance from the present but really existing nevertheless. We have here no other alternative but to follow with Kant the second postulate of empirical thought, which defines reality as that which is bound up with the material conditions of the experience, that is with sensation. But sensation or sensual perception does not mean only *present* sensation. Kant spoke of the "series of the possible sensible perceptions" in order to make the connection of reality with sensation in general and not merely with the actual sensation in the present.

6. See R. G. Collingwood, "Some Perplexities about Time," in *Proceedings of the Aristotelian Society* (1925–26), p. 149.

Therefore if the past was once a present, i.e. an occurrence bound up with an actual sensation, there is no power capable of abolishing its reality. How could a later moment convert a reality into a nonreality? The chief defect of Collingwood's theory is that it identifies reality with the present. This is due to the fact that he conceives reality to be bound up with one dimension of time instead of with time in general. Since Collingwood and Croce are not concerned with the relation between the category of time and historical time, they neglect the conceptual background of historical time and confine time to a single dimension only. The jump into a theory of history without due consideration of the relevance of the time factor obscures the view of historical time. This is one of the main faults of the historicist trend: It speaks in the name of history, but it may be doubted whether history is well represented by its historicist advocates.

Here one may refer to Paul Weiss' attempt to safeguard the reality of the past and to find an adequate expression for the ontological status of the past.[7] He sees that the fact that the past has a different mode of reality from the present, that the past is "closed," for example, does not turn it into something occupying a different ontological position from the present, e.g. that of an ideal in contradistinction to the reality of the present. We learn from his theory that one may not abolish the various shades of reality so as to be left only with the alternatives of either a real present or an ideal past. Yet the question remains whether this theory does not allow that there may be an *absolute* past altogether disconnected from the present. The past in fact is essentially relational; its meaning depends, at least partially, upon the present which contemplates it. We may

7. See Paul Weiss in *The Review of Metaphysics*, June 1952, December 1953, and the present author's observations, *ibid.*, June 1953.

therefore ask, at least in terms of historical time, whether
there can be a past as a sheer fact, apart from the meaning
bestowed on it, as this theory assumes. Past is closed as
time, but since the past contains a meaning the factor of
meaning is responsible for the proximity of the past to the
present, that is to say for the relative openness of past to
present. We have to find our way between the historicist
position blurring the distance and the ontological interpretation stressing the distance in terms of the closed nature of
the past. Historical research is possible because the two dimensions are related in their meanings. Historical research
is worth while because the two dimensions are separated,
being rooted in time, and it is worth while establishing con-
tacts on the basis of separation. The view which sees only
the contact makes historical research trivial, in spite of
its concern with the nature and central position of historical
research in the map of knowledge. The view which stresses
the separation makes historical research impossible, because
it maintains the process directed toward the future and
does not provide justification for reflection turning back
to the past.

10. We may throw light on this aspect of the relationship to the past from another point of view as well. Historical research dealing with the past may also be applied
to consciousness concerned with time as such. The relation
to time will be in this case a historical datum or a factor
implied in the datum as datum. For instance, historical
research is concerned with eschatological expectations of
the end of the world, with chiliastic movements centered
around a date of a particular meaning, etc. In all these
cases we do not face a vague event in the past but an event
in the past, the content of which is determined by temporality inherent in it. In such cases time is not only a bridge
between events but a content as well. Yet it is not empty

or pure time which is the forthcoming day of judgment, the second coming of the Messiah, etc. We have here a composition of meaning and temporality characteristic of historical time in general. But it is obvious that when we deal with an object, the content of which is characterized by a specific temporal consciousness, we do not identify this temporal consciousness implicit in the object of research with the consciousness of historical research dealing with that object. The consciousness of the historical research deals with the remains of that temporal consciousness in the past insofar as they exist in the present, but the temporal consciousness qua object of research in itself lies beyond the present. It lies in the past where it has an existence of its own, enclosed in itself and meaningful on its own merits. Where the object is temporal in its very content and not only in its position within a causative order, we clearly see the double relationship of affinity and distance existing between the present and the past.

To sum up this part of the discussion, the relationship between the present and the past rests on a construction. This construction is evident from the fact that we start with the present which is later and not with the past which is earlier. We convert the ontological order of time into an order structured from the point of view of historical considerations. From the point of view of the ontological order the French Revolution, for instance, does not appear before the Napoleonic Wars, because the occurrence called the French Revolution has a self-sufficient existence within time, without an inherent relation to subsequent occurrences.[8] The sequence of occurrences is a determination

8. Collingwood would consider the two events as one and the same event, as in his example of the murder of Caesar and the Battle of Actium ("Some Perplexities about Time"). But this view is characteristic of Collingwood's refusal to consider the time factor as a primary one in the nature

bound up with the assumption of a chain of events needed
for historical consciousness and meaningful in it. Here
again we find the dual relationship to the past: It exists
in a relation to the present as what appears *before* the present, and it exists on its own in the dimension of an occurrence which was *once* a present in itself. We encounter
here again the two aspects of time in general: succession
and duration. From the point of view of succession we determine the order of earlier and later, i.e. which is the
past which precedes the present, because of the capacity of
this past to explain the present. From this point of view we
discover the relationship between the dimensions of time.
But from the point of view of duration we discover the
individual term within a sequence, and in the case before
us we arrive at the past in its self-sufficient existence, i.e.
we dwell on the present of the past. The dual relationship
between the present and the past reflects and materializes
the two aspects of time in general. Succession of time
provides for the contact between the dimensions, while
duration provides for the possibility of a detachment of one
dimension from the other. Duration in turn serves as the
basis or support of the meaning of the past in its own terms.
The aspect of duration as the aspect of time does not exhaust the status and essence of the historical event under
consideration. It only provides the necessary time factor for
the synthesis between time and meaning.

---

of a historical phenomenon. Therefore a difference in time position is for
him not relevant in terms of the content of the events. If we stick con-
sistently to this view, nothing could prevent our looking at the whole of
history as one prolonged event once we detect the meaningful connection
between the partial events composing history. Hence unless we consider
the time factor as constitutive the whole historical sequence may become
as a set similar to the series of the natural numbers, which although following one another do not follow one another in time.

11. An observation might be made here regarding what is usually called historical progress. Historical progress presupposes the notion that historical time possesses a clear center in which all the paths converge and toward which all the paths lead. But it has been made clear that historical time has a moving focus, that is to say it is focused on in the present. The status of a focus is accorded to the present not owing to its peculiar *content* but because it is the *dimension* of the datum. The relationship between the present as the dimension of the datum and the past as a dimension safeguarding the meaning assigned to the present cannot be one between a lower stage and a higher. The relationship between them is a correlation and not a ladderlike gradation. Further still, the present has two meanings: It is the dimension of the datum and the dimension of the occurrence. As the dimension of the datum it is the present of our own actual present, but as the dimension of the occurrence it is not only a dimension of our own actual present but also the dimension of the past in its status as a creator of our own present. The access to the past is through the datum existing in the present. But the present can be seen as a prolongation of the past, still not as a sheer dimension of time but as a dimension of meaningful data. It is not feasible to assume, as in the theory of progress, that our present, as the dimension of the occurrence bound up with ourselves, represents a higher stage than the present of our ancestors. Our present is at most *richer* than that of our ancestors, since here in our present their present and ours meet, or their present is encapsulated insofar as it was historically productive. Yet this cannot lead us to say that ours is superior in terms of values. One should not see historical time as a progress possessing a direction or an upward movement. Historical time has a moving and an accumulative focus. The present

is not the exclusive property of anybody; every hour of the present, every *historical* hour, is richer than previous ones and therefore different from them—but not superior.

At this point we may rightly introduce a distinction between historical *achievement* and historical *progress* proper. If I set for myself, or if a society sets for itself, a goal, for instance the conquest of the desert, the achievement of that goal may be considered as progress. But this kind of progress is actually an achievement of a goal from the point of view of the subjects, be they individuals or societies, who set this goal for themselves. The progress in this sense is relative to the subject concerned with the goal and is an achievement. But talking about historical progress implies talking about the historical process as a whole, about something which is immanent in the process itself and relevant to the universal subject of history. Progress is supposed to be relevant to a subject who would experience the total course of history as an individual or a society may experience the achievement of the determined goal they set for themselves. Yet from the point of view of the historical process there are differences between generations and enrichments of experiences, but no progress proper can be encountered. Practically we see that when we talk for instance about technological progress we actually talk about achievements in a particular field. Talking about progress is actually talking about goals realized, like that of improving the standard of living. Yet we know that the achievement of a goal, as in the case of technological development, need not automatically mean historical progress in the total sense of the word. The distinction suggested before between achievement and progress is fundamentally related to the ontological difference between fragmentary courses of events, connected to specific goals and experiencing subjects related to these goals, and the total rhythm of history considered from within by a universal subject and not from the position of a particular experiencing subject.

Not to see the difference between our own achievement and the progress of history in general is somewhat similar to not seeing the difference between our own interest and the general consideration not attached to any partial interest. The naïve shift from the partial achievement to the total outlook amounts to a fallacy of "misplaced totality." It is precisely the task of a philosophical analysis, rooted as it is in total (synoptic) outlook, to see this difference and to remind us about the limitation of the achievement point of view when projected onto the realm of history in general.

We may put differently the criticism of the idea of progress. This idea presupposes *a*) that in a particular present something is realized which is an absolute value or a universal value or a value from all possible points of view. It presupposes *b*) that there is a subject experiencing this realization, or that the very progress creates with its own course the total subject experiencing the all-round value. Yet it is clear that the process of historical time precludes the elevation of any particular present to the level of the point or basis of realization of something which surpasses historical reality, i.e. the absolute value inherent in the progress. The same process in time precludes the fixation of a universal historical subject, because to be a subject is to be an experiencing and reflecting being. To be experiencing and reflecting makes the subject a particular subject within the process and not one breaking the process and asserting itself as a universal subject. The piecemeal nature of historical process and the piecemeal position of the subject experiencing the perpetually given present permit the idea of a piecemeal achievement and preclude the idea of a total progress.

Similar considerations apply to the common concept of historical decline. This concept too can at most point to a limited perspective, i.e. decline of the West, decline of religion, etc. In such a limited perspective we clearly deal with a subject matter or a concern (West, religion) and look at the process from the point of view of this subject matter or concern of ours. But there is no justification for dealing with decline in general, isolated from a specification of what declines. The concept of total decline differs more from the concept of achievement dealt with before than from the concept of progress. The logic underlying the concept of progress underlies the concept of decline. The difference is one in direction but not one in the outlook of the fundamental nature of the historical process and the relationship between past and present in the process. Hence a historical achievement may mean a decay of some institutions worth while on their own merits, as when technological achievement sweeps away handicraft. The concept of achievement allows for this ambiguity, but the concept of progress or of decline does not.

It is traditional to distinguish between the epistemological-formal approach to history and the metaphysical-material, the one dealing with historical knowledge and the other with the process itself. Unless I am wrong this distinction must be abolished, for history is, as has been shown, essentially a union of the two aspects though not an identity of them. We do not object to the ideas of historical progress and decline by affirming that the actual historical facts overthrow them. We object to them by showing that an analysis of the concept of time in history, as the coordinate of facts and not as an event or a setting

of events, shows that there is no room for the ideas of progress and decline in terms of historical consciousness proper.
These ideas cannot be historical conceptions based on
the epistemological and the ontological essence of history. They presuppose the isolation of the aspect of historical process from the aspect of historical consciousness;
they also presuppose the clear, single, directed determinability of consciousness by process or in the sense that there
is a clear direction in the process; consciousness has only
to recognize it as it is. But consciousness of the process is
always a consciousness within the present and not the consciousness of what the process will have accomplished in
the future. All these fundamental considerations have to
serve as a criticism of the idea of historical progress—and
not some material facts, like poverty, which make this concept contradict facts. To put it sharply, the idea of historical
progress defies the fundamental features of the nature of
history. It is not an idea of a conception of history but
rather an import of some extrahistorical consideration to
history or a superimposition of wishful thinking on history.
Sometimes it appears as imposing wishful thinking and
sometimes as transferring plans and projects from the sphere
of deeds to the sphere of the process in its objective course.

12. We may turn now to the aspect of future as a
dimension of historical time. The past appears in history
through the medium of cognition since the bridge to
the past is stretched out from the present and the data in
it. In contrast, the bridge to the future is stretched out
from the present as the dimension of occurrence and
decision. The future exists in relation to the present. The
existence of the past and its meanings depend upon
the *consciousness* of the present; the existence of the future
depends upon *occurrences* within the present which as
occurrences go by definition beyond the present. Here too

we must distinguish between the two meanings of the future or between two aspects contained in it, namely the complete future closed for the change introduced by the historical occurrence and the future built up by the occurrence itself.

Tadeusz Kotarbinski formulated the problem of the future in a somewhat paradoxical way.[9] He asked, Does not something already exist in the future? Can next summer not cease to be, since it is already in existence? Does it not exist before its actual appearance? Yet, are there not parts in the future which do not yet exist? It is possible to assume that the death of a hero already exists in the future; but the manner of its occurrence, the circumstances, and the historical factors which play a part in that occurrence are not fully independent of the deeds which shape the future. These features of the future depend upon actual historical occurrences directed toward the future.

This distinction between the two aspects of future can be put in the following way. Perhaps it is desirable to draw boundary lines between those occurrences found in the existential, the biological, or the physical field and other occurrences which are *historical proper*. Those found in the former exist even before they have occurred; a Russian winter, for example, appears at a specific time of the year and is an established fact before it actually occurs in a particular year during a military invasion of Russia. But within these occurrences which constitute a quasi-framework there appear *historical* occurrences in the strict sense of the term, for example the impact of this winter on Napoleon's invasion of Russia. These latter occurrences exist in historical time in its strict sense, i.e. within the tension between the present and the future. Thus with respect to the future, historical time appears as contained in an

9. In an article in the Polish periodical, *Przegląd Filozoficzny*, 1913.

embracing setting in which there is some room for historical occurrences as well. In other words, the future appears in regard to historical occurrences both as a background and as a content shaped by it. The future as a background belongs to the framework, physical, biological, etc.; future as a content and as a content only belongs to historicity itself. This distinction between the two aspects of future is indifferent to the notorious problem of determinism. We do not stress the freedom or dependence of historical occurrences on what preceded them causally. We do stress the fact that the future in itself provides some room for historical occurrences proper which plan, build, and shape it.

In the relationship of the present to the future we may therefore distinguish three interacting attitudes.

a. Against the background or within the framework of physical, biological, etc. occurrences the actual decision in the present can maintain toward the future a single relation only, that of *readiness* or *preparedness* toward what is due to occur. Here readiness appears as a passive attitude, i.e. not as creating the future but as taking into account factors within the framework which are independent of the decision, for example the fact that the winter will come regardless of the tactical decisions of Napoleon. The decision to invade the country consciously or unconsciously takes this aspect of the future into account. But in doing so it introduces into the activity of going toward the future something of the nature of consciousness and reflection. Thus the relation toward that aspect of the future which is unshapable by the historical—in our example military—operations is not a relation rooted in decision. It is a relation rooted in reflection, that of taking into account and knowing what is due to occur irrespective of our own decisions and deeds. We said before that the relation toward the past is one rooted in reflection, because the past as existent can be only known and not shaped. From this point of view we may observe a partial analogy between the past and the future: The unshapable aspect of the future, though it did not yet actually occur, belongs as it were to the already existent past. And having the nature of the past as existent (through dwelling in terms of dimensions of time in the future) this aspect of the future evokes a relation of reflection similar to the relation evoked by the past. Reflection in this case amounts to taking into consideration.

b. Our decisions are concerned with those things and events which will occur within the framework of the already existent future. What shall and what can we do in the framework of the given fact that winter will come anyway? The existent framework of the future draws a line between what is only possible and open to our own shaping and intervention and what is beyond our capacity to change and hence has to be taken for granted. The relationship toward the future is one of knowing not only what already exists but also the possibilities within the given framework of what is beyond the possible. This kind of knowledge related to the line of distinction between the given and the possible affects our decision and directs it. One of the main problems facing a historical agent is to know where this theoretical distinction between the closed and the open, between the existent and the possible, is to be applied. Winter is an established and unavoidable fact. But a historical agent may try to utilize the established fact for his decision or he may try to act by means which would overcome the difficulty implied in the existent fact. The facts as facts cannot be undone; but the position of the facts in the total context of a historical deed may be open to a historical shaping. It goes without saying that political decisions depend very much on this kind of reasoning and weighing of the established facts and factors (for instance the geopolitical situation of a country), and in terms of these it utilizes or overcomes what is changeable within the situation. To put it differently, the framework to be taken into account is not only a framework; through the historical agent it becomes a deed, or at least may become a part of the historical deed. The planning of the future makes the given framework active, as it were. The historical deed activates the passive background of the future.

c. Unlike what is open to decision, i.e. what can come into existence through the act of decision and its direction, the relation toward the future is not one of sheer reflection. It is a relation adequate to the active character of the decision and as such a relation of *intention* and *planning*. The future appears from this angle as the dimension of the object of planning, and the decision is directed toward the materialization of plans. The aspect of *knowing* remains always in force, but it is interwoven in this case in the aspect of *decision*, as active interference in the course of events. Even so, the future does not exist outside all relation to cognition. Only the moment of the decision as such can be conceived as a pure occurrence, while its content, being a projection and planning of the future, contains elements of cognition. Here we can agree with that side of Marx' view according to which there is no practice devoid of theory. Practice is always circumscribed by the cognitive framework, though the framework does not make the picture itself nor, in our case, eradicate practice. In all the attitudes toward the future an aspect of anticipation is inherent by the very fact that the future is the horizon for the process beginning in the present. The attitude of readiness (under *a* above) is an attitude rooted in anticipation, causing the adjustment of the present to what is due to occur in the future. The attitude of taking into account (under *b* above) is in a way more than sheer anticipation, because in this attitude the future is not only the horizon but becomes also a factor in the consideration and deliberations of the present. The attitude of planning goes beyond that of taking into account; here the very horizon of the future is built up and thus not the given horizon is taken into account but the present creates the future by its own means.

13. There is a complexity of relations between a historical consciousness dealing with the past and a decision directed toward the future.

a. Historical consciousness implicitly presupposes the existence of the future as a dimension in which new historical data are due to be discovered and thus to be used by a future historical consciousness. Historical consciousness supposes that archaeological or documentary remains can and will be discovered in the future. Thus it is aware of the possible relation of that future to the chronological past already dealt with in existing historical research. These new discoveries are likely to change the historical view already formed and held. From the point of view of historical knowledge, being as it is an *open* knowledge, the future appears to indicate what Whitehead called the dimension of incompleteness. We may be more specific on that. The awareness of the future makes any approach to data existent in the present incomplete, one to be completed in the future. Because of this critical reservation or anticipation, historical consciousness is a consciousness of a datum in the present, while the future appears in regard to it as a dimension of a new present possessing new data. From this point of view time is the change of the future into a past.

b. The actual present occurrence influences historical knowledge. The future appears in regard to historical knowledge as the dimension of a new present. Knowledge therefore takes into account the new present not only in its capacity of enriching the historical material already in possession by providing new data but also in its potentialities for shaping the historical understanding itself. The new present will be a meaningful situation which is due to throw light on the past; the present often guides the understanding of the past; the future is a potential present and as such has to be taken into consideration by the historical research in the present. The anticipation of the future accompanies not only the existence in the present but also the research undertaken in the present. This research anticipates the future in the sense that the future as the dimension of data and as the dimension of actual meaningful occurrences must influence historical research either by making it incomplete or by making it listen to meaningful occurrences to be encountered in the present of the future.

c. Insofar as historical understanding emerges from the present and is itself a part of the present, it affects the occurrence and becomes a factor shaping the tendency toward the projection of the future. Marx saw this point, but he identified consciousness as such with the position it holds within the occurrence. He treated the actual decision as though it were only an expression of the occurrences. This is a rash identification, for consciousness does deal with the past and becomes related to the future only indirectly. We have no right to change this indirect relation and make it into a determination of the present by the future. Theory is apt to be a part of practice, but it is by no means identical with it any more than the future is identical with the past or the investigation of a datum in the present is identical with the actual occurrence in the present which projects into the future. We always encounter consciousness; we do not always encounter an occurrence. This creates a kind of preponderance on the part of consciousness which is *related* to occurrence but is also *independent* of it. Practice has theory in it, but theory is more than practice and oversteps its boundaries. This preponderance of theory is again related to the fundamental fact that all the attitudes toward the future have an anticipatory component. Thus they have to some degree the cognitive component of awareness. But only some of the attitudes, and mainly that of decision, have the practical component of planning. Thus there is no escape from the reflective attitude. To be sure, this attitude does not exhaust the field of anticipation but is always there.

This point has some bearing on the problem of historicism so extensively discussed in our generation. The presupposition of historicism is that reflection is meaningful and valid only in the setting of its occurrence. This is so because of the fundamental assumption of historicism that the process creates the reflection on it and that there is no independence on the part of reflection. But the analysis of historical knowledge proves the opposite: Reflection transcends the situation; it oversteps occurrence both toward the past and the future. Paradoxically the examination of the nature of the various aspects of historical knowledge does not prove historicism but rather proves to be a starting point of a criticism of it. Historicism gained strength not from a conceptual examination of the nature of historical knowledge but from a kind of "shadow atmosphere" created by the flood of historical research. Historicism makes reflection sink into the circumstances where it occurs. But—to put it in metaphysical terms—man is more than his circumstances, and historical consciousness is an activity of man as a partly sovereign being. Historical consciousness is rooted in the reflective attitude which is present in the direction toward both the past and the future. Historical consciousness is not a part of the process only, because it has its roots in consciousness which is not historical only.

Collingwood suggested the connection of the dimensions of time with modal differences. He saw the present as a mode of reality, the past as a mode of necessity, and the future as a mode of possibility.[10] *Prima facie* this sounds plausible. The past cannot be reversed and therefore may be considered necessary; the future is open to shaping and hence may be considered to be possible. But on a closer examination we see that within the future there is an aspect of necessity in all those sides which form the framework of occurrences; for example, the fact that a historical agent is bound to die is, in existential terms, a necessary fact which cannot be changed and thus cannot be historically shaped. An aspect of possibility is implied even in the past, however, because the past appears in regard to the present not directly but in its connection with consciousness. The past is never complete from the point of view of consciousness. Just because the past is the dimension of meaning (it explains through its existence the essence of the present) it cannot and should not be identified with necessity. On the contrary, if we follow the guidance of the modal differences we might with equal justice identify the past with possibility, since an essential meaning of the past is to be open to various possible interpretations.

We are, however, unable to accept the details of the conception that establishes connection between the dimensions of time with modal differences, nor can we accept the general view. Here we find another attempt to base his-

10. R. G. Collingwood in "Some Perplexities about Time," p. 147.

torical time, or at least the dimensions of it, on content. Yet actually no other way is open to understand historical time but by exhausting the meaning of history. History in its two meanings manifests itself in the essence of historical time and its dimensions. Historical consciousness is concerned chiefly with bridging the distance between the present and the past, while historical occurrences are connected chiefly with the transition from the present to the future. The structure of the dimensions of historical time reflects the essence of the sphere of history as a realm of occurrence stretched toward the future and as a realm of reflection directed toward the past.

14. If we wish to sum up this analysis of historical time we must again emphasize the distinctive trait of the *construction* that is carried out in terms of historical time.

a. The first step in the process of construction is the assumption of an order of "earlier" and "later" within the historical process where the earlier is a factor explaining the later. It has been said above that the localization of the French Revolution had nothing to do with its being an event preceding the Congress of Vienna. This localization is a result of historical investigation, which places the events in the order of a series of preceding and following. Historical investigation, interested as it is in the order of preceding and following, is thus related to the very essence of time qua form of succession. It interprets succession as a relation of preceding and following. On the basis of this the historical order of causal or meaningful relations is laid down. The procedure of construction in the case under consideration lies in looking back on succession from the point of view of the later stage and in establishing a series connecting the later with the earlier.

b. The construction of earlier and later is made from the standpoint of the later, namely the present. We are always investigating the antecedent of the present. The assumption of the order is thus connected with the contraction of the extent of time. In other words, not every succession in time is the object of historical investigation. Here, in the assumption of an earlier and a later and in establishing a series between them, a transcendence has taken place beyond the pure temporal order, and an order of content is built up. Historical investigation determines the French Revolution as "earlier" in regard to the "later" Congress of Vienna since a relationship of content or meaning exists between the two occasions. Historical investigation is not interested—so long as there are no other data which compel it to be interested—in establishing a relationship between the work of Confucius and the Congress of Vienna, although from the mere chronological point of view the sequence of earlier and later holds good in this case too. The chronological order becomes a historical order only owing to the presence of material or meaningful relations. According to this relation we construct a fragment of a temporal series closed between two meaningful events.

c. The fragmentary temporal series is built of qualified events, like the French Revolution and the Congress of Vienna. Between these two events a great many others took place, but historical investigation is interested only in a certain number of them. Only these are included within the series which is limited by the two main events. Historical investigation, by establishing a temporal series between these two events, tries to discover their sequence and continuity in terms not only of time but of meaning too. The sequence in time serves as the given basis for the historical construction but is not identical with it. Historical investigation establishes a sequence of its own on top of the given sequence.

In other words, the sequence and continuity are not pure within pure formal time. Within historical time we assume discontinuous qualified events but try to explain them by continuity. This continuity is never given and is never safeguarded; its dependence on pure time as form of succession cannot be a guarantee of its historical relevance. Historical investigation establishes for itself, through its own means, a continuity employing material principles such as the principle of causation.

Here we envisage one of the peculiar features of historical time. Kant held that temporal succession is the *schema* of the principle of causality. Once the temporal succession has been perceived, a causal relationship between the situations is built up according to the principles of causation. The aspect of time is provided for in transcendental aesthetics and is in a way prior to the aspect of causality dealt with in transcendental logic. Transcendental logic in Kant's sense provides the categories which are realized in the sequence of time, while the aspect of sequence is established in the first place. In contrast we notice that with reference to historical time we cannot rest on the succession or on the perception of it (even when we disregard the fact that past events cannot be *perceived*), as in the case of Confucius and the Congress of Vienna, for instance, where there is a temporal order of sequence between them and still no historical order of dependence of the latter event on the former. The material relationship between events establishes a succession of its own. The idea of succession, derived from the form of time, allows us to establish the material relationship as a superstructure for the order of earlier and later of the events in a sequence. This second order on top is one of meaningful dependence between the events. Thus the dialectical character of historical time becomes manifest again; it has an aspect of time established by meaning, as well as an aspect of meaning rooted within temporality. If we conceive historical time through an analysis of historicity as containing temporality and through an analysis of pure time qua form of succession and duration, we can significantly distinguish three functions of time in history:

a. Time is the *background* or condition of every historical assumption, since time is the form of succession and duration. Every historical assumption presupposes this form and is hence a priori related to time.

b. It is the *medium* for every historical assumption since such an assumption depends upon the order of preceding and following assumed between the two qualified events. It gives a specific meaning to this order, besides that implied in the order as such. Through time we establish the specific historical relation between events, which is more than sheer sequence. In other words, for a historical assumption the aspect of sequence in time is relevant to the extent that this assumption interprets the sequence in terms of time as one in terms of meaning. This leads us to the third aspect.

c. Time is not only the passive framework of history; it is also the *content* of every historical assumption, since no issue under consideration is historical, even in terms of its content, apart from its position within time. The time position is a part of the content and not only the condition for assuming contents. Talking about a historical event, World War I, for example, we *a*) presuppose time as such as the background of our investigation and *b*) use the series of events between, let us say, the establishment of the German Empire and the outbreak of the war. We place the war within this series of time, making this series an explanation of the event under consideration, thus turning the sequence in time into a medium of historical explanation.

And lastly *c*), we see the position of the war in this series (1914) not as an external feature in terms of the historical meaning of this event, but as an expression of the content of the event in the sense that the whole series of events becomes as it were concentrated in the particular event. We start with time as the background and approach more and more the inherence of time in the events themselves, either as a medium for their explanation or as a component of their content.

The analysis of historical time centers around the distinction between the dimensions of time. Human social existence is related to these dimensions and as such it is a subject matter for social science. We shall deal now with the attitude of social science versus the attitude of history and thus attempt to establish their respective positions toward historical time.

CHAPTER 4

HISTORY AND SOCIAL SCIENCE

THE ATTEMPT to throw light on the relation between history and social science will be linked up with the description of this relationship as it is presented in modern sociological research.[1] This analysis will start with an elucidation of the presuppositions underlying the relations between the two domains. From there it will proceed to the explicit relations between them. On the basis of these two investigations I shall try to arrive at a formulation of a positive and systematic set of relations between the two domains and thereby add some aspects to the description of the nature of historical knowledge.

A. *The Implicit Relationship*

1. Sociology has sometimes been defined as the theory of the common life of man. This definition, understood in terms of principles, may lead and actually has led to an attempt to lay down some a priori conditions within consciousness itself for the given fact of the common life of man. The idea is to find roots for social reality in consciousness as the ultimate source of all attitudes. The assumption which underlies such a regression to consciousness seems to

1. Our analysis is based mainly on German sociological research since there the issue has been dealt with from various points of view. Attention should also be paid to the works of Morris Ginsberg, Robert MacIver, and Talcott Parsons.

be that we cannot be satisfied with the fact that common life is a given and encountered empirical fallacy. Hence we have to show that the common life of man is a necessity, since it is ultimately rooted in the realm of consciousness and that of the a priori. Max Adler, for instance, tried to go this way and sought to elevate the historical fact of human common existence to the level of essences. How could this be done? Adler thought that the concept of the universal validity of knowledge, which is in itself an epistemological concept, implies the plurality of subjects. There must be, he thought, a plurality of subjects for whom the validity of knowledge holds good and to whom it might be applicable. To be valid in terms of knowledge implies to be valid not for one single man only but for the rest of us too. Hence it was his assumption that the consideration of the nature of true knowledge leads us intrinsically to the realm of human social existence, which is supposed to be identical with the plurality of subjects engaged in valid knowledge. The idea of valid knowledge related to consciousness demands the empirical human reality of society or community. Or, put differently, the idea of valid knowledge is and can be empirically realized in social life, because the concept of validity requires the plurality of existent human individuals.

This theory actually amounts to the assumption that the common life of man, which is historical common life of course, is but an empirical concretization of an a priori presupposition for universal, or at least intersubjective, validity of knowledge. The historical existence is not an independent or primary sphere but one rooted in a source which is intrinsically above this existence. Or in other words historical common life is not the primary self-sufficient datum of social science, though this view is not oblivious of the empirical fact that the direct immediate datum of sociological investigation must be an empirical datum and therefore a historical one.

The reason for this search for supra-empirical sources for an empirical fact seemed to be the very attempt to place human social existence in its historical context above the level of empirical facts. The reason is to be found in the attempt to look at social existence from an essentialist point of view and to show that social existence is not simply a sheer fact. This theory therefore faces the difficulty of determining the precise nature of the relation of concretization between the a priori datum in consciousness and the empirical datum in history. It must show not only that social existence is rooted in consciousness but also how it is that consciousness goes over from its a priori status to the realm of empirical and historical facts. The theory is ultimately unclear on a fundamental issue: Is universal validity of knowledge realized in the sphere of plurality of empirical subjects living socially together? Is this realization a necessity? Or is there perhaps only a parallelism between universality on the one hand and plurality on the other? In the latter case there is no essential transition from the ideal a priori realm of consciousness and knowledge to the realm of empirical social life. There may be an analogy but not a dependence of the empirical on the a priori.

The difficulty faced by this quasi-Platonic theory can be clearly seen in what is as a matter of fact its tacit assumption: that a *plurality* of subjects is identical with human *common* life, that is to say that subjects related to valid knowledge are ipso facto subjects having mutual relations outside their relation to knowledge. But this is certainly not a necessary consequence. We all may have a relation to a poem we read and appreciate; yet we do not have a relation to each other in terms of reactions, institutions, patterns of behavior, etc. in which we are empirically involved. What holds good in terms of our relation to a poem holds good in terms of our relations to valid knowledge. Valid knowledge may be knowledge for a plurality of subjects, yet this plurality does not automatically create society proper, understood as a pattern of common existence.

But actually sociological research does not rest on any such a priori supposition. It refers to a given fact of social life and does not try to explain its a priori sources in a domain above the empirical, but is engaged in studying the nature of the structure of the empirical domain itself. In the very description of its datum, sociological investigation is bound up with the assumption that this datum as a human reality is a historical reality. Hence the common sociological attitude presupposes that the sphere within which sociology finds its material or its datum is actual human existence, i.e. the domain of history.

2. Furthermore the connection established between sociology and history appears even more clearly from a different point of view. Once we ask the question as to the core or basis of social existence, which is the actual and not the hidden supra-empirical subject matter of sociological investigation, we intend to put our finger on the primary datum of social existence. Max Weber, for instance, and a great many sociologists who followed his line, thought that this datum is not to be found in society as a substance but in social action, i.e. in the process of human existence and behavior itself. He therefore took sociology to be a science dealing with human activity in its various guises. Concepts pointing to collective entities such as "state" or "association" are, he thought, from the sociological point of view but categories of various modes of mutual activity between human beings. Proceeding from the same starting point Georg Simmel drew the conclusion that society is not a *substance* but an *occurrence*. Soci-

ology is for him an empirical science which starts with the empirical assumption of the existence of social life of men and attempts to understand the phenomena composing this life. We may therefore look at the general concept of "society" not as an ontological determination of an independent substance but only as a general description of an empirical datum. As this is an empirical datum it is not a *being* but a *becoming*, not a *thing* but a *function*. It seems to be the epistemological presupposition of this theory that in experience we encounter not substances but processes. Hence the description of the nature of sociology as a branch of empirical knowledge must place the subject matter of sociology in the proper context of empirical phenomena qua processes.

This view leads to the conclusion that the sociological datum is to be conceived of as identical with historical activities, occurrences, or functions. The datum or the material with which sociology is concerned is then not different in its ontological essence from the datum or the material of history. Hence this conception is bound to presuppose that the historical datum in itself is an occurrence. To be sure, this is a presupposition which must be rejected in the light of what has been said before about the historical datum.

Yet the occurrence is not given except in the scene of occurrence itself and for one who is actually engaged in it. And since this scene is, in terms of time dimensions, of the present, some sociological theories arrived at the conclusion that the very subject matter of sociology is the present. Through this device they tried to retain their reference to what they assumed to be the historical datum.

Yet it must be observed that in these theoretical suggestions one encounters a confusion of concepts. As a matter of fact the concept of occurrence is employed here in two different senses. On the one hand occurrence appears as opposed to being, just as function is thought to be opposed to substance. Hence the sociological theory on this view rejects every approach to social existence which looks at society as at a static object existing independently of and beyond the historical process in its perpetual change. On the other hand the concept of occurrence or function is opposed to the concept of a self-consistent collectivity existing independently of the concrete relations between individual human beings. Society is conceived of only as the network of the various relations between these human beings. Thus there is no clear difference made between two sets of opposite concepts: substance versus function and collectivity versus individual¹ human beings. The term occurrence is taken as covering both processes and individuals. In any case the idea of social substance is rejected as a legitimate sociological idea because it connotes both the status of a being and a status of a collectivity independent of individuals.

This confusion of concepts, which throws some light on the epistemological naïveté of some of the sociological theories, makes it nevertheless clear that as soon as sociology confines itself to the empirical realm it actually takes for granted the historical datum. The tacit intention is to emphasize that the sociological datum is virtually identical with the historical occurrence. In this case the connection between history and sociology would lie in the sphere of the existence of the datum and its nature. From the point of view of the status of the datum there would be no difference between the two branches of knowledge, which are nevertheless separated from each other at least technically or in terms of a division of scientific labor. The relationship between history and sociology turns out to be one of a concern with the common datum. The questions

which theories of this kind necessarily meet are two: *a*) Is
the description of the historical datum adequate, whether
or not the datum understood historically can be turned
automatically into a datum understood sociologically?
We notice here that sociological theories have to interpret the historical datum with the view of its serving as
the sociological one. *b*) The second question is how to
justify two approaches, i.e. the historical and the sociological, to the same datum. The theories which rely on
the alleged self-understood relationship between the two
branches are too naïve to answer these questions, especially
the second one.

3. The sociological datum is historical; it does not therefore remain a shapeless activity or a mere function. Max
Weber pointed out that the meaningful nature of this
activity was manifold and that it thus had been conceived
of from various angles. The several attempts at clarifying
the qualitative nature of the sociological datum are in
reality attempts at clarifying its many meanings. Only
through the various meanings attached to and conceived
in it does the vague sociological datum become an object
proper and thus the subject matter of sociological research.

It might be worth while mentioning some of the classifications of the qualitative plurality of the sociological objects. We may then be in a position to get some relevant
hints as to the relationship between sociology and history.

a. Toennies tried to express the plurality of the sociological objects in the following way. Sociology is concerned with:

1) *Social relations,* such as marriage and the various
forms of family life, the relation between workman and
apprentice, king and ministers, representatives and electors,
etc.

2) *Totalities* of social and political relations indicated by various terms such as society, nation, classes, etc.

3) *Social associations* such as unions, organizations, cities, villages, states, etc.

4) *Social norms* as they manifest themselves in the spheres of order and right, mores, etc.[2]

This conception, if examined from the point of view of its implicit supposition, is actually an attempt to understand social activity as it manifests itself in various spheres and as it shapes itself in various forms, thus acquiring various meanings. Hence Toennies attempts to conceive of the common datum of sociology and history as possessing specific qualities. The plurality of the qualities ceases to be an accidental or sheer arithmetical fact and becomes justified in the social realm. But the real problem of all attempts of this kind is what is the relationship between social activity as such, the pure activity as it were, and the various meanings in which it embodies itself. The question is whether we assume that the datum of sociology, identical as it is with the datum of history, is classifiable from the outset into the four categories, or whether it is the sociological approach which attaches the four meanings to the shapeless datum by classifying it in accordance with them.

b. Let us consider in turn the classification proposed by Pitirim Sorokin:

1) Sociological theory describes the distinctive biological, psychological, etc. traits of every human-social phenomenon (anthroposocial).

2) It clarifies the causative or functional relationship existing between social classes and the various branches

2. See Ferdinand Toennies, *Soziologische Studien und Kritiken* (Jena, 1925–29), 2, 63, 430.

dealt with by the moral sciences or humanities, for instance the relationship between economics and religion.[3]

The objective of this classification is to stress the particular status of the sociological domain within the general scope of the domain of history. This is done by pointing out that sociology deals with the *permanent* factors which are indispensable for social life in any form. Sociology on this view also deals with *some* of the historical phenomena, called social phenomena proper, such as classes, and with *some* other historical phenomena considered to be manifestations of the spirit, as for instance religion. Thus sociology deals with the "antehistorical" (obviously "ante" in the logical sense of the term) factors, such as the biological or psychological factors shaping human existence, and with elements within history proper, such as different forms of the relationship between society and the phenomena of spirit. But here there is an implicit presupposition that without the historical background there would be altogether no basis for the sociological considerations. A regression takes place as it were from the historical occurrences proper to the antehistorical permanent factors of social life. But it is obvious that there is no possibility of and no sense in an elucidation of the biological and psychological factors shaping the social existence without the starting point being placed within the historical realm and without the presupposition of the givenness of historical data. The primitive society, for instance, in which we attempt to point out and to isolate the biological and the psychological factors does not cease to be a historical reality because of the isolation of some of the factors active in it. Since it is a historical reality it lends itself to an analysis directed by the interests of

3. See the contribution in the collective volume, *Soziologie von Heute*, ed. by R. Thurnwald (Leipzig, C. L. Hirschfeld, 1932), p. 46.

sociology; since it is a historical reality it may call for the sociological approach. The sociological approach presupposes the historical nature of its subject matter.

There is no possibility for an investigation of the relationship prevailing between social classes on the one hand and ideologies and religions on the other without a presupposition that all the phenomena involved in this network of relations are on one and the same plane. Hence we ought to search for the causal or functional relations between the different phenomena, since they dwell in the common, that is to say historical, plane. In other words, since the classes as well as the various forms of spirit are considered to be historical data we may be justified in trying to determine the relations between them and make this determination the proper task of the social sciences. Here again the sociological approach thus takes for granted the historical nature of the phenomenon and proceeds with its specific approach on the basis of the tacit presupposition. Sociology, according to this doctrine, deals with:

1) The detailed *description* of various social objects, such as family, state, orders, etc.

2) The *comparative* description of the various objects.

3) The *causative* analysis of a reality which has come into being.[4]

The first two parts of the above classification connote only that the sociological approach is to be applied to some specific historical data and that this approach endeavors to conceive of them by the method of description or comparison. We will discuss the third part of the above classification in connection with the problem of sociology as a science of the present.

To sum up, in all these conceptions as to the subject

4. Karl Mannheim, *Man and Society in an Age of Reconstruction* (London, 1940), pp. 165–6.

matter of sociology an implicit relationship between history and sociology is presupposed. No serious attempt has been made to define the ontological essence and status of the sociological datum. The various attempts intend to determine only the particular quality or content of the sociological objects as against history. History is taken for granted as the background of sociology. But all these theories fail to explain how and why history fulfills this function and further whether or not there is a clear distinction between the historical and the sociological aspect.

4. Formal sociology, as understood by Georg Simmel, undertakes to put the issue out of the scope of the common sense identity of the datum of history with that of sociology. It shifts the center of interest from the *matter* of human common life to its *form*. The form abstracted from the actual common life lies in a sphere which cannot be identified with that of history. Hence the concept of society, according to this view, contains two different denotations. On the one hand society denotes a unity of individuals maintaining a kind of mutual relationship between them. From this point of view people usually talk about what is called the "human material." But on the other hand society denotes the sum of the forms or relationships through which and within which society in its former denotation actually exists. This double aspect of the concept of society may be compared with a similar distinction in geometry. "Ball" denotes, on the one hand, a material possessing a particular shape or form. But on the other hand from the point of view of geometry the stuff it is made of is disregarded and ball denotes the particular *form*. Only because it has this form does the material become a ball in the strict sense of the term.[5] Applying

5. Georg Simmel, *Soziologie* (2d ed., Munich and Leipzig, Duncker S. Humblot, 1922), p. 8.

this example to the sphere of sociology we may say
that in the various social groups differing from one another
in their aims, historical settings, and means, we still may find
some common ways of behavior. They are common only
from the formal point of view, regardless of differences
rooted in their particular-historical situation. In the various
social groups existing in the different historical settings there
are to be found the relations of ruler and subject, com-
petition, division of labor, imitation, party systems, representation, etc.[6] Sociology in this view does not deal with the
qualitative plurality of the historical material as in the
theories discussed before. It aims to maintain its neutrality,
as it were, toward the historical reality insofar as the specific
quality of the individual events is concerned. It takes the
forms out of the actual reality and makes them self-consistent and self-contained. Historical reality contains the concreteness of these forms, existing in singular situations and
inherent in singular configurations. But sociological research
does not deal only with the elements which are not specific
for any particular situation. It deals with forms and hence
with the common elements present in various situations.

Yet even according to this view sociological research
is meaningless—short of a presupposition of its connection
with historical material—as it presents itself in particular
situations. Sociological research adds to the material a perspective of its own which is not contained in the material
as such and which is not dealt with in historical research,
namely the perspective of form. Compared with history
sociology appears as a branch of knowledge which establishes an object as having a specific status of its own. This
object, compared with one in history, is, as it were, removed
to a different plane. Sociology thus releases its object from
its intermixture with concrete facts and analyzes it in

6. *Ibid.*, p. 7.

its purity. This release of the object is of course a method-ological device and does not connote the idea that the object is placed in a domain of reality other than that of history.

The significance of the formal sociological approach for the epistemology of social science lies in its making evident that history and sociology—in spite of their common empirical data—have different perspectives. But the formal approach does not stress sufficiently the particularity of the historical perspective and the mutual interdependence of the two perspectives. It looks at history as at a mere datum of sociology, without making clear how, in spite of this, the two perspectives are interrelated. Paradoxically it does not elucidate the importance of the sociological per-spective for the historical perspective. History is considered as mere material for sociology, and sociology is not turned into a methodological device for the sake of historical re-search, as when, for example, a study of historical events illuminates the forms of government which are embodied in them. The perspective of the forms of government belongs to formal sociology proper; yet this perspective is—or at least can be—a tool in historical investigation, and this in spite of the material essence of the latter's interest. The formal theory describes the relation between the two branches as one-sided. Sociology needs history, but in this view, paradoxically enough, the question is not raised as to whether history needs, or may need, sociology. In the frame of reference of formal sociology we remain within an antithetic distinction of form versus matter. This dis-tinction once assumed becomes methodologically rigid. To be sure, formal sociology offers a starting point for an examination of the relations prevailing between history and social science in terms of principles, but not more than a starting point. The antithesis of form and matter is assumed on the basis of the relationship taken for granted between the two concepts, which amounts to the relationship taken for granted between history and sociology.

5. From a completely different point of view a relationship between history and sociology has been maintained in the theories defining the subject matter of sociology in terms of time. Sociology is then considered as investigating the present. According to this view we no longer deal with the sociological datum in its ontological core as action, nor do we take into consideration the qualitative plurality of its datum according to the various classifications. Even the form of the datum is disregarded. An element of content in its concreteness is set up as the subject matter of sociology, though content appears here as a segment of time. This position has several interesting features.

a. One branch of sociology is connected with the investigation of the present. Unlike all the other directions of investigations discussed before, this aims at describing all the circumstances and the situations of a society within a determined period of time. R. Steinmetz, who described this investigation, called it sociography. The term *graphy* used instead of the term *logy* seems to imply the substitution of description for analysis. The present is then conceived of from the point of view not of the forces shaping it but of the actual situations apparent in it and described accordingly.

In line with sociological naïveté no justification is to be found in this account for the special position occupied by the present. Sociology should deal with various aspects of social life, and social life in the present is but *one* of these possible aspects. The restriction of sociology to the present is based only on an arbitary decision. Therefore sociography cannot be released from the methodological problem involved. No exploration, not even a description,

can be carried out without presupposing some set of concepts. Sociography needs concepts, and these can and
must be furnished by a discipline outside it, i.e. sociology
proper. The selection of the objects and the formulation of
the phenomena which are to be described presuppose a
relation to some concepts and principles of sociology. From
the point of view of the problem before us as to the relationship between social science and history, we may say that
breaking up historical time into fractions and making the
present an object of description are impossible without
first providing a justification for these steps in the concepts
of sociology in general. Hence the problem of the relationship between history and sociology arises again: What
position does the present hold in sociology, and how is it
possible to draw a line between the position of the present
in history and its position in sociology? Since history
sometimes deals with situations and circumstances in
the present—contemporary history—is it necessary to
clarify the difference between a history of the present and
a sociographical description of it? Clearly the confinement
of the interest of social science to the present points to
the necessity to elucidate the relationship between history
and social science, at least from the point of view of the
position of the present in the two branches of knowledge.
Either the distinction between the historical and the social-
science approach to the present is a matter of importance
(and then the position of the present has to be explored),
or it is only a technical distinction and then there can be no
demand on the part of social science to consider the present
as subject matter worthy of special consideration.

b. A step forward is made by those theories which maintain that dealing with the present is a genuine and distinctive feature of sociological knowledge. Sociology is, in this

view, supposed to be the scientific self-consciousness of a
reality in·the present.[7] Sociology determines what forces
shaping social life are at work within the present, what
trends of development of a society or state prevail in the
present, what decisions confront us as men living in the
present, what new forces in the present and what kind of
change are due to occur.[8] The progress made by this theory
is to be found in its attempt to consider sociology as a theory
of actual reality. It knows that actual reality is a reality
in the present and that actual life is always of the present.
It knows that the connection of sociology with the present
is not accidental or arbitrary. Life, it recognizes, produces
a reflection of itself; theory is therefore concerned with
an actual substratum which lies within life in the present.
The sociological investigation of the present is not a result
of an isolation of a fraction of history. It is in this view the
result of the very structure of life and its direction.

This theory is not free from the difficulties which face
sociography. Freyer, for instance, who stresses the necessary
relation of sociology to the present, argues that the object
of sociology is to understand the structure of the present and
not merely to describe the facts of the present. Sociology
must investigate the various strata of reality to be encountered in the present. But then the inevitable question arises:
Whence does sociology derive the concepts of structure
and the nature of the strata which are to be discovered within the present or which are to be employed for the sake of
understanding it? Does sociology determine that the
present has a particular structure because of the *composition* of the factors of the various strata in it, or because
of the very essence of each of these strata, even when con-

7. Hans Freyer, *Einleitung in die Soziologie* (Leipzig, Quelle and Meyer,
1931), p. 10.

8. *Ibid.*, pp. 28, 149.

sidered *individually* and not in their totality as a composition? Where are the limits of the present as an object of investigation? These questions are not answered by the mere statement that the relation to the present and the interest in it are a distinctive characteristic of sociological investigation.

It is thus not enough to declare that the investigation of the present is a genuine sociological investigation. Man is always close—the theory goes—to himself and always deals with what is close to himself. Such a declaration in terms of closeness may perhaps throw light on the genesis of sociological interest. But it is clear that a methodological analysis of the concepts employed in sociology must find, or at least look for, an objective explanation of the position which the present holds in sociology. In this case no other way is open except that of starting with the fact that there is a conceptual affinity between the investigation of the present and any other sociological investigation, such as one into the nature of statehood or of economic activity, etc., which are sociological issues par excellence. But there must be presupposed a conception of historical time to the extent that the present occupies a special position within historical time. The idea that sociology is related to the present thus requires at least two assumptions: *a*) the assumption of a sociological theory which provides in its structure the concepts to be used for the exploration of the present; *b*) a philosophical theory of time which provides a concept of the present and explains, in terms of the present, the possibility of its being explored in terms of social structures.

c. Indeed, sociological investigation has grown out of the discussion of the problems of a specific present (that of the first half of the 19th century) and an endeavor to solve them. This distinctive feature in the essence of sociology, bound up with the driving forces which created sociology, has been explained by Siegfried Landshut.[9] The impulse toward the creation of French sociology which originated with St. Simon and Comte, and German sociology which is rooted in Hegel's theory of law and in the theories of Lorenz von Stein and Marx, is to be found in the present of the first part of the 19th century and its problems. It is an exaggeration to assume that, since the origin of sociological investigation is rooted in a particular social situation marked by the tension between the concepts of freedom and equality, every sociological investigation is necessarily bound up with this tension. What is relevant is the nature of the connection of a problematic situation with a definite historical present.

Sociology arose from the perception of the particular situation of European society and culture. A new object for investigation was created by the effort to establish new means for overcoming the crisis of European society and for creating a new integrated culture.[10] Indeed this aspect of the nature of sociology is significant for two reasons. First of all, insofar as one is permitted to draw conclusions from the history of any science regarding its conceptual structure one may draw them for sociology as well. The origins of sociology may then point to the idea of the connection existing between the approach of social science and the present as a dimension of special status and interest. And secondly—and this aspect is even more significant—we can look at sociology as a branch of knowledge conditioning the changes in the present situation and focusing toward the incipient future. This implies that sociology is the science of the present as projected into the future. We then

9. See his book, *Kritik der Soziologie: Freiheit und Gleichheit als Ursprungsproblem der Soziologie*, Munich and Leipzig, 1929.

10. In his later works Karl Mannheim shared this opinion.

arrive again at the assumption of the connection between sociology and some of the dimensions of historical time.

d. In this field we find another similarity between history and social science: The point of departure of sociological investigation, like that of historical research, lies in the present. The two branches of research in their capacity as empirical investigations acquire their data in what is essentially the dimension of data, the present. Therefore the question arises as to the difference between the two attitudes toward the present.

After all that has been said on the implicit relationship between the two branches it seems to be plausible that history always remains the material background of sociology in terms of content as well as in terms of the time factor inherent in the subject matter of sociology. The presupposition of this background is of course necessary for any sociological conception, though the disaster of specialization tends to drop the awareness of the background, let alone the knowledge of it. What is clear is that the presupposition of the inherent relationship is not enough, and explication is needed here as elsewhere.

We are bound to proceed now to an elucidation of the difference between the two related and yet different attitudes, since we cannot be satisfied with a vague feeling of both the differences and the similarities between the status of the present in history and in sociology respectively.

B. *The Explicit Relationship*

1. The above survey of the implicit relationship existing between history and social science was bound up with the analysis of their respective data. With the second part of our analysis, exploring the explicit relations between them, we meet with a genetic fact: Sociology has grown out

of the philosophy of history. Some problems in the philosophy of history, such as the nature of historical "development" or of the laws of the process and its meaning, have been shifted over from the philosophical sphere and have been given a sociological treatment. Unfortunately the methodological problems involved in this legacy have not been clarified in the bestowing of it.

Some modern sociological systems continued to identify the philosophical-historical approach with the sociological. Franz Oppenheimer, for instance, used to think that sociology was a universal theory of the social development of mankind. He therefore undertook to clarify the nature of the transition from the primitive to the developed stages of civilization. He tried to demonstrate the function played by the state in that transition. In this development he did not conceive of periods for their own sake but only as illustrations of the general sociological principles which explain that main transition. This conception is bound up with the assumption of an end toward which the development proceeds—the establishment of a society of free men. Sociology in this view differs from the historical approach because sociology provides the total outlook as to the meaning or end of the historical process.

2. We face here a general trend, i.e. the sociological approach to history, an approach which finds its expression in an investigation of the successive stages of historical development. These stages are not explored for the sake of their detailed and individual features. They are investigated in terms of their general trends and structures. Such an approach to history is emphasized in the so-called "sociology of culture." The important innovation of this approach, which is indicated in Jacob Burckhardt's reflections and which has been clearly formulated in Alfred Weber's sociology of culture proper, is that it conceives of history as

a complete structure of meaning. The sociological approach to history is in this view an investigation of this structure and of the factors and strata creating it.

From the point of view of content though not of the time order, the first step was already suggested by Franz Oppenheimer. The sociological investigation of history aims at an understanding of the genetic connection between various stages of historical development. Sociology attempts to understand the cultural-historical stage of the present by linking it with the genetic process of the cultures which have emerged during the entire historical development. It envisages a general scheme of historical development of a particular pattern or confines itself to a pattern within a single society of people. This approach is represented also by Spengler and Toynbee, though it appears sometimes or pretends to appear not only as a study of civilizations but as a study of history proper. As a matter of fact, because of this pretension to discern the meaning of the total historical process this view turns into a historical or pseudohistorical prophecy as we witness in Toynbee's later volumes. Here we note also an increasing use of sociological categories, an attempt as it were to create not only a total view of history but also a "synopsis" of history and sociology.

But this is an extreme case. More sober theories suggesting the meaning of the process are more modest in their statement of the patterns of the development of history. To be sure, the discovery and the statement of the pattern seem on these theories to be a sociological task, at least from the genetic point of view. They suppose that we are bound up with a fundamental rhythm of succession insofar as the process occurs in time. But their main concern is not with the process as one of succession but with its structure. Hence these theories made a step forward, at least in terms of methods, in the concern with structure not as representing the chronological order but as encompassing meanings and quality. Then we may see history as a structure marked by strata of historical creativity or by constant factors active in the process. These factors in turn can be conceived of as various spheres of human creativity. This is what Jacob Burckhardt did in connection with the "three powers" of historical reality, namely state, religion, and culture.[1] These were, on the one hand, the main domains of human activity manifesting themselves in the course of history and, on the other hand, the main forces shaping historical reality. State and religion were thought of as striving to acquire validity within human reality (although they were in turn products of that reality), while culture as a domain and a historical factor was viewed both as a totality of spontaneous expressions of spiritual and moral life and as a set of factors affecting the material side of human life.

Burckhardt was of course aware of the distinction between his investigation into these three powers and the usual fact-finding approach to history. This distinction may be compared to the difference between a picture in its totality and the isolation of several forms from this totality. Burckhardt's powers occupy a special position in the totality of the process, since they represent the main forms and contents of historical activity. In any case the direction toward the isolation or at least the stress of forms converts Burckhardt's approach into a consideration of the structure of history as a totality. This structure is actually a complexity of both domains and factors. Religion, state, and culture are actually domains of activity and factors shaping this activity by furnishing it with its distinctive qualities. They are both channels of human activity and its causes, contents and causal factors as well.

1. Jacob Burckhardt, *Force and Freedom*, ed. by James Hastings Nichols (New York, Pantheon, 1943), p. 105.

The same is to be said with regard to the conception underlying Alfred Weber's sociology of culture. He drew a line between his approach and that of the philosophy of history, saying that he was not interested in discovering the meaning of the historical process.[2] But we should add to this negative aspect a positive one. The meaning of the historical process is replaced by the structure, and the end of the process is replaced by architectonic considerations. In this structure of the historical process Alfred Weber points out the three strata: *a*) There is the stratum of *social process* which contains both the geographical and the climatological conditions of social life and the forces of instinct and will sponsoring social life. *b*) There is the stratum of *civilization* proper, in which the technical and rational forces of society are in action and in which society reveals and cultivates the forces through which it aims to dominate nature and build up the rational, practical world of man. *c*) There is finally the stratum of the movement of *culture*, in which each society expresses its latent irrational forces. In this realm it is not the domination of the outside world but the manifestation of the hidden inner content that is decisive. Its main embodiments are religion and metaphysics.[3]

We shall not consider the details of this conception, since we are interested not in evaluating these details but in analyzing their main trend in terms of our objective, in terms of the view of history that sociology is bound to assume as soon as it expressly states its concern with it. Weber made an attempt to understand the realm of history as a structure built of three strata, each marked by a distinctive qualitative characteristic in terms of both its content and its social function. Sociology, in this view, is interested in

2. See Alfred Weber, "Principielles zur Kultursoziologie" in *Archiv für Sozialwissenschaft und Sozialpolitik*, Vol. 47.

3. *Ibid.*

this structure and in the processes which comprise it. Furthermore, it does not consider the underlying laws of the process; it does not bring us either to the determination of the relationship between two variable factors or to an assumption that may lead to any deductions as to the particular events in a certain class of events. In other words, sociology is not concerned with the problem involved in the immanent structure of history as a successive-meaningful structure, determined by and related to the essence of historical time. The subject matter of the sociology of culture is thus not the meaning of the process qua process. Its objective is to detect the strata of human existence in general either as coexistent or as placed in a vertical order. Thus we find in the sociology of culture the introduction of a legitimate sociological approach to historical existence. History in this theory is a meaningful object, it is considered from the outset to be a meaningful totality and not a shapeless datum.[4] Since history as a totality is the subject matter of the sociological investigation, this investigation is not interested in qualitative processes as such but in the strata and the domains of a totality. The very introduction of the concept of totality or, to put it more cautiously, of the *aspect* of totality, is the innovation of the sociological approach. The sociological approach conceives of the historical totality as a pluralistic structure. The discovery of this plurality beyond and in addition to the plurality of facts and events ordered in time and possessing the individual meanings qua facts and events—this is the contribution of the sociology of culture. Alfred Weber (and it seems that here we may find a difference between his conception and the hints to be found in Burckhardt) sees this not as a plurality of powers of activity and causes but as one of

4. Alfred Weber, *Ideen zur Staats- und Kultursoziologie* (Karlsruhe, 1927), p. 8.

domains which are channels of human activity. The channels do not have a causal status in the historical process.
Every historical constellation can thus be understood as a
composition of the different domains pointed out by the
sociology of culture. The domains in turn are disconnect-
able when looked at from the ontological point of view, but
in actual life they appear as compounds. Any particular
historical or social situation is only an interplay of these
three domains. From this point of view the three domains
represent the permanent factors of the process, again factors
not in the causal sense but in the sense of ways of historical
activity.

If one would sum up the contribution made by the sociology of culture to the understanding of the relationship
between history and sociology in terms of categories, one
might say that the sociology of culture considers *history*
and not the shapeless *datum* of history. It presupposes history to be a sphere of process and research, and it establishes
the sociological structure proper above or on the foundations of history in its two denotations. The meeting between
history and sociology takes place not within the "pure" core
of human activity but within the domain of meanings.

Sociology in this view does not pretend to regress from
history to what is antehistorical. It presupposes history and
analyzes it only in terms of domain and not in terms of
the specific relationship between the specific events.

Yet the sociology of culture must be subject to criticism
precisely from the point of view of history, for it looks at
history in its totality as its subject matter. Without the
perspective provided by the sociology of culture, history
would remain a *process* only and would not become a *whole*.
Therefore we must examine how it is possible to conceive
of a process as a whole, or else where and on what grounds
the borderline is to be drawn between interest in the process

proper and that in the whole. Let us formulate this question
from the opposite point of view: Is it possible and conceivable that the process will undermine the whole as defined
by the distinctions provided by the sociology of culture?
Further, is there no chance that the process will shatter
this structure of the three strata, namely social process,
civilization, and culture? Is it a priori inconceivable that
the process of history may create new forms and domains
of human activity, in addition to and instead of those already existing and outlined in a system of the sociology of
culture? As a matter of fact this problem has not been
raised, let alone solved, by the sociology of culture, mainly
for a technical reason, since this theory intended to be a
science and not a "science of sciences." Yet there is also a
reason of principle, since this theory does not take into consideration the moment of the human decision in the present
directed toward the future—the decision which may ultimately create new forms which the sociological investigation will be compelled to explore, in spite of the fact that
these forms may not and need not fit into the existing
scheme of forms. This shortcoming of the sociology of culture, put forward from the point of view of history, turns
out to be a shortcoming in terms of sociology proper, since
history may create new forms to be ultimately investigated
by sociology.

To put this criticism differently, the sociology of culture
presupposes history as a whole. In this presupposition it
turns history into a closed whole, in the sense that the domains of human-historical activity are supposed to be permanent, existing in history forever. Here the import of the
sociological aspect not only presupposes history but even
changes the outlook on history, because it introduces the
aspect of permanence. History is not only presupposed but
also bound by the aspect of sociology. The *methodological*

relationship existing between history and the sociology of culture turns out illegitimately to be a *material* relationship with a preponderance of the sociological view. All this, to say the least, cannot be taken for granted.

From the sociological point of view it must be objected that the sociology of culture has taken into consideration the *patterns of the process* only and ignored the *patterns of institutions*. The sociology of culture deals with economics, laws, states, etc. at most from the point of view of their position within one of the three domains of human activity but not from the point of view of their intrinsic nature and function. Thus it does not investigate the structure and meaning of the various social institutions. In other words, the sociology of culture analyzes the strata composing the historical whole, but it does not analyze the special relationship between each stratum and its manifestations and the factors composing it. It investigates the totality and neglects the elements in terms of social institutions. It makes, as it were, the naïve presupposition that the structure pertains only to the totality and not to its parts. This may eventually lead to a notion that the total structure is created by factors which do not have a structure of their own.

3. Yet sociology, at least in its programmatic outline, did not confine itself to this kind of determination of its relations to history, where the aspect of pattern is put forth versus the aspect of process. Sociological theory suggested a different approach as well; sociological concepts are seen as fulfilling a function of premises or presuppositions for the sake of historical research, or at least for the sake of the history of culture, the latter being one of the branches of historical research. Sociology, it has been held, maintains toward the history of culture a specific logical relationship because it is thought to be for this field a "fundamental

science." [5] It is here assumed that historical research precisely because of its historical nature is bound to presuppose a systematic discipline, and that the sociology of culture fulfills this function, at least with regard to the history of culture.

To be sure, historical investigation in the various domains of its concentration, statehood, economics, religion, technology, etc., depends in the last analysis on assumptions as to the content and essence of these domains. Without a presupposition as to the content of statehood, for instance, and the political activity comprised in it, it would be quite impossible to investigate the history of political events. It does not matter at all whether this systematic presupposition is explicitly made by the historian or whether it is assumed as a matter of a plausible understanding of the meaning and nature of the events at stake. According to Kantorowicz' theory, culture proper is the domain to be added to the other domains of human productivity, which in turn are to be presupposed as systematic disciplines for the sake of the history of culture. Being systematic this discipline has to be investigated sociologically. Hence the sociological approach to culture, in contradistinction to the historical approach, is tantamount to a systematic investigation. Just as the theory of government lays down the concepts which are the axis of any investigation of political events, sociology of culture should furnish the concepts which would enable us to investigate activities which are cultural. History in this view is no longer just shapeless material for sociology but a field of application of systematic sociological concepts.[6] We do not start from the historical material and then proceed to the sociological concepts, as

5. Hermann Kantorowicz, "Der Aufbau der Soziologie," included in *Hauptprobleme der Soziologie, Erinnerungsgabe für Max Weber* (Munich and Leipzig, 1923), 1, 76.

6. *Ibid.*

is naïvely assumed in accord with the way the actual or psychological process of formation of concepts occurs. In fact, in terms of the logic of the concepts we start from sociology and then proceed to history. It seems that the pattern established here is similar to the relationship between mathematics and physics. Just as physics is the field of application for mathematical concepts and theorems, so the history of culture as an empirical investigation is the field of application for a theory, that is to say the sociology of culture as the fundamental science. The relationship between the branches of knowledge turns out to be a double one: *a*) between the systematic branch and the historical one; *b*) between the approach in terms of principles and the field of application. The sociological branch, in terms of the sociology of culture, represents the systematic approach and the approach exploring principles, while the historical branch represents history proper as the field of the empirical facts to which the principles are to be applied.

There is certainly room for doubt whether the relationship between pure and applied science, like the relationship between mathematics and physics, can be a pattern for the relationship between a systematic and a historical discipline, since the two sets of relations are quite different. The model of the relationship between the *pure* and *applied* cannot be transplanted to the relationship between the *systematic* and *historical* branches of knowledge. The historical field comprises both the state and the political events, to the extent that the systematic investigation of the nature of the state deals with a historical reality. The approach may be systematic but the reality it refers to is historical, unlike the case in mathematics where the relations, numbers, and orders are not in the plane of the empirical facts dealt with in physics. Hence with regard to history and sociology the former is not simply a field of application for the latter.

Yet this conception signifies a methodological advance

since it looks at the relationship between sociology and history in terms of a functional relationship between a principle (sociological concepts) and that which depends on that principle (the understanding of the detailed historical events in their qualitative aspect). The introduction of the functional point of view into the scope of the discussion is certainly relevant; in fact it enriches the field of the theory of sociology, if compared with the point of view of the plurality of strata or domains emphasized by Alfred Weber in his sociology of culture. The very fact of a functional analysis moves the discussion from the scope of naïve assumptions to the realm of a more precise epistemological or logical analysis. This in itself indicates a clear step forward in terms of a theoretical analysis. The theory is not free from certain difficulties, however, which must be pointed out in addition to the previous argument.

a. The functional relationship assumed to exist between history and sociology is understood to go in a single direction only. For it is assumed that sociology provides a foundation for historical investigation and not vice versa. This assumption depends on one which has already been mentioned, that is to say that sociology, as distinct from history, is considered to be a systematic discipline. Yet it goes without saying that sociological concepts employed as principles or as presuppositions for historical investigation are in their material aspect concepts of historical content, like city, community, the Renaissance, etc. They are concepts derived from the historical approach to human reality and would be meaningless without this, precisely because of their essence as material concepts. Material concepts have to have their origin somewhere, and it is clear that their origin lies in the "fertile depth" of experience, i.e. in history.

The question must be asked whether the distinction

between a systematic approach to historical reality and a historical approach proper can fit the epistemological situation of the relationship between history and sociology. This may perhaps fit the relationship between history and philosophy, since philosophy puts the contents in a systematic way within the entire scope of human activities. But sociology cannot take over the task of philosophy although it sometimes appears to do so. Sociology cannot replace philosophy because it deals only with a specific aspect of human activity, i.e. the common life of men. Sociology is certainly not historical in the way history proper is, but it is not systematic in the sense that philosophy is. Hence sociology cannot be understood simply as a systematic science over against history. The relationship is at least more complicated, and the complexity makes us state the nature of sociology more modestly than it is stated in the theory of the sociology of culture. Both are historical, and the difference between them must be sought within the common domain of history.

b. The concept of culture employed in Kantorowicz' theory is not sufficiently clarified in its material sense with regard to the historical features implicit in the very content of culture. From the outset he sees the concept of culture as sociological, while its historical nature is omitted or at least not dealt with. Yet culture is rooted and inherent in the souls of individuals living in it and shaped by it. Only this intrinsic connection between individuals and their culture, and the fact that generations of individuals are bearers and maintainers of the values and habits composing a specific culture, makes it a social power and hence worthy of sociological study.

This is one aspect of the historical nature of culture which prevents us from considering it as a fundamental concept in opposition to history and historical concepts.

The second aspect is connected with the immanent rhythm of culture in its relation to human beings living in it. The individuals in a culture are at once spontaneous in it and receptive of it. Martin Buber has shown that culture is ambivalent in its nature because it comprises the aspects of creativity and tradition simultaneously.[7] Tradition connotes here the material connection between the generations, and as such historicity is not just a starting point of the methodological analysis of culture but a characteristic of the content of the concept itself. Hence a theory which places culture as it were above history is mistaken insofar as it also defines the functional relationship between them.

c. It seems that this suggestion as to the status of sociology in relation to history is based on the implicit assumption that the theory of culture necessarily means sociology. In Alfred Weber's view there was no room for question on this point, since he attempted to describe only the ontological position of the sphere which he called culture and which was understood as the emanation or expression of the irrational creative forces of society. He traced culture back to its sources and also noted the specific rhythm of its process. But in a theory assuming that the history of culture presupposes a sociological theory of culture it is thought that sociology has the task of investigating the material essence of culture. Alfred Weber attempted to explore both the social sources of culture and its transcendence beyond the social process which he viewed as identical with the biological growth of society. This theory remains within the limits of the historical whole and its strata. But against the idea of the sociology of culture as a fundamental science we have to maintain that both the sociology of culture and history are principal or fundamental

7. Martin Buber discussed this problem in his Hebrew essay, *Al Mahutah Shel Tarbut* (The Essence of Culture), Tel-Aviv, 1944.

sciences, and accordingly we can see an ontological community between them. The common subject matter of the two is society; this gives rise to culture and culture exists within the process of society. Hence we are entitled to attempt to conceive of the process with the help of the concept of culture. Without this presupposition of an ontological community between the domain of history and that of sociology there would be no basis on which to build the functional relationship between them. Thus the question arises again as to how this bifurcation into sociology and history is brought about and where the difference between them is to be established, once the relationship in terms of a principle (sociology of culture) and what depends on the principle (history of culture) can no longer be maintained.

The lesson we can learn from this discussion is that the relationship between history and sociology is a methodological one. As such it is bound to depend on the functions of the related fields. But this functionality is not exhausted by the theory which considers sociology as a systematic condition and supposition for historical investigation.

4. Nevertheless, this view of history as conditioned by sociological concepts in their capacity of forming a fundamental science implies an important methodological consideration. This consideration is not to be identified with the particular expression it has previously received nor is it to be restricted to the idea of culture.

Systematic concepts are to be distinguished from historical ones. They are general; historical concepts are individual. If we compare Society with a given society here and now we evidently shift from general to specific concepts. As Mannheim observed, the discussion of Society is not historical but "deductive." Even if we employ not

the concept of society in general but more concrete sociological concepts such as city, village, family, etc. we still
deal with general concepts. These are to be distinguished
from specific concepts such as the city of Florence in the
era of Machiavelli, the Roman family, etc. The latter can
be the concern of history.

It is usual to define the difference between a historical
and a sociological investigation as the difference between
a concrete description of a given city, for instance, and a
typological and comprehensive description of cities in
general. Such a distinction is made by Pitirim Sorokin and
various other sociologists. The observation of the difference
between the sociological and the historical investigation
is bound up with the assumption that historical concepts
are always individual concepts. General concepts are used
to help us conceive of what is typical and general in the
processes. Thus the difference between history and sociology turns out to be that of extension of the respective
concepts. To the functional difference put forward before,
a formal one, in terms of extension, is added.

Actually there is an overlapping between the functional
and the formal aspect. The general sociological concepts
have to condition the historical concepts, which in turn
describe individual objects, and they perform the function
of conditioning precisely because they are general concepts.
There is a reverse conditioning too. History with its data
and its individual concepts is a *conditio sine qua non* for
the formation of the general concepts of sociology. We are
unable to form the concept of a city as such or the type
"city" without first describing the Greek polis, the city
in the Middle Ages, in our modern civilization, etc. The
formulation and the formation of the sociological concepts
depend on a prior formulation and description of historical
concepts. Historical concepts provide material for the

sociological. The functional relationship gives way to a relationship of strata built on top of it. It seems that at this juncture we find the logical and systematic place for Max Weber's theory of Ideal Types. This concept offers a synthesis of the formal with the functional aspect by employing sociological concepts over against historical occurrences and facts. This synthesis seems to be the background for the formation of the concept of the Ideal Type. To be sure, I do not intend to suggest that Weber arrived at this theory of Ideal Types by means of a synthesis between the two aspects. Historically all the theories, or almost all of them, are related to Weber and have absorbed his main trend. The discussion of Weber's contribution to the solution of the question of history in its relation to sociology is placed here, because our concern is mainly systematic. Hence the elements are put forward before the analysis of Weber, who combines the various elements in a rounded picture.

5. The Ideal Type, as compared with the particular historical phenomena, is a general concept. To be sure, the feature formulated in an Ideal Type is not to be arrived at by considering a number of phenomena and seeing what properties are common to all of them. The concept and its traits are acquired by isolating a particular feature from a qualitative phenomenon possessing many features. The sociologist considers the isolated and the specifically stressed feature as essential. For instance, from a variety of traits and features of the capitalist economy he separates an essential feature, or one considered to be such, say the rationality of the economic process. With the help of this he looks at the various historical phenomena and deliberates whether or not they are to be listed as belonging to the capitalist system. The Ideal Type is therefore a general concept achieved through a one-sided emphasis on some single

feature. It is not a picture of a given reality but a "utopia" —as Weber himself put it. For Weber the task of the actual investigation in the field of sociology is to determine the degree of proximity between the actual historical reality and the distinctive features used in the formulation of the content of the Ideal Type, or else its task is to determine where and to what extent the reality departs from the Ideal Type.[8] The Ideal Type is therefore a concept of methodological heuristic validity only. It is obtained from an observation of given phenomena by one-sided emphasis, and then it is brought back to the individual historical phenomena as a measure for describing and understanding them. The Ideal Type is "released" from the reality of the existing facts and occurrences so that we can compare the reality of the facts with a type abstracted from them.

The mutual dependence of the Ideal Type on facts and of the facts on the Ideal Type is one of the chief innovations of Weber's theory. The Ideal Type is a rational construction and has a methodological function to perform with regard to the phenomena. The more rational the type, that is to say the more constructed it is, the greater is its disposition to fulfill the methodological function it is supposed to fulfill. Weber formulates this difference between the Ideal Type and the individual phenomenon by saying that the more alien is the type to the world, the better able is it to fulfill its task.[9] This emphasis on the distance of the type from the actual world implies that rationalization is a methodological tendency or an assumption only and not a force within reality itself. Weber explicitly cautions against confusing the boundaries be-

---

8. Max Weber, *Wirtschaft und Gesellschaft* (Tübingen, 1947), p. 3; English trans. by A. M. Henderson and Talcott Parsons, *The Theory of Social and Economic Organization* (London, 1947), p. 92.

9. *Ibid.*, p. 10 in the German text; cf. English trans., p. 111.

tween these two aspects of rationality.[10] He is aware that
when he stresses the rational character of the activity
of capitalism he consciously omits the irrational factors
present in it as well, such as passions, errors, miscalcula-
tions, etc., which certainly affect the actual activity within
the realm of reality. But his emphasis on rational activity
enables him to delimit and to identify other extraneous
factors precisely as being irrational. He understands or at
least points to the irrational nature of these factors by
means of his rational principle.[11]

Weber himself stresses the tension existing between the
methodological pole of rationality and the irrational factors inherent in the individual historical phenomena. But
actually the tension between them is only half of the
story of their difference. They are interrelated. We are in
a position to know what rationality is like, for instance when
expressed in the pursuit of an economic end, since we can
contrast it with irrationality as expressed in other activities
which are not motivated by rational driving forces. We
can point to irrational factors since we have the well-
defined Ideal Type of rational behavior. The Ideal Type
in its methodological function is, as it were, an index of
itself and of its opposite as well, if I may introduce this
paraphase. Thus the interdependence between the Ideal
Type and the phenomena is a bridge between the poles.
This might give a somewhat dialectical interpretation of
Weber's theory, yet it seems to be legitimate.

Because of this interdependence, the theory of Ideal
Types is confronted with the task of finding a justification

10. *Gesammelte Aufsätze zur Wissenschaftslehre* (Tübingen, 1922), p.
195. In Toynbee's theory of civilization one does not discern a clear understanding of the status of civilizations—of whether they are tools for historical description or else real historical entities.

11. *Wirtschaft und Gesellschaft*, p. 3; English trans., p. 92.

for abstracting one particular aspect rather than another. Weber himself was aware of this problem and therefore could not always insist on the purely methodological character of the Ideal Type. The difficulty implicit in Weber's theory may be formulated in this way: As a methodological device the Ideal Type is alien to the actual world. But in order to be an Ideal Type for the understanding of the individual phenomenon it cannot be entirely alien to the world. Weber himself said that only those rational constructions in which some proximity to reality can be observed are sociological types of an actual occurrence.[12] Thus the Ideal Type can be formed only when it is rooted in given historical facts. It is alien to the world, but its alienation is one of emphasis and is not due to its existence in an ontological sphere of its own, separated in a Platonic way from the actual. Thus the Ideal Type is a sociological concept, whereas the actual facts in their qualitative denotation are represented by historical concepts. We may restate the position by saying that in Weber's theory the sociological concepts must differ from and yet approximate historical concepts.

Again, there is a need here to point out one essential assumption regarding the conceptual background of the determination of the relationship between the Ideal Type and the actual individual facts. Without the assumption that the facts are meaningful in themselves there would be no basis for the formation of the Ideal Type, since it emphasizes a feature already existing in the facts. The common background both of events and of Ideal Types is the meaningful character of human activity which is embodied in the historical facts and is understandable by means of the Ideal Types. Weber deals in his sociology with the meanings of human activities. He draws a line between

12. *Ibid.*, p. 6.

those meanings and the meanings which demand absolute validity for themselves, like those of logic, ethics, etc.[13] He endeavors to conceive of the meaning involved in actual human experience as an end toward which the given activity is striving.

The chief points of Weber's theory are the stress on an aspect and the construction of an *Ideal* Type according to the aspect stressed. Such a construction is possible because the substratum of his methodological procedure is to be found not in a shapeless process but in human activities, necessarily directed toward objectives and therefore meaningful on their own merits. In other words, the empirical meaning rooted in behavior or in a historical activity is the basis for the rational construction of a meaningful concept embodied in the Ideal Type. While the structure of the world is one of space and time, the Ideal Type is a construction dwelling in the timeless sphere of methods. In Hegel's language we may say that the Ideal Type lies in the "shadowy world" of methods and does not exist in the actual world of historical facts. But the historical facts themselves are meaningful. Hence the Ideal Type is to be released from them by means of emphasis and is to be applied to them by means of methods. Weber's conception oscillates between the poles of inherence in historical facts of the meaning stressed in the Ideal Type and the emancipation of the Ideal Type from historical facts. The inherence is in terms of contents while the emancipation is in terms of the status assigned to the contents; this could serve as a description of the oscillation present in Weber's doctrine.

To put it differently, the Ideal Type is alien to the world if viewed from its ontological plane, but it is close to the world by virtue of its genesis on the one hand and its

13. *Ibid.*, p. 2.

application and function on the other. It seems that it is precisely here that Weber has made a decisive step toward the understanding of the real relationship between history and sociology, in spite of the fact that he perhaps did not fully realize the consequences of his step. Sociology is both bound up with and distant from history, in a way similar to that in which the Ideal Type approaches and departs from the complex facts. But both closeness and distance presuppose a fundamental community between the two domains of history and sociology.

It might be proper at this juncture to make one further observation as to the nature of the theory of the Ideal Types. In a way, the trend expressed in the concept of the Ideal Type is close to that of formal sociology, since in forming an Ideal Type we separate it from the historical-material concreteness. A similar separation is performed by formal sociology in releasing the sociological concepts from their historical, that is to say material, texture. Yet it is necessary to distinguish between the two forms of separation employed in the two theories. This distinction may hint at the necessity for considering a complementary relation between them. In formal sociology the separated element is arrived at through an abstraction from the material context, such as the forms of rule and obedience, and establishes itself as an independent domain, that is to say as the sociological domain proper. In this theory there is a clear-cut distinction between the material-historical domain and the formal-sociological. Weber's system does not offer a clear-cut duality of this kind, however, but rather a comparison. This feature is methodologically expressed in the emphasis on the one trait of the given historical phenomenon, by way of which sociological concepts qua Ideal Types are formed. The Ideal Type is a *meaning* only; the historical contents are both facts *and* meanings. The stress is not on the formal elements but on the meaningful one which is inherent in the facts themselves. The formal element as formal is merely *constructed*; the meaningful element is separated from its full context and is not sheer construction. Weber's position has a rather nominalistic touch, whereas formal sociology has in a way a more realistic bias. This difference accounts for a further one: Formal sociology stresses the clear-cut difference between the material and the formal, while the theory of the Ideal Type has rather to recognize the gradual transition from what is both fact and meaning to what is a meaning only.

Since the sociological concepts are acquired by stressing the meaningful features of the facts, they cannot be concepts which establish a self-contained dimension. They always need the historical environment in which they have grown and from which they are isolated. The Ideal Type is not, for example, city in general but a city in the Middle Ages; it is not nation in general but various types of national life, etc. This distinctive trait of Weber's theory appears most clearly in the fact that Weber substituted for the two concepts of society and community what he called "*tendencies* toward society and community" (*Vergemeinschaftung, Vergesellschaftung*) respectively. Thus he put forward the historical nature of the various and fundamental forms of social existence. The historical nature of those forms comes to the fore in the fact that they are considered to be *tendencies* and not closed self-contained *realms*. The awareness of the historical origin of the forms of social existence is always present in Weber's discussion of them, unlike the formal sociology which starts with historical facts but tends to build up objects with a power of their own.

Weber sought for methodological concepts but did not

give up their ontological correspondence with historical reality. This has been expressed above in the idea of the closeness of the Ideal Type to meaningful facts. The formulation of the nature of the relationship between sociology and history rests on the solution of whether it is possible for concepts to originate in the investigation of given facts whose meanings can be considered to be independent of the facts. Thus we come back, though on a higher level, to the problem of the relationship between the general concept and the individual fact.

From another point of view it can be shown as well that the theory of the Ideal Types tends to maintain their close relationship with historical reality. The various concepts of collective entities such as state and association are, according to Weber, categories of different manners of human social behavior. They are descriptions of the interrelations of activities of individual men.[14] The Ideal Type is to be applied to forms of activity, provided that the activity is rational in its essence, i.e. directed toward a goal. Weber tries to draw a line between his own theory and all those theories which look at society as a self-sufficient substance existing *in se*. He therefore endeavors to reduce society and its various manifestations to actual activities of men. But he also tries to conceive of what we may rightly call the "differential" of the historical process, namely the meaningful human activity. Therefore when he deals with man's connection with a social order or with a social institution he intends to stress the existing *chance* that men should behave in a specific well-defined manner evoked and stimulated by specific motives. Here again we encounter a closeness between the meaning of the historical phenomenon qua phenomenon of active human beings and the meaning of sociological concepts. Human

14. *Gesammelte Aufsätze zur Wissenschaftslehre*, p. 415.

beings in their actual behavior act according to certain chances. The chances of their behavior are inherent in the situations. It is the task of sociology to separate the chances, that is to say to investigate the ways of behavior rather than the actual concrete individual behavior here and now.

To sum up, Weber attempted to analyze ways of behavior rather than the inner structures of the various social institutions. He did not consider the institutions as forming a stage comparatively higher than that of the individual historical phenomena. He analyzed various forms of government in their qualitative essentials (monarchy, charismatic rule, etc.) but did not separate the institution of government from these qualities nor try to determine in detail the structure of the government qua government in addition to its various historical qualitative appearances or even typological manifestations. Precisely this step, lacking in Weber's theory, has been made by formal sociology. Weber tended to exhaust the nature and the content of the historical phenomenon in its differential, i.e. in meaningful activity. Then he integrated the phenomenon in a meaningful whole constructed by means of the content of the Ideal Type. His "universe of discourse" always remained the universe of history. We do not therefore find in Weber's system what is as a matter of fact the central sociological category, i.e. the category of a *social framework*. Weber attempted to conceive of the phenomenon in its inner meaning; he consciously left out of the picture the other complementary aspect which is the main basis for sociological investigation proper. To take an example, the activity of governing involves the possession of power. Yet the relationship between the activity of governing and the possession of power is always double. On the one hand the acts of governing imply the possession of power, but on the other the acts of governing take place within a social framework of possessive power and imposed rules of conduct. The activity of governing, as it were, absorbs the framework in itself by turning it into its own meaning and content. When Weber speaks of the chance that people will actually behave in a certain way, it is clear that he does not refer to an individual activity. His theory looks at activities as exhausting themselves in themselves. As such, they are not placed in a framework. Weber did not sufficiently consider activity as a single fact within a whole that is both the content of the individual activity and a framework in which this activity and other individual activities are placed. The state, for example, is not only the meaning of activities called political but also their encompassing framework. Activities not considered in terms of their being encompassed in a framework are, sociologically speaking, in a void.

Each political act, for instance, has a political meaning since it *intends* by definition to shape government on the one hand and *takes place* within the framework of politics on the other. Had Weber considered the aspect of framework or institution implied in sociological concepts he would have paved the way for an investigation of a new dimension, in addition to the historical, in the proper meaning of the term. Yet on this decisive point Weber's theory unfortunately remained bound up with some trends in German philosophy of history (Rickert), and he accordingly tried to maintain that sociological concepts were individual because of their historical origins. In order to maintain the historical aspect of sociological units Weber neglected the aspect of framework and overstressed unduly the aspect of meaningful activities. To be sure, the aspect of framework does not replace that of activity but is to be assumed in addition to and for the sake of it. This is only an indication of the importance of the consideration of the sociological unit as a framework, in order to advance some critical observations of Weber's doctrine. The problem in its broader implications will be dealt with systematically in what follows.

The individuality of sociological concepts differs from the individuality of historical phenomena as the organization of a city in the Middle Ages differs from a single market day in any medieval city. But in spite of this difference, which is a difference in emphasis, the individual character of the sociological concepts has been maintained in Weber's theory. One may therefore claim that a sociologist of Weber's stature remained, in his methodological considerations, still within the field of history on which he built only a superstructure. In his methodological analysis he did not arrive at an adequate description of his own work and did not provide the epistemological justification for the concepts actually employed in his detailed sociological work. These shortcomings of his theory, if compared with his practice, are due to the one-sided emphasis he placed on the aspect of the meaningful activity, while neglecting institutions and frameworks within which the meaningful activity comes into being.[15]

6. The attempt to describe both the difference and the positive relation existing between history and social science by employing the paired concepts of individual and general is connected with the assumption of a ladderlike structure of gradation in which the general concept is supposed to be above the level of the individual concepts. Facing this theory is the problem of the relationship of the points on this ladder. In the beginnings of sociology a solution to

15. It seems to me that this is the decisive step made by Talcott Parsons which brings him beyond the frame of reference of Weber's conceptual apparatus. Cf. Parsons, *The Social System*, Glencoe, Ill., 1952.

this problem was suggested by Comte. He distinguished between the statics and the dynamics of society, assuming that one and the same process can be regarded from both points of view. As a matter of fact, Comte does not explicitly identify statics with sociology and dynamics with history. But the distinction he makes is significant for our discussion since it contains the kernel of distinction which will be developed in the following lines. Social statics attempts to discover the laws of society in its quasi-"resting" situation. It tried to understand the interrelation and the structure of a social configuration, to detect the external factors (climate, natural environment) and the internal factors (economic relations) which form this configuration. Social dynamics in contrast tries to outline the social history of mankind.[16]

This distinction might serve as a basis for a differentiation of history and sociology which applies the perspective represented by sociological investigation to an isolated fraction within the historical process. This distinction is to be found in some modern, even nonpositivistic theories. It has been pointed out for example that historical investigations deal with the *growth* of nations while sociological investigations are concerned with the *being* of nations. The being of nations is not thought to be a sphere placed outside the process of the growth and independent of it. It is a particular situation defined in a methodological way only, by means of the fragmentation of the comprehensive historical process. The being of nations is not a given fact but a product of a construction localizing the process, making it, as it were, stand still and converge at a particular moment. It is a static situation of mankind or a part of it, not given naturally but explicitly introduced

16. See H. B. Acton, "Comte's Positivism and the Science of Society," *Philosophy*, 1951.

and constructed by the perspective of sociological investigation and the methods employed by it. The new aspect provided by social science as against that represented by history is explicitly and clearly a methodological construction, that is to say an interpretation of the historical data.

This view was formulated somewhat differently by Friedrich Gottl in his analysis of the formation of the concepts of social science.[17] Gottl pointed out that social science considers an occurrence in its equilibrium, while history considers it in terms of the innovation it introduces or in terms of the novelty it represents over against the entire process. It seems as if Gottl intended to point out the cognitive step that logically precedes the cutting up of the process and to give an indication as to the nature of the distinction between the process and the fraction isolated from it. The process is taken to be a stream of novelties and changes related to these novelties and brought about by them. In contradistinction to the nature of the process the situations within the process are established through methodological devices which disregard the novelties and the changes inherent in the process as process. The concept of a situation presupposes that some stability exists within the process and that situations manifest this stability in concreto. From the point of view of architectonics stability implies that the process comes to a standstill and acquires equilibrium. The equilibrium immunizes the situation, as it were, against the ongoing process, or at least isolates the situation for a while from the texture of the process. Formal sociology stressed the isolation of formal ways of behavior from the texture of the process, while Gottl's view stresses the isolation of material situations from the ongoing process. For instance, he would say that history

17. See Friedrich Gottl, "Zur Sozialwissenschaftlichen Bergriffsbildung," *Archiv für Sozialwissenschaft und Sozialpolitik*, Vol. 28.

proper is concerned with the changes which occurred in the life of the English people in the 19th century, while social science seeks to understand a particular situation of the English people in a particular segment of the 19th century and therefore disregards the variety of the transient events which compose the process and tries to give a description of a static constellation. Yet it is obvious that the equilibrium does not exist outside the process or above it. The aspect of the equilibrium is only a result of a conceptual reflection and its procedure. Though the process is given the equilibrium is constructed, and thus we arrive at a conclusion—to which Gottl does not point clearly —that social science is *more constructive* than history. This additional constructive nature of sociology is understandable. Since the presupposed realm is history or since the essential character of human events lies in their process in reality, any outlook which brings process to a standstill and builds a dimension on top of the presupposed realm essentially and consciously employs a procedure of construction. Situations are not given; they are built by constructions.

Gottl went a step further in the same direction: Since social science endeavors to conceive of situations, the only methodological way open to them is *not to consider* changes and novelties. Thus the underlying approach of social science is connected not only with emphasizing the constructed *equilibrium* but also with pointing out *permanence* within the process as well. Yet when we try to translate the idea of permanence into terms of time we encounter the notion of recurrence. The permanent element, by the very fact that it is permanent and not confined to one specific point of time, is apt to recur at different points of time, that is to say it is apt to reappear at various historical periods. Thus the distinction between historical and sociological reflection is eventually a distinction between the consideration of novelties on the one hand and that of recurrences on the other. From the point of view of historical reflection we deal with the variety of events and changes, while from the point of view of social science we deal with permanence or, to put it more cautiously, semipermanence. From the point of view of social science we are entitled to speak of the English people as "a unity, the permanence of which is identical in the repetition of the occurrences." Thus sociological investigation stresses the aspect of situation as the first stage of its methodological procedure and as its second step stresses the aspect of permanence against the background of historical process. We may add (although this has not been explicitly stated by Gottl) that the consideration of human social existence is characterized by a tension between novelty and permanence as two aspects of one and the same reflection. This tension is as it were dissolved into the two partial aspects, which are in turn dealt with in two branches of knowledge, history and sociology respectively.

This conception, the sources of which are to be found in Comte, has certainly enriched the conceptual apparatus of social science with particular reference to the problem before us of promoting a better understanding of the relationship between history and social science. Yet it seems that the problem cannot yet be dismissed, and several observations are in order for the sake of a systematic conception of this relationship.

a. In this conception we do not find a sufficient explanation as to whether and to what extent a relationship exists between equilibrium and the employment and application of general concepts; for example, whether the situation of the English people implies distinctive traits which enable us to form general concepts, such as society, state, industry, etc. In other words, whether the aspect of permanence carries with it the aspect of generality, or whether the recurrence is confined to a particular historical process. If the latter is the case then we may note recurrences in the history of the English people but may not apply the concepts of state, industry, etc. to the histories of other peoples as well. Clearly such a view is a narrow one and would confine sociological investigation not only to segments of time—i.e. situations as against processes—but also to segments in space—i.e. the English people over against other peoples. The notion of situation and permanence may be a foundation for building some general concepts. Via these concepts we not only bring the process to a standstill but also enlarge its scope, taking into account different situations and dealing with them by way of the general concepts.

b. This conception deals with the logical basis for constructing a sociological description of fractions isolated from the total process. But we are not yet instructed as to the actual concepts by which this isolation is carried out in the practical research of social phenomena. We have to find the material concepts employed when describing a sociological situation. The procedure of bringing the process to a standstill in the form of a situation is again only a starting point. This procedure paves the way for the sociological consideration but is not identical with it; it is instrumental for the sociological consideration, but the consideration proper begins where the procedure ends.

c. What is more significant, the very mutuality of the aspects of novelty and equilibrium has not been elucidated. Equilibrium in this view is a product of a deliberate omission of novelties, innovations, and changes. The question must therefore be raised as to the possibility of understanding novelties occurring within the process merely by proceeding from the aspect of equilibrium and contrasting equilibria with novelties as they appear in the historical process. We understand novelties by comparing them with equilibrial situations created constructively, as we understand situations in terms of the changes and novelties which came to a standstill in the situations. The two aspects are functionally interrelated.

d. It has not been clarified whether a relationship exists between the situations conceived as a process of coming to an equilibrium and the concept of the *present* as a specific subject matter of sociological investigation. No attempt has been made in this theory to include the present in the legitimate scope of the general notion of situations, that is to say to explore whether the concept of the present can be considered as a situational concept as well, in spite of and in addition to its character as a fraction of time. To be sure, the aspect of a fragment of time is implied in the aspect of a situation. But when we deliberately move to the aspect of the present a fragment of time becomes explicitly a situation. Hence it is imperative to deal with the question of the status of the present in a theory of sociological concepts.

7. The difference between the two aspects represented by the two branches of knowledge is also hinted at in the distinction between the vertical and horizontal phases of the process. The aspects of novelty and equilibrium were distinguished against the background of time. The vertical and the horizontal phases are distinguished by direction. In considering human life from the historical point of view we consider it in terms of its vertical continuity, and from this point of view we reflect upon the stream of occasions in time; in considering human life from the point of view of sociology we reflect upon the horizontal con-

tinuity as a surface upon which human life takes place. In other words, actual human life is to be considered from the angles of both the world behind us and the world which is contemporaneous with us as beings engaged in reflection about our actual life.

If we translate the distinction between the two aspects from the neutral methodological language into the language of the relations between actual human beings we may say that within the comprehensive historical world, which is the common background of both historical and sociological investigations, we may distinguish between two spheres: Conceiving of an occurrence as taking place between two definite dates in two different dimensions of time (past and present) we are concerned with history; conceiving of the relation between wills of human beings and the forms in which these wills embody themselves we are concerned with sociology. Thus the distinction between the vertical and the horizontal lines is identical with the distinction between the relations of human generations on the one hand and the relations between actual human wills on the other. Here again some indications as to that doctrine are to be found in Hans Freyer, and yet the connection between the relationship of actual human beings and their wills and the aspect of the present (which is the dimension of the situation as it is eventually shaped between the wills and by them) is not yet clarified.

We must come back to the distinction made in the first place between the world lying behind us and the contemporaneous world.

This distinction presents the same difficulty indicated above (par. 6) in connection with the difference between novelty and recurrence of events. Does not the consideration of a relationship between generations involve at once a consideration of a relationship between human wills?

Relations between wills embody themselves in forms such as states, associations, classes, churches, etc. Must we not take advantage of these forms once we want to understand the relationship existing between human generations, that is to say the historical relations? The connection existing between actual wills is in itself a link in the chain of generations and therefore becomes necessarily part of the vertical line. Thus the distinction between the two directions of consideration can be a basis for an outline of a theory of the relationship between history and sociology. Yet the dialectic involved in this relationship must be stressed more clearly.

8. So far we have discussed the various forms of the suggested relationship between history and sociology from the point of view of concepts and methods in use. It has turned out that sociology looks at history as a system. It makes history the material substratum of its concepts, or else turns its own concepts into instruments for the understanding of history. We have examined so far some of the main attempts to solve the problem of how the immanent transition takes place, as a result of which history as the domain of occurrence makes and justifies a reflection on it —both a historical reflection, in the narrow sense of the term, and a sociological one.

This picture of the various systematic attempts to clarify the relationship between history and sociology will lack completeness if we omit another of its features, one which refers to *contents* rather than to *methods*. The objective of sociology in this view is supposed to be to promote the understanding of the historical process from within. This can be accomplished, according to this assumption, by showing that the subject matter of sociology proper, that is to say society, is a cause or at least a factor in the historical process. Sociology thus brings to prominence an entity which is in itself a historical factor, i.e. which shapes the historical process. As such sociology hands over to history a concept or a set of concepts which is to explain the historical process itself in its material content, direction, and dynamics. Any sociological theory assuming this is connected as a matter of fact with the presuppositions of Marxist philosophy. This is so even in the case where such a theory is opposed to the specific content of Marxist philosophy and to the consequences drawn from it. The main Marxist assumption is that there is an ultimate stratum of the historical process and that the specific dynamics of and in this stratum account for the dynamics of history. Society—analyzed as it is in Marxism (and this particular way of looking at society is the specific feature of Marxism)—is this ultimate stratum. Hence the sociological outlook discerns as it were the historical rhythm. This Marxist approach was taken over by many theories which were non-Marxist in their details. The main feature is the suggestion that the subject matter of sociology, i.e. society, is a historical factor in terms of the contents of the historical process.

There may be an even more radical position in line with this theory. What appears as a sociological approach to history and as a sociological attempt toward an understanding of history is actually an attempt to present society as the only empirically given and empirically detectable factor active in the historical process. According to this view, whatever exists and is active in the historical process is in the last resort a manifestation of society and derives its momentum and shaping capacity in and from it. Society is not only a historical factor but as the ultimate stratum of history it is also the *fundamentum reductionis* of history. "Sociologism" is but an expression of this bias, sometimes vaguely formulated and sometimes held vehemently because of the impact of social problems on human life in our age. Again, every such approach to society as the causative factor in history is linked up with Marx' doctrine that we have to understand the circumstances and the conditions of men by looking at them as outcomes of human activities. And further it is assumed that human activity is essentially a social activity. According to such a view sociology provides an instrument of understanding and a sound basis for any historical research proper, since sociology considers the world of historical objectivations as being a product of society.

We have to distinguish between this form of the relationship supposed to exist between history and sociology and the forms discussed above. There our aim was to show and examine where and how it is possible to find within the historical occurrence itself and through historical reflection referring to it the point of departure for the formation of sociological concepts. It was assumed there that the domains of both historical occurrences and historical reflection are given. From these two given facts we are supposed to be permitted to proceed to sociological investigation and to justify it in terms of epistemological principles. In brief, this was a problem of *methods*. In contradistinction to this methodological approach we find in the sociologist bias a suggestion allegedly enabling the sociological investigation and its concepts to penetrate into the historical domain itself since in this view it is sociology which furnishes historical investigation with means for understanding the subject matter of history, i.e. the historical occurrences. In other words, sociology presents its own *subject matter* for *investigation* (in terms of methods) as the *active subject* of history (in terms of real forces shaping the process) and suggests to historical investigation that it carry out and uphold this transition from the *object*

of research to the subject of action. Opinions may differ
as to the material essence of this object, that is to say
as to what real forces are active in society and maintain it.
But according to the assumptions of this theory there is
no difference of opinion regarding the very status of the
object of sociology in its position within the historical
process. History is a manifestation of society—this would
be a résumé of this doctrine.

But here all the problems discussed before as to the conceptual apparatus of sociology arise again. Sociology presents its own subject matter as the *subject* of history. Yet
this subject matter is a topic for investigation and therefore subject to its methods and concepts. We are bound
to ask: If not in history, then where does sociology find
the data for establishing its subject matter, and what is
the ontological nature of this subject matter if it is not
determined by the place it occupies in the realm of history? Sociology attributes to its subject matter a status in
a particular methodological dimension either as form or
as Ideal Types or as situation. But in the theories discussed, now stemming from Marx at least in terms of
their direction, sociology seems not to be satisfied with the
methodological approach and with the steps taken in order
to uphold the sociological approach as far as it goes. Sociology proposes to turn its object, established by *methods*, into
the *ontological* subject of the historical process. Marxian
sociology, which so vehemently opposed any metaphysics,
accusing it of being just "mystification," turns out then to
deal with society as *the* historical subject and thus takes
a hypostatic turn, which in itself is characteristic of metaphysics. Society is a historical reality and as such a composition of events and occasions. Turning society into the
subject of history poses the problem of the relationship
between the subject of history and history itself where

the subject is active. Hence all the questions as to the relation between the historical aspect and that of social science creep in again. Precisely because the metaphysical turn does not separate society from the historical process there is no escape from the consideration of the relationship between the sociological approach concerned with society and the historical approach concerned with the process.

In any case, there is no way of evading consideration of the relationship between history and sociology in terms of categories and principles, since the naïve—though true —assumption as to the material relationship existing between them does not itself suffice and needs justification.

C. The Concatenation

1. Our preceding discussion makes quite evident the difficulty and perplexity of maintaining the distinction between the domains of history and sociology. Nevertheless it does seem that this distinction, at least in principle, can be maintained. This can be done in spite of the fact that the actual investigation in both domains does not exactly follow the strict line of demarcation and sometimes upsets the systematic effort to make the matter clear in terms of principles.

To begin with, let us point to one distinctive line characteristic of social reality following from its connection with the wills of human beings. There were sociologists who held that social institutions were institutions of human wills only and not also of meanings. This distinction cannot be maintained in fact. In upholding the connection between meanings and the psychic aspect of social reality as borne by human wills we still say that one pole of the comprehensive social reality must be psychic. Social reality is essentially connected with psychic occurrences and acts, and these can be designated in various forms or from various points of view as to their material nature—will in general, agreement, acknowledgment, mutual attraction between the human beings involved, the feeling of distance or closeness between them, etc.

Yet this connection of social reality with specific psychic acts cannot exhaust the full nature of the former. One may try by a method of "psychological reduction" to base social units on psychical acts. But essentially such a reduction annihilates the social reality qua *social*. If we assume that the core of social reality lies in wills or is rooted in feelings of agreement, etc., we do not yet take into consideration that this will or that agreement is embodied in a particular form. Because of this particular form there are differences between the acknowledgment characteristic of personal relations between two friends or lovers and that characteristic of the impersonal relations of a man dwelling in a comprehensive social sphere like a city or a state. Furthermore, there is a difference between the meanings of acknowledgment of the social order expressed, for example, by a man living in a Greek polis and by a modern man living in a state with a mass population and a complex structure of sociopolitical relations. An essential characteristic of a social institution is henceforth the interaction of a psychic act and its particular embodiment in terms of the historical position and the specific meaning of this embodiment. This embodiment gives to the psychic act its particular quality and its particular meaning which make it significant beyond the personal realm. A psychological reduction of the social reality is as impossible as the reduction of a language to the few elementary sounds composing it. The social institutions are not mere intermixtures of psychic acts anymore than a language is merely a mixture of phonetic sounds. Social institutions are historical ones carried by various acts, just as languages are universes of words and meanings carried by elementary sounds. Only the historicity of a social institution turns it into a meaningful whole, just as the context of words turns a language from an aggregate of mere sounds into a domain of meaning. The psychic acts are parts of the domains of social institutions as sounds are elements of language. Social institutions are composed not only of elements but of complex patterns as well.

This psychic aspect characteristic of every sociological unit may be called the *functional* aspect, since its essence lies in the psychic historical process inherent in it. But the sociological unit has another aspect too, well described by Hans Freyer. We can agree with his description even if we eventually arrive at a systematic conclusion opposed to his. Freyer's explanation is that the sociological unit is not merely functional—or, according to his own terminology, a process. But such a unit has another side too, that of crystallization and stability. The sociological unit, in spite of its immanent historicity, is stable or at least quasi-stable. One finds here another expression of the distinction between the static and the dynamic aspects. But the emphasis is placed on the crystallization which emerges from the dynamics of historical occurrences. Freyer spoke of these forms of social reality as "forms which grow out of life." [1] In a metaphorical way he described them as vaults established by the process of life. We cannot accept the introduction of the term "life" into this context, since the functional side of social reality in terms of the process inherent in this reality is not just life. This aspect of the social reality is historical and therefore meaningful in itself. It is thus a stratum above life. The historical aspect of social reality as a composition of acts and meaning

1. See Hans Freyer, *Einleitung in die Soziologie*, p. 81.

transcends life in this sense. Therefore the aspect of stability and crystallization in social reality acquires a particular denotation. The historical meaningfulness of the various social acts is made to flow into the sociological meaning of the forms, units, and institutions in which the acts take place. When, for instance, we speak of the meaning of the act of acknowledgment of the order of a polis by a citizen of Periclean Athens, we understand that this act of acknowledgment has a particular historical meaning, rooted in the connection with the particular social and political order that is being acknowledged. The particular order of the polis as a social and political form comes to the fore here in its two aspects: This order is a content inherent in the actual historical deed performed by actual citizens, deeds expressing the dependence on and the subjection to the order. Yet this order is also the framework *encompassing* the historical deeds as they are actually carried out, by the citizens of Athens for example, since the order of the polis is not only a meaning inherent in the acts but a framework as well. As a framework the order becomes a common sphere for all the citizens and ceases to be a private "monadological" sphere of a single citizen of Athens and his subjective intentionality. The common sphere which is essential to the nature of sociological institutions has as its characteristic the concrete manifestation not only of the inner meaning of an act but of an embracing framework as well. We conclude that the historical occurrence as the functional aspect of a sociological unit is meaningful due to the connection of this unit with the framework in which the occurrence is placed. This unit becomes sociological proper, since it is carried by a meaningful occurrence possessing an intentionality toward the framework.

In different terms, the historical occurrence as viewed

by sociology is always bound to be intentional, directed toward the meaning through this intentionality only. Hence the social unit is always one of a higher level, the fundamentals of which are rooted in the intentional occurrence lying on the lower level. Through this intentionality the act ceases to be a vague, sheer psychic event. The occurrence becomes historical due to its tendency or intentionality toward a sociological framework, and this framework in turn is a real unit since it is rooted in the real historical occurrence. An example will throw some light on this relationship. A state is not given and existent in the sense that its citizens are. The state exists as a meaning of the acts of actual human beings living in it and acting on it. But it exists also in the sense that these beings will and intend it to exist. In the meaning of their deeds there is inherent this independent status of the state as encompassing all the deeds and all the acts of intentionality. The state is both inherent in the meaning of the deeds and encompasses these deeds. The meaning itself provides, as it were, for the status of the state as a framework.

If the sociological unit lies on an upper level as compared with the actual historical events, we do not from the outset limit the number of levels placed above the level of the historical occurrences. We assume, for instance, that the acknowledgment of the citizen of Athens directed to his social order presupposes his polis. The polis serves as the framework which renders meaning to the act of acknowledgment and attachment, and it is the polis which transforms these acts into concrete historical acts, such as participation in the assembly, in the jury, etc. In saying this we do not imply that the intention of the citizen of Athens is confined only to his polis. We are in turn entitled to analyze this polis and to dissolve it into its various elements. From the point of view of the concrete meaning

as it appears on the horizon of the actual citizen it is
a Greek polis, city-state. But being a framework it is also
a starting point for an analysis which carries the polis
beyond its *prima facie* meaning as an object of the historical intention of a concrete citizen of Athens. The Greek
polis can be looked at in turn from the point of view of
a more general and comprehensive scheme of social orders.
Hence as a framework the polis can be considered not only
in its relation to the actual citizen of Athens but also in
its relation to other frameworks, in this case to other sociopolitical units.

Here essentially two ways are open before us. The framework may be looked at in a comparative manner, i.e.
we may compare the structure of the polis with the organization of a city in the Middle Ages, or with that of a modern
city in a modern state, and the like. In this case we still
consider the various forms of social order against their
concrete historical backgrounds. We regard them not as
meanings immanent in historical occurrences, however,
but as frameworks existing side by side, or we try to understand the genesis of these frameworks as they emerge one
out of the other because of certain historical factors.
There is still another way open to us: We may try to
understand the nature of the framework as framework, that
is to say to analyze the social order or the state in general.
In this case we could explicitly transcend the limits of comparison, which leads us to what may be called a comparative study of social institutions, and arrive at a quest for
the *phenomenology* of these institutions.

Or to put it from a different point of view, if we consider
the frameworks as such and compare them with one another
we still remain within the scope of the qualitative plurality
of historical reality. To be sure, we look at this plurality in
terms not of the acts producing it but of the frameworks

supporting it. Yet there is still room for the investigation of the genesis, i.e. of the process of coming into being of the various social orders, since our goal in this case is still to understand the real relationship existing between the various consecutive social orders. We still deal with history, although with history on a second level—not with the genesis of a particular historical unit but with the genesis of the various social units. In this case we do not write the history of the polis but a history of political orders. But in addition, placing the historical investigation on a higher level yet still keeping it in the universe of discourse of history proper, we may introduce another aspect. On the basis of the historical investigation into the various social units we set up an Ideal Type. With regard to this Ideal Type the various social frameworks are on the one hand material data and on the other hand illustrations of a certain structure inherent in them. Thus only since the social unit implies an aspect of framework or, more accurately, since the meaning of a social unit depends on its being a framework for the various acts and events, the way is open for an investigation of society as a particular subject matter connected with but nevertheless separated from history, namely the investigation carried out by social science.

2. This conception of the social units as frameworks has some affinity with Paul Tillich's concept of *Gestalt* as applied to social reality. Tillich argues that the usual systematization of sciences based on the distinction between laws (natural science) and events (history) needs a third link, i.e. that of Gestalt. As examples he offers the organism as the subject matter of biology and society as the subject matter of sociology. According to this suggestion every Gestalt draws a borderline between itself and a different Gestalt, but there is a common lawfulness among all the Gestalts which are of one and the same kind. Each organism

is distinguished from the others but there is still a lawfulness common to them all. The interconnections within
a Gestalt form a closed system. Space and time exist within
it; as a closed system it is therefore a figure in space. This
can be easily observed in biological and sociological units,
for they occupy places. Time too is present in the Gestalt,
since a Gestalt grows both individually and within its
species in the transition from one stage to another of
its career.[2]

Tillich calls our attention on the one hand to the character of a society as a unit closed in itself and on the other to
its existence within process. However, we must observe that
Tillich in a way exaggerated the similarity of a social to
a biological unit. He pointed out that the historical process
occurs within a Gestalt, but he did not sufficiently emphasize the decisive fact that it is the historical process
which builds up the social unit as a Gestalt. Therefore the
social unit is a *product* of the process as well as a historical *producer*. These two functions of a social unit are
possible and compatible since this unit is both a meaning
inherent in acts and a framework *embracing* acts. As a
meaning the social unit exists in the acts and occurrences
directed toward it, and as a framework this unit furnishes
particularity and content to these occurrences. The biological example would serve here as a bad guide. In an organism—even when it is considered teleologically—a single
occurrence has no meaning and certainly does not possess
the consciousness of its meaning, since a single physiological
occurrence as such does not have an intentionality toward
the totality of the organism. According to teleological
theory a single physiological occurrence is connected with
a *telos* and serves it; in contrast, an occurrence in the social

2. Paul Tillich, *Das System der Wissenschaften* (Göttingen, 1923), pp.
23, 78.

realm comes within the scope of consciousness—let us recall that to be unconscious is still to be in the realm of
consciousness but to lack actual awareness. Therefore a
social occurrence has the meaning of *taking part* in a totality of a social unit, which is both meaning and framework.

Again it seems that a parallel is to be found here between
this dual relationship characteristic of the structure of a
social unit and the structure of language; any single expression put in a linguistic form has a meaning only insofar
as the structure of the particular language in which it is
expressed, its logic and inner form, are contracted or concentrated as it were in this concrete and actual expression
as brought forth here and now. This expression has a
meaning since it constitutes a *part* of the totality of the
particular language and since it *occurs within* that totality.
The whole of the language appears both as the reservoir
of meanings and as the totality of all the actual and possible expressions of these meanings. The actual expressions tap this reservoir by the very fact that they occur
within the whole of the language but are not identical
with it and do not exhaust it. A similar structure of relations is applicable to social activity and social units.
Political or economic acts, for instance, introduce political
and economic meanings into these particular acts, since
those performing the acts *take part* in these meanings. But
these acts *take place* within the spheres of politics or economics respectively. This interconnection between the aspect
of taking part in (meaning) and the aspect of taking place
(framework) seems to be the characteristic trait of the
inner rhythm of the social unit and points to the relationship between history and sociology. History is thus concerned with acts of taking part while sociology is concerned
with the institutions through and in which the acts take
place.

The problem of the theory of the state, says Herman Heller, is how to conceive of the state in its growth as a structure. For on the one hand the state exists only when men in particular situations allow it to exist through actual acts of their wills, and on the other hand these acts have an order and connections of their own through which they become particular units of a totality of acts, namely the state. It is only because this structure possesses a permanence that the theory of the state gets its subject matter. But since this permanent structure is again subject to continuous changes it is impossible to consider it closed. It must be seen as being open; history is a passage. Therefore it is necessary that the theory of the state should conceive of what is coming into being in what has already come into being, i.e. in the trends of development to conceive of the structure of the state.[3] Heller in the above-paraphrased passage dwells on both the static and the dynamic aspects within the state. We can go further and say this holds within *each* social institution as well and not within the state alone. If structure is the aspect of stability prevailing in spite of and within the change, the state is the structure of political life.

We may be in a better position to determine the methodological position of the concept of structure if we take account of a *threefold* rather than a *dual* composition of social institutions: act, meaning, and framework. The structure of any particular state or of state in general, of a city in the Middle Ages and of city in general, imply an aspect of permanence since they are institutional frameworks. They also imply an aspect of change since they are meanings inherent in historical acts to be defined against the background of time and process. It is obvious that the aspect of meaning and framework respectively are not two

3. Herman Heller, *Staatslehre* (Leiden, 1934), p. 51.

different data placed on two different ontological levels. They are two aspects of one and the same object. The difference between them depends only upon the perspective of the investigation. If we consider a social unit historically it appears as the meaning of an act. If we consider it sociologically it comes to the fore as a framework.

3. The social unit qua framework for the historical act is capable of being historically conceived of as the permanent element in the event. In emphasizing the aspect of the framework of occurrence sociological investigation hands over to historical investigation a constant element. The concepts of polis or of city, state, etc., as indications of particular frameworks, are or may be for historical investigation indications of constant elements in actual occurrences. Since the framework can be set up on different levels, either as polis or as state in general, as a city in the Middle Ages or as city in general, and so on, the constant element in turn cannot be independent of the particular setting within which we proceed with the actual investigation. If we localize our investigation within the setting of Greek history, for instance, the concept of the polis can be looked at as the institutional aspect and thus as the constant element. But if we go beyond this particular setting to the history of political life in general, the concept of the polis itself is conceived of as the datum or as an illustration of the concept of the state in general. The aspect of framework appears in this case in terms of the state in general as the comprehensive institution and thus as the permanent element vis-à-vis the historical process. Here the constant element in the process of events is no longer historical-qualitative (polis) but structural-sociological (state), isolated or abstracted from the realm of the qualitative occurrences. Indeed there is always an alternative the investigation faces in this field. We may legitimately deal

with the history of Greece and then use the concept of polis as the framework, or we may deal with the structure of the polis from the point of view of the concept of the state in general and thus not deal with Greek history in general but with the history of the polis or the political organization in particular.

Yet this alternative is not an arbitrary one and does not depend only on the decision of the investigator or the scholar. The concept of the polis is connected with the concept of the state in general, since with respect to the state in general polis is a meaningful, that is to say historical, reality existing within a sociological framework. What is conceived of as framework on a lower level can in turn be conceived of on a higher level not as a framework but as a meaningful historical reality. This again is an indication of the fact that an institutional framework is not a self-contained ontological entity but a methodological concept. In any case, even the determination of the concept of the polis is impossible without having recourse to the concept of the state, just as it is impossible to determine the concept of state in general if we disconnect it from an elucidation of the various types of political reality or separate it from actual historical types.

Since in this conceptual building up of a relationship of history and sociology we distinguish between the *levels* of history and sociology, we are able to locate the positions of their different social functions respectively. In regard to Greek historical occurrences, for instance, the polis is the framework. In regard to political occurrences in general the polis is in turn an occurrence while the framework is set up on a higher level, being namely the concept of the state or of politics in general. We can treat other social concepts in a similar way. As we ascend the scale of concepts we may consider the lowest or the narrowest as the content or meaning inherent in occurrences. The occurrences in turn are comprised in frameworks which are "higher," that is to say wider, concepts in the scale. In considering, for instance, the activities of a Greek polis we analyze the activities of those living in this polis, activities which take place in and derive their meaning from it. Here because we consider a narrow scope of activities the narrow polis is the framework. In considering the activities of the state in general, however, we analyze the activities of various states in their historical expressions, since the data for the state in general are the various historical types of the state. In this case the polis which is a framework considered from the narrow point of view becomes a sum total of activities or a shorthand description of them. In this capacity polis is the historical-meaningful occurrence or a set of occurrences while the state or regime in general becomes the framework. The very distinction between occurrences dealt with historically and institutional frameworks dealt with sociologically is a relative distinction, i.e. related to the point of view.

This structure, described as one of levels, may also be described as one of concentric circles. The circle of occurrences lies within a framework, while the particular framework lies within a wider framework, just as polis lies in the wider circle of the state in general. From the point of view of the wider framework the narrower can be considered to be an occurrence and thus to belong to the realm of history.

In a way the main question confronting sociological investigation is connected with difficulties inherent in this concentric structure. This problem may be formulated in the following way: Is there a final, all-inclusive framework? If there is one what is it? Is the social framework ultimately contained in a nonsocial framework, such as the

sphere of climate, biology, nature, cosmos, etc., more comprehensive than the social-historical domain? Or if it is
assumed that an ultimate framework exists and is identical with the social domain, what is its nature? Is it a framework only or is it at the same time a domain of both occurrence and framework? The dialectical approach considers
the comprehensive circle as a composition of the two
aspects. If we say that mankind is the most comprehensive
circle of social life, we treat it as both a framework and
a content, both as a sociological unit and as having a history. The history of mankind can thus be considered
a meaningful process which is located within the limits of
mankind where this history actually takes place. Clearly
the confinement to the human framework is the first step
accomplished in this consideration. The reason for this
confinement may lie in the fundamental contention that
history is a human affair and the ultimate framework of
history has to be human as well. This contention may be
put differently as a harmony between the occurrences and
their framework in terms of their ontological status.

A further consideration is that both historical and sociological analysis show that human reality as it is envisaged in
experience does not have this structure of concentric circles,
coexistent in a *static* way. Actual experience encounters
clashes and collisions within human reality. Hence the comprehensiveness of only one circle becomes at most a historical-social ideal indicating in what direction it is proper
to organize human reality through the process of grouping
the variety of trends and units in it. We envisage here an important theoretical fact: Sociological investigation through
its adherence to the concept or aspect of a comprehensive
framework of human social life may furnish historical investigation with more than only methodological means. It
may even set an objective in terms of content, in order

to indicate the course of the historical process in terms of its goal or ideal. The comprehensive framework in its status as the supreme meaning of the process may be set as the ultimate value and goal in regard to any particular historical occurrence. The ultimate human framework does not indicate in this case any given institution related to the meaning of the occurrences in the present. It rather indicates the human future. In other words, if there is at all an ultimate framework this framework ceases to be an institution and becomes a goal.

It may rightly be said that the relationship between the historical and the sociological aspects proper is the core of Marx' doctrine. According to Marx the totality of mankind organized as a unity becomes the objective goal of the historical process. This totality as the most comprehensive framework, being as such a sociological concept by its very logic, becomes the ultimate station in the historical process of events. But if we analyze this conception in a methodological manner, i.e. from the point of view of the implied justification of the relationship between history and sociology, we are bound to come to the conclusion that it is by no means inevitable that we look at the *social* totality as though it had the highest historical value and thereby convert it into an ultimate historical stage. To be sure, in Marx' doctrine society itself becomes both an occurrence and a framework. But different forms of totality are possible and certainly conceivable, for instance the religious invisible ecclesia of Christianity or the cosmos as a whole. But it is also possible and conceivable not to employ the concept of totality at all and to consider historical reality in its limited scope as a continuous process. The step made by Marx in converting the total framework into a content of actual history does not rest on purely methodological grounds. Actually Marx takes for granted the very employment of the notion of the human framework qua society of organized mankind. He further takes for granted that the actual process of history leads to this framework and hence that there are in the actual process representatives of the total framework. The historical place and role of the proletariat is, in this theory, due to its position as the given representative of the future unity of mankind, i.e. of mankind as a framework.

It is clear that all these considerations are not based on a historical analysis as they pretend to be. They are rather based on certain evaluations and decisions, as follows:

a. Marx considered totality to have or even to be the highest value. This is a notion which Marx inherited from Hegel. But for Hegel it was a metaphysical notion, that is to say applied to the all-embracing reality. Marx contracted the field of his outlook to history and still used the concept of totality. He dogmatically assumed that history is a totality and did not consider the possibility that the fact that history is human does not mean that whatever there is in the human realm is a priori historical. He did not consider the possibility of distinguishing between the historical aspect and the aspect of totality, which in this sense may be the cosmos. Yet in case there is no a priori identification of the human with the historical and of the historical with the total, there may still be room for a "world loyalty" of man. Man as human is historical but can be more than historical, transcending history toward reason or toward a cosmic view. The fact that all these possibilities were omitted in Marx' doctrine are due to the fundamental perplexity characteristic of this doctrine: It wanted to confine the outlook to the historical sphere and yet to retain the notion of totality. Hence it identified, overhastily to be sure, the course of history with totality.

b. The hasty search for totality leads to the consideration of history as a product of society. Here again there is no necessity to identify the course of history with the course of *society*, as there was no necessity to identify the course of history with totality. Yet because of the first identification there occurs the second one: Society provides, as it were, the aspect of totality inherent in history, turning history into a whole. Again this step could have been taken only through the identification of the human course with the historical qua social course. This can be clearly seen from the fact that Marx assumed the need for criticism of religion as the presupposition for criticism of society. Since the religious totality certainly trespasses on the historical realm in the sense that it places man in the cosmos and not in history alone, religion had to be criticized for the sake of the total historicity of man.

At this juncture it seems proper to return to Max Weber's theory of the formation of the concepts employed in social science. Weber's aim was to translate the sociological concepts in their aspect as frameworks of historical occurrences into historical concepts indicating meaningful occurrences. There is no better example of this tendency of Weber than his attempt to define the concept of a nation. He did not find any other possibility for defining this concept save by indicating the aspiration characteristic of communities which regard themselves as nations, namely their striving for statehood. It may be assumed that behind this sociological attempt an *ideological* approach is to be detected (connected with German history), but this does not matter for the purpose of our discussion. The significant thing is the methodological approach exhibited in this theory.

Weber turns the sociological concept of a nation into a content of the historical process, assuming apparently that this aspect exhausts the nature of the social unit considered. He tried to conceive of a social unit as a condition and a pattern for the particular behavior of individuals. This indicates that he was aware of the fact that the behavior within a social unit is not arbitrary but has a particular structure pattern imposed by the social unit. But Weber did not dwell sufficiently on the ambiguity of this structure's being both the structure of a behavior and a framework surrounding it. For the two concepts of Toennies in which the aspect of framework is implied (society, community) Weber wanted to substitute two parallel functional concepts connoting processes (the *tendency* toward a structure of society and the *tendency* toward a structure of community) and thus to indicate only the meaningful direction of the historical occurrence without shifting over to the domain of sociological concepts proper. It may be justly said that from this point of view the two theories, that of Marx on the one hand and of Weber on the other, offer two opposite poles of sociological approach in general. With Marx historical investigation is integrated in sociological investigation, whereas with Weber the sociological concepts which have to be considered as indications of frameworks are ultimately dissolved within concepts describing the historical occurrences. Actually these two main sociological theories represent the disintegration of the interplay of the two aspects. The one theory dissolves the interplay in its bias toward the aspect of sociology while the other dissolves it in its bias toward the aspect of history. In addition to their body of information and to their stature as two great theories, they lay bare in an "ideal-typical" form the two elements of sociological investigation in general. Yet we cannot say that the two theories represent systems established by the pattern of the real relationship between the two elements, since they actually emphasize only one of the elements and thus are bound to be one-sided when they ought to be based on a real dialectical set of relations, or at least on a set of complementary relations.

Hans Freyer, who has been quoted before, grasped the ambiguity inherent in sociological concepts. He tried to bring it into prominence by emphasizing that social units are both *stages* in the historical process and *strata* of the social reality in the present. The concepts of society and community, for instance, signify for him two stages of a historical development in terms of time. They are stages in the development from the social form in the Middle Ages to that in the modern urban era. But the two forms of social life are for him also two types of contemporary social existence, since an era distinguished by the structure of society also contains "islands" built up of the elements of community. Thus the forms of social existence are both forms that came into being in the course of the historical process and structures of present existence. The task of sociological investigation is to explore the structure built up from these strata, which in terms of history came into being one after the other.[4]

This program contains a significant indication as to the nature of the social forms, though it seems to me that the conclusion has not been formulated with due precision. If we try to formulate the issue in a stricter way we must point to the structure of sociology in terms of its presuppositions and the concepts of social struggle. Though Freyer says that the reality of social life is built up in strata of social structures, it is actually built up in coexistent circles. Within the social reality of industrial society, for example, there can and actually do exist narrow corners of life-enclosed circles, as it were, such as families, peer groups, clubs, etc.,

4. Cf. Hans Freyer, *Soziologie als Wirklichkeitswissenschaft* (Leipzig and Berlin, B. G. Teubner, 1930), p. 217, and also his *Einleitung in die Soziologie*, p. 126.

which are not based on the fundamentals of the industrial society. The description in terms of strata does not bring to the fore the fact that the various forms are actually contemporaneous, although in terms of history they do represent various consecutive stages.

It would be wrong to assume that the social reality of any present situation is built up in a *static form* from coexistent strata and circles. Perhaps the term "strata" is again not adequate for the description of the structure dealt with. Social reality is to be considered as a structure of strata if looked at from—as it were—a geological point of view. Thus, for instance, we see a big city as built upon small towns or a technological economy as built on an economy of handicraft. But a social reality contains in every situation some decisive, overwhelming, or predominant features as well, so that in a particular period of time one social form preponderates over the others. In this case the subordinate form—like handicrafts in industrial society— is not only a foundation but also, since it still continues to exist, a kind of island in a big ocean.

The theory of the pluralistic structure of society as composed of strata points in a way to an underlying idea of progress. Here progress means the victory of the later form over the former. But the theory which looks at the plurality of social existence as a structure of circles is closer in its description to the actual and the possible tensions between the various coexistent forms of social life. It must be assumed that the subordinate strata are capable of prevailing against the upper strata, and that they can overcome the existing social structure. If we look at the situation on the basis of a model of concentric circles we will see that one circle—for instance that of industrial society—prevails over the others, and that there are other circles as well which may possess a tendency toward expansion. In terms of a social situation this means that an actual struggle occurs within the surrounding and the preponderant circle. To sum up, in the structure of strata the various forms are built one *on the top* of the other, while in the structure of circles they are built one *within* the other. The theory based on the model of strata considers the subordinate stratum to belong to the past, while the theory based on the model of circles puts forward the plain fact that though the circle is subordinate it still is a part of one and the same present— if not of a universal present then at least of a specific fragment of it.

In social struggles each of the involved partners attempts to convert the content of its aspiration into the framework of the entire social existence. Each partner tries to objectify his aspirations and goals, to make them cease to be sheer aspirations and aims and become institutionalized in the objective and objectified ways of life and patterns of existence of a given society. The historical-meaningful content of the various aims intends to be established beyond its original position of a sheer aim carried by a conscious tendency of actual human individuals. In the struggle to establish aims as an objectively existing factor of social life, the tendency is to shift the aim from the domain of occurrences to the domain of frameworks. If, for example, a worker strives for a working day of eight hours, and he does so in a social reality which still is not formed according to his goal, he actually strives to make his goal a constitutive element existing objectively, that is to say as an institution in the social reality. Once he achieves his goal the content of his struggle becomes a part of the social landscape. As such it can be taken for granted and no longer needs to be advanced by a social struggle rooted in the acts of intention of actual human beings. Thus the process of social struggle may be considered in terms of its structure as an attempt to shift from historical-meaningful occurrences to the realm of institutions, which are sociological concepts, embracing as it were the processes of the occurrences. The aims of historical processes are to cease to be only aims in order to become social institutions.

Here one comes across one of the few really significant contributions of the social outlook on the historical process. If the sociological outlook is related to the concepts of frameworks and institutions this outlook is capable of presenting the meaning of what is usually called "progress" as that line in the historical process in which goals and trends get established in institutions, that is to say where contents of an aim acquire a permanent existence that is taken for granted. Yet the sociological conception of progress understood precisely is limited to certain data of the historical process only, i.e. data which are genuinely capable of becoming or being converted into frameworks, such as those bound up with the economic or biological sides of human life. It may be said that there must be some kind of an affinity between what can be a framework of human historical existence and those aims that become a framework of that sort. The strife for economic achievements or for the biological safeguards of human existence can be institutionalized because of its nature and content. Hence a struggle of this sort can be placed within the movement of the shift from the historical aspect of the process of human existence to the social aspect of institution. As against this kind of movement, the development of ideas or the stages of development of any branch of knowledge cannot be conceived of as involved in this transition from the realm of intentions, consciousness, and aims to the sphere of frameworks and institutions, since these data are of a different nature. The content of knowledge does not constitute the aim of organizing human-historical existence, as is characteristic of those aims which are established in the course of the historical process as social institutions. This point will be taken up later.

From what has been said several conclusions are to be drawn.

a. The sociological conception of history is able to explain at most only how ideas grow or how sciences are established against the background of the historical transition from the content of an aim to the content of a social framework. But this conception is unable to render the means for understanding the specific rhythm of the movement of the ideas themselves and of their intrinsic nature. One of the main fallacies of any totally sociological consideration of history lies in the confusion of the boundaries between the approach to the *background* of ideas and the approach to the rhythm of *ideas as such*. Sociological theories of history sometimes tend to the naïve assumption that the means we apply to explain the emergence of ideas in some social settings are to be applied as means of explaining the contents of ideas and their validity. In this case sociology becomes sociologism, parallel to the conversion of psychology into psychologism.

b. It is not feasible to transfer in a simple way the conception of progress, as defined above, from the domain of human-social existence to the domain of ideas. The structure of the domain of ideas is one of regions lying next to each other. There is a "progress" in the realm of ideas when new issues are discovered, such as the question of permanence within the manifold of phenomena as a philosophical issue. But this progress by no means carries a replacement of the former issues within itself; the new discovery does not make the former one pointless or obsolete. This applies even to what seems to be a victorious development, as for instance the establishment of modern science. Even in this case there is no sheer replacement of the former by the latter. We witness the criticism directed against the quantitative approach in the realm of nature, as for instance that of Goethe against Newton, or in the different realms such as psychology, psychiatry, etc. The development in this field is different from the development let us say in the economic field, where industrial achievements make former ways of economic behavior obsolete, even if we would like to retain the former ways of economic activity, as technological industry replaces various forms of handicraft.

c. In the third place, no progress in the realm of ideas makes one particular idea established in the sense to be found in the social realm, where an issue gets the authority and the status of an *external-objective* factor, like the institution of the eight-hour working day. In the realm of ideas there is no trend toward that sort of objectification. Ideas remain ideas—this is their weakness and their strength. Yet this essence of the realm of ideas imposes an a priori limitation on any sociological approach to ideas. No sociological approach can disregard the ontological peculiarity of ideas simply by converting them into social facts. This invasion of sociology into the realm of ideas must impose on ideas the essence of social facts as establishing an institutional framework. Yet such a sociologism in the realm of ideas is essentially precluded by the very definition of this realm and the elements composing it. Sociologism—and historicism—gains from the lack of a clear notion of the different fields of human activity. Hence it takes for granted that all the fields are on one and the same level and can be treated as social facts. Furthermore, because of the importance of social life in the modern era and the visible achievements of turning aims into institutions, the tendency is to advocate the notion that whatever is human is essentially a social or historical fact. Again the necessary distinction between levels and fields of human activity related to a phenomenology of these levels frustrates any attempt at blurring the boundaries between them. The phenomenology of the facts and events turns out to be a criticism of some modernistic trends based on the nebulosity and vagueness of the conceptual and analytic approach.

4. Some approaches to the problem of sociology emphasize the fact that the present is the subject matter of sociology. Still there is no approach which would try to make the present the exclusive subject matter of sociology, in disregard of the other subject matters such as social forms, institutions, etc. The methodological issue which must not be avoided here is clearly this: Is the connection between the various subject matters of sociological investigation an accidental or merely a technical one, or is it connected with the genesis of sociology insofar as sociology was originally founded as an investigation of the present situation and expanded the scope of its interest in the course of time? A theory confining itself to the genetic aspect cannot recognize the systematic relations existing between the various branches of sociological investigations. But it seems that the practical sociological investigation which combines a concern for the present with a concern for social institutions was justified in its very assumption of a connection between them, although it often did not provide support for it in terms of categories and principles. We shall try to offer such a justification.

When dealing with historical time we came across the concept of the present. The present there was considered to be one of the dimensions of historical time. It was made clear that the concept of the historical present is both a dimension of the historical datum and one of historical decision. Now we face the problem of the meaning of the present within the domain of sociology. The solution of this problem implicitly carries with it the answer to the question regarding the position of the present as a subject matter of sociological investigation and its inner affinity with other well-established subject matters of social science, such as institutions.

A possible suggestion might be that sociology conceives of the present as a structure and as a framework. It conceives of a particular fragment of *time* in the same way that it conceives of the historical process in general. From the sociological point of view the present is not a moment. It cannot be conceived of as a moment since the moment is the meeting point of the actual living and experiencing individual subject with his world. Since sociology is interested not in the individual living subject but in the "togetherness" of subjects, the individual and subjective moments necessarily expand and accumulate in volume. Sociology conceives of the present not in terms of its subjective aspect of a meeting with the world but as a situation, that is to say as a composition of factors forming a social unit. In conceiving of the present as a situation sociology from the outset shifts the particular fragment of time from its subjective status to an objective domain. Nevertheless the present qua objective situation does not become a sheer historical datum which calls for historical reflection proper. Sociology establishes a domain of its own, an intermediary one between the present as a subjective dimension of decisions of human individuals and the present as the dimension of the datum, to be reflected upon from the subsequent historical point of view. Sociology conceives of the present both as a fragment of time and as a situation, and it is here that we find the real innovation of the sociological approach to the present. On the one hand the present is the *content* of actual existence for the human beings living in it, and on the other hand it is the *framework* of their existence. The present is both meaning and framework. This duality in the concept of the sociological present gives way to an identity in terms of structure of the sociological concept of the present with the sociological concept of the meaningful frameworks, in general.

To put it differently, sociology points to the fact that the actual historical existence of men occurs in various spheres such as cities, societies, states, economies, etc., which are actually frameworks of men's activity. It points to another fact as well: Actual human existence occurs in another sphere, not defined in terms of content (cities, etc.) but in terms of the present. The present itself, in addition to the spheres of content included in it, is a sphere on its own merits. Sociology thus turns a dimension of time into an institutional framework and gives time, as it were, a meaning of space.

The present is a framework but also the locus where the other frameworks are contained. Within the present, states and cities, economies and churches, societies and communities, etc. exist; there exist within it all those meaningful frameworks which are again by themselves subject matters of sociological investigation. Actual human beings exist and act within these frameworks which in turn exist in this present. But still the present itself is also a framework. The difficulty inherent in sociology is to be found in its task of clarifying the relationship existing between these particular frameworks which have contents—let us call them again institutions—and the present as having the position of framework and forming an institution in its own right.

Is the present as a framework, having a structure and pattern of its own, always and everywhere a composition of the *same* institutional frameworks? From the point of view of historical occurrence all that has occurred exists, yet we know

that not all that has occurred has historical relevance since
it does not leave actual traces to be discerned within the
present, and from the position of the present. It is obvious
that this is the case regarding particular events. But the
question might be posed whether this is also true with reference to the social frameworks. These frameworks certainly
exist in history, yet we may ask whether their existence implies that they always exist as actual shaping factors in
history and appear at all times and in all places as constitutive factors of any historical fragment whatsoever. Even
when we assume that not every *event* has a historical relevance we may perhaps have to assume at least that every
social *framework* is bound always to have historical relevance and hence to be always active in every present and always in the same direction.

Stated differently, we may say that any present is a composition of frameworks. What is the difference between
the various presents? Is it a difference in terms of content,
like the difference between the economic system of a city
and the economic system of a state, or is it a difference of
social stratification such as that between castes and classes?
Or do we have to assume that the difference between the
various presents is one in terms of the very factors composing them, such as the difference between a present shaped
mainly or entirely by religious factors and another one
shaped mainly or totally by political or economic factors?
Must the relation and the proportion between the various
components creating the total framework of any given present be the same at all times and at all places, assuming that
the components as such appear in every social situation?
Or can we assume that there is a framework of the present
in which, for instance, there is to be found a preponderance
of political institutions, whereas in a different present there

has been or will be a preponderance of religious or economic frameworks?

In all these questions only empirical sociological research is entitled to say the decisive word. Yet it is clear that empirical research is conditioned here by posing these fundamental questions. These questions touch on problems of categories and principles. The conception of historical materialism made a far-reaching decision on this point. It assumed dogmatically that the present of the industrial society is to be found in all historical periods and situations. Since the economic factor was supposed to be decisive in the present of industrial society—that is to say in our own present—this factor was considered as decisive in any historical situation of the past. Hence historical materialism tried to put forward the permanent factors of history qua causes of any historical situation and qua causes of any historical change. Against this view it has to be maintained that there is no a priori necessity for transferring to every other present the *present* present of our own—that present which serves as the starting point of historical materialism, that is to say the social situation of industrial society. If we transfer the findings of the sociological investigation of our present to the presents of Pericles or of Jeremiah, and if we search for the factors which shaped their respective presents, assuming them to be like the factors shaping ours—for instance the predominance of the class struggle—we unwarrantedly suppose that the structure of every present is bound to be the same. On this view the difference between one present and another is thus a sheer chronological one, i.e. merely one of position within the order of time. It may be said that this naïve transfer of our own present abolishes the autonomy of all presents and maintains only the autonomy and the meaningfulness of our own present.

By pointing out that the sociological present is the framework of man's activity and therefore has a structure of its own, we have implied that both the present of the past and that of the Samoans in our era have a structure of their own, unless actual research shows an identity or similarity with the composition characteristic of our own industrial present. The methodological task of the sociological investigation is to understand, say, the present of the population of Samoa. More exactly its task is to look at the present of the past as a structure established by its immanent formative factors. But this investigation must not assume as self-evident that our own present has to be projected into that of the past and serve as the pattern for every analysis of a social situation in it. We have to be restrained and grant every present which is a true subject matter of our concern the benefit of uniqueness. Since there exists the danger of projecting our present into every present we have to go the other way around: First we essay the supposition that there are immanent and unique factors shaping the present under consideration, and then we compare them or identify them with the factors active in our own present.

We encounter here an interesting confusion of the sociological and historical approach to human reality. This transfer of the structure of our own present—even assuming that this is actually its structure—to the structure of the past is no longer a properly sociological outlook. When we say that in Jeremiah's present the religious factors did not possess an independent value or a formative power of their own, we do not consider the situation of the past (that is to say, the present of the past) from the inside, by taking into consideration its inner shaping forces and factors. We look at this past *historically* and try to discover the hidden factors which affected it and which are embodied in disguised religious forms. We look at the past from the traces it left in our present; hence we assume or pretend to know the past better than it knew itself.[5] Yet when proceeding in this way we no longer consider the present of the past as a structure. We consider it as a historical fragment traces of which are found through an analysis of the occurrences which took place in the past. But then the sociological approach passes beyond its legitimate boundaries and thus ceases to be sociological altogether. This victory of sociology —and we find many examples of it in modern literature— is virtually a Pyrrhic one.

The distinction between the historical and sociological approach must be maintained since this distinction is ultimately rooted in the essence of historical time. Historical investigation starts with the present by looking at it as a message from the past. It conceives of the present as an objectivation of past occurrences. In contrast sociological investigation is interested in the present for its own sake and is concerned with the objectivations of the present as they manifest themselves within the scope of the very present which creates them. Sociology is primarily concerned not with the study of the genesis of the state or of social classes—though practically it deals with this—but with the *function* of the state and with the actual *position* of the classes within a given society. To be sure, historical investigation, dealing with the genetic aspect, may sometimes serve as a useful tool for sociological investigation, just as the findings of sociological investigation are sometimes used by historical research. But this interrelation, which certainly places difficulties in the way of a systematically clear-cut differentiation between the two approaches, does not nullify the distinction.

Within the flow of historical time we encounter two

5. See again on this point Leo Strauss' criticism of historicism as stated in his various works.

different directions, one based on the relation of the *present to the past* and the other on the relation of the *present to itself*. Historical investigation relates phenomena over a line or in a series, the line leading from the past to the present; sociological investigation conceives of its objects as placed in circles or as included in frameworks. The series characteristic of the historical outlook stems from the openness of the present toward that past and from the openness of the past which enters into the present; whereas the circle characteristic of sociology is connected with the relation of the present to itself, with its movement beyond itself, a movement carried by deeds in the present. Sociological investigation is thus evidently bound up with the concept of a whole, for the present, like any institution considered as a sociological phenomenon, is a whole. Historical investigation, if we wish to cling to its proper meaning, is the investigation of the present through its past; hence it does not know the concept of a whole, for a whole, as it were, closes time. But time in history is open. Closing creates a framework; it is henceforth a sociological and not a historical device.

5. The present is a structure and like other structures is a legitimate and justified subject matter of sociology. This leads us to a further aspect of the *globus intellectualis* of sociology. When we speak of the subject matter of sociology we think of two aspects: Society is the totality of the functions of common life and the totality of the forms in which these functions are embodied. Society produces the functions and is at once their totality. It is both the foundation and the building as such, both the source and the whole. The functions emerging from it are still contained in it. It is not by accident that there is a problem as to whether the state is a legal or a sociological institution, even though this distinction cannot finally be maintained. We may con-

ceive of the state as a legal reality by disconnecting it from its social source, but the state, even in its formal-legal aspect, exists within the comprehensive social reality. From this point of view it does not possess a sociological *content* but rather fulfills a sociological *function*. In other words, the sociological approach leads us to look at society as embodying itself in objectivations like government, law, economics, etc. It tends to consider these objectivations as the totality of social life. But society is both the producer of these objectivations and their comprehensive totality. The intrinsic difficulty of sociological investigation is connected with this double-sided approach to one and the same reality. This can be stated in a different way as well. We have distinguished before between society as the producer of objectivations and the objectivations themselves. Does this distinction have any ontological significance? What is society in its narrow connotation as merely the *producer* of objectivations? Is there a society void of objectivations, or does society itself qua producer of objectivations contain them in itself beforehand? Actually society as a producer of objectivations and forms accomplishes the act of production by these very objectivations, just as thought expresses itself in thoughts, and yet only through thoughts can we know what thought is like. For instance, society produces government, law, economic life, mores, etc. But it produces all these through its process which contains in itself forms of government, law, economic activity, ways of life, etc. This inner affinity between the producer and its products must lead us to a conception which will avoid the error of supposing that we can penetrate to the last source of human reality and by means of sociological investigation place this reality on its foundations. This conception of "placing on foundations" (by means of a sociological reduction) assumes that there is a primary function, that is to say an exclusive function, which builds the social existence. Vulgar materialism sees this primary function in sheer economic production, disregarding Marx' own observation of the difference between the work of bees and that of human beings. Marx intended to convey the idea that the economic deed is filled by thought and that even at the core of social reality there is a passage beyond mere economic function in the narrow sense of the term. The sociological reduction pretends to arrive at this conception of the primary, fundamental function of the economic factor as producing human society and determining its structure and historical course, because it assumes that the factor which is first in *time* is also first from the point of view of function. We find here again a confusion between the sociological and the historical approach. The economic factor, assumed to explain the *genesis* of society, is supposed to be the factor which determines the actual *existence* of this society. Granted even that economic activity, as Marx thought, brought about the progress of human life from the animal to the historical status, we must not conclude that the economic factor as *genetic* is *eo ipso* the *fundamental* factor of society.[6] When we consider the genesis of society we intend to come back, as it were, to the zero point preceding the various objectivations of social reality. In that case the zero point must furnish the point of departure of the objectivations. But when we consider the structure of a society we conceive of it as a whole, producing objectivations through the already produced objectivations. In this case we must accept the circle rounded by this approach. This circle is an instance of Rosmini's *circula solida*, rather than *circula vitiosa*.

In sum, there is no room in the present for the earlier

6. Cf. the present author's "Marx's Thesen über Feuerbach," *Archiv für Rechts- unds Sozialphilosophie*, Bern, 1951.

and later. All the factors in the present exist together, are included in the present, and maintain it. The present is a composition of various domains of human activity, but it is itself a composite factor with the special capacity of uniting various domains into a total situation. The present becomes a space itself and a space of spaces, similar to society, which is a framework of itself and a framework of frameworks as well.

This suggestion as to the relation between the approach of social science and the perspective of the whole calls for one qualification: The notion of the present as a whole does not imply the consequence that there is one total present. The total present has no social meaning for the simple reason that it cannot be humanly encountered. Totality is a notion, an idea, but not an object within actual human experience. The meaning of the suggestion as to the sociological approach in its relation to the present is that even a partial present—and there are only partial presents, for instance the present of one generation, the present of a group of immigrants, etc.—all these, while explored sociologically, are looked at as wholes embracing the different factors and phases of human existence, biological, psychological, economic, cultural, etc. The present as a whole is again a piecemeal whole and not a total one.

6. "Sociology deals with objects toward which we maintain an existential relationship, completely different from the relationship we maintain toward the mainifestations of spirit." [7] Sociology undertakes, according to this view, to understand our own decisions as social beings. From the sociological angle man directs questions to himself and comes to understand his own behavior immanently. This conception, as summarized in the above quotation, is justified to a large extent, but precisely for this reason the issue

7. Freyer, *Einleitung in die Soziologie*, p. 114.

must be formulated in a more exact fashion. Let us ask in the first place how sociology is capable of comprehending our own decisions. Where do we find this relationship of sociology to decisions? In the light of our previous discussion we may point out now that since sociology is, among other things, a science of the present, it deals also with the present acts of men, that is to say with the decisions or deeds resulting from them. Sociology tries to conceive of the dynamic decisions within the situation of the present since these decisions are a part of that situation.

Two aspects have to be emphasized here: 1) The decisions dealt with by sociology and the social deeds stemming from them are actual and therefore present processes. 2) Since they are actual and present processes they take place within a dimension of reality which is, in regard to them, a framework or a situation. The statement as to the existential or willing character of the decision or the deed confuses the full meaning of the concepts of decision and deed as dealt with sociologically. By saying that the deed and the materialization resulting from decisions take place within the framework of the present, we assume at once that they are integrated in a particular meaningful framework which lies beyond the subjective realm. They are not just vague decisions or contentless acts of realization seen in their shapeless core. They are from the outset deeds full of content, and this content is furnished to them, for they are related to a social structure and embedded in social situations.

Once again we encounter the threefold structure discussed before: 1) the process (acts or functions as such); 2) the meaning inherent in the process; and 3) finally the framework where the process takes place. In any decision or any act of materialization we can detect meanings and directions. They are constitutive deeds; they build the present and are themselves built by the composition of the various structures forming the present as a compound social situation. A social institution thus cannot exist apart from its relationship to actual human beings. It is necessarily based on the polarity of man as the producer of deeds and acts of realization on the one hand and the objective structures qua framework on the other. The anthropological reduction—that is to say the pretence of analyzing the setup of all the structures with man as their foundation—is excluded by the very essence of the sociological approach. Sociology builds its structure presupposing man's maintaining a relationship to the objectivations, and not on a presupposition of "pure" man. The objectivations here appearing as social institutions and situations are constituted by man and constitute him as well. Hence the main sociological category is that of reciprocity, since the conceptual structure of sociology is a circular one. This reciprocity is but a formulation of the circular structure characteristic of the relationship existing between man and institutions. Merely raising the well-known question as to whether man builds society or whether society builds man indicates that an attempt has been made to dissolve the tension characteristic of the sociological approach, i.e. the tension between living man and the frameworks of his life. Such an attempt to disregard the tension is bound to fail since it contradicts the very nature and logic of the sociological approach to human reality. Eugen Rosenstock-Huessy rightly distinguished between sociological and historical knowledge as a difference between knowledge arising from participation in a *deed* and knowledge arising from participation in an *experience*. In trying to conceive of the present reality—and first of all the reality of our own actual present—sociology takes part in the activity of the present (participation in a deed). History, which tries to conceive of the present through a distant reality or of a distant one through the present reality, establishes relations between distant and alien factors. Therefore it is able to *conceive* of but not to *take an active part* in a given situation.

Here again the dialectic of sociological knowledge, bound up with the essence of the present, is brought to the fore. Every decision occurs within a specific present; the present is hence the framework of a decision. Yet a decision is essentially directed toward the future. It aims at actualizing something which does not yet exist. The *act* of actualizing is present, yet its *intention* is directed toward the future. Since sociology conceives of the structure of the present in its relationship to the act of decision it must assume the provisionality of this structure. By definition the present intends to cross the limits of the present.

The social structure is ambiguous; it is a given structure since it is present; it is also distant since it is a structure to be established in the future and to be maintained by passing beyond the present. The present being a present of actualization implicates the incipient future. The social structure is open toward the future precisely because it is a present structure. The man of action in maintaining the present structure at once changes it and replaces it by a new one. Again we come back to the relationship with history. Historical investigation deals with data in the present by explaining them through their relation with the past. Sociological investigation deals with the present situation and as such it is bound to see it also in the light of the future which is about to come. Thus the distinction and the determination of the relationship between history and sociology is ultimately linked up with the nature of historical time.

It is usual to point out in the literature devoted to the history of sociology that sociology grew out of the philosophy of history and Hegel's philosophy of law. Generally the starting point is thought to be Hegel's analysis of the "bourgeois society" as presented in his *Philosophy of Right*. But in the light of the former analysis we can expand the notion of the intellectual and conceptual origins of sociology. Sociology is opposed to the very outlook of Hegel's philosophy of history (but is, as a matter of fact, already envisaged in his *Philosophy of Right*) for it offers a new aspect of human reality, namely that of the present directed toward the future. As against this the philosophical approach to history as clearly conceived by Hegel—and for very sound reasons of principle, not because of Hegel's social relations with the Prussian state as is sometimes suggested—was bound up with the investigation directed from the present toward the past. The trend inherent in the sociological investigation of the present naturally includes in its scope the aspect of the future state of society. The discovery of the aspect of the future paved the way for the investigation of human deeds as directed toward the future. The discovery of the dimension of the future, however, which was indicated in the various shades of opinion expressed in Hegel's school, opened the door to a perception of the present as a whole containing the seeds of the future, that is to say as a sociological present proper.

7. The social sciences, dealing with human collective existence, with law, the state, etc., rest essentially on history and on historical research. History is that sphere in which the occurrences conceived of as characteristic of society, the state, the nation, etc. take place. But the social sciences do not confine themselves to occurrences in history and do not content themselves with understanding them through the dynamics of the past alone. Although states, nations, etc. are products of the historical process and are necessarily involved in it, the social sciences aim

to understand them as *given* and aim at investigating their structure as units and institutions. In the social sciences the dynamic conception, being the cornerstone of their very innovation, is linked up with the static aspect, which removes the subject matter of, say, sociology from its historical surroundings. The social sciences do not content themselves with an indication of the functional position of their subject matter in history. The addition of the static perspective inherent in the perspective of framework implies essentially the employment of the concept of subject. The state, the nation, and so on, which within the scope of the historical approach connote function or composition of relations within a process, become in the social sciences subjects of features, properties, attributes, and trends. By this procedure the social sciences give their objects a quasi-independent status. To be sure, this status is actually only a methodological consequence of a change from a dynamic perspective of the process to the static conception of institutions in which the process takes place.

These objects are embedded in historical processes and therefore cannot be isolated from the process. From this point of view they are not subjects but compounds of relations. But they are conceived of as active subjects once we consider them as subject matter of the social sciences. To be sure, we do not in actual research adhere strictly to the demarcation line between historical and sociological investigation. Yet from the point of view of principles this demarcation line has to be maintained.

To put it differently, what is conceived in history as a *system* of functions is conceived in the social sciences as a *subject*. The social sciences resting on historical research accept the domain of history as a datum and regard historical occurrences as something to be taken for granted. Historical reality being the basis of the sociological approach becomes concentrated as it were and turns into a subject possessing properties. The task of sociology is held to be that of exploring these properties and the ways of life in which they express themselves. The domain serving as the foundation (history) becomes a subject in regard to and from the point of view of what is built on it, although within its own limits—in our case the limits of historical consideration proper—it is only a system of functions.

Such a relationship as that existing between history and the social sciences is characteristic also of the relationship between history and biology. What in history is a biological subject is, from the point of view of biology, only a set of functions. In biology we do not penetrate beyond the scope of functions to their alleged ultimate bearer. For instance, biologically Napoleon is defined by his organic functions and morphological expressions and not by the properties he has qua subject. But from the point of view of history, since history is an *additional* stratum built *upon* the biological, the set of functions is conceived of as a being contained in a closed subject. Historical understanding does not again split into its functional elements the subject taken for granted. It borrows from biology its sum total, though biology itself may not present its findings as concentrated in a sum total. The fact that history takes advantage of biology enables or entitles history to sum up via the concept of subject that which biologically is not summed up this way. *What serves as a basis becomes a subject in regard to what has been established on that basis.* In this structure of relations between the various spheres of knowledge, parallel to the various strata of existence, the category of subject has only a relative meaning. It owes its meaning to the stratification of existence or to points of view: The stratum on top of the basis looks at the basis as at a subject. The subject is meaningless within

a single detached realm and becomes meaningful only
from the angle of the stratum which employs the concept
of the subject. To state it differently, the basic stratum
is a subject for the higher one and its function as a subject is assigned to it by the higher one. To be a subject in
this field is to be related to what is in a different realm
from the subject itself.

The historical occurrence and historical reflection are
the *rationes essendi* of sociological investigation. The social
unit exists insofar as the historical occurrence is conceived
of as a present framework. But on the other hand sociological investigation can be employed as a methodological
aid for historical investigation proper. Historical investigation borrows from the sociological its concepts such as
state, city, economics, religion, etc. in order to explore the
occurrences and select from them those events with which
historical investigation is concerned. Political history for
instance investigates those events whose meaning is political,
i.e. determined by their being integrated in the framework
of the state. Sociology thus hands over to history the frameworks which can be employed as principles of selection of
the events to be investigated. Hence sociological investigation fulfills the epistemological function attributed in
some philosophical schools to values and their application
to historical events. The connection of the historical
process with values is subjected to criticism, since it imposes
on historical research a dependence (which has to be proved
to exist) upon elements which are not elements of knowledge proper. In addition, and this is decisive, this dependence on values is not necessary for the methodological task
of providing a guide or a criterion for the selection of events
to be investigated in historical research. There is certainly
a problem as to the values the historical process is or is not
aiming at. There is also a problem about the authority and

even inescapability of the evaluation of historical events and agents. But these problems cannot be decided on the narrow methodological issue, since it has been suggested that through value concepts such as culture, religion, etc. we know which historical events are to be explored by historical research. For the sake of providing a criterion for the selection of events which are the subject matter of historical concern it is sufficient to put forth the following principles. The subject matter of historical concern is those events which shaped the present and are henceforth of general interest. Sociological investigation possesses from the outset concepts of general interest, since these concepts apply to the social-collective existence of human beings. The assumption is that the attachment of human beings to institutions in which—in terms of the foregoing analysis —their activities take place enables us to use the concepts of institutions as a guide in the selection of historical events which are to be studied historically. What is public is usable as a principle of selection in historical research, which is concerned with public events. The advantage of substituting for principles of selection based on values those based on sociological concepts is clear; when pursuing this line we remain in the scope of empirical knowledge and do not shift over to so different a field as the sphere of values. We employ principles of selection which are not alien to history since they are placed on the same *ontological level* as history, although their *epistemological* or methodological level is different. History becomes a mirror of itself and we do not overstep its bounds. Max Weber realized this point, and therefore proposed to substitute Ideal Types for values. Yet he made the Ideal Types an intermediate stratum between that of history and that of values. This was not needed, for the historical and the sociological domains are connected in root, that is to say in the decisions of men, which actuate the process and maintain its structure. These acts are directed toward the future. Against the background of this ontological unity there exist both a difference and an interrelation between history and sociology. All this does not preclude the historical evaluation and its position. What I meant to stress is only that in the domain of knowledge of historical events there is no need to jump at once from events to values on the basis of a methodological consideration.

The possibility of taking advantage of the categories of sociological investigation in the historical field must not be confused with a sociologization of history. The tension encountered in a particular situation, as for example the tension between the executive and the legislative power in a state, cannot be projected onto every historical period under consideration. It cannot be taken for granted a priori that this tension is an essential characteristic of statehood as such, merely on the basis of the fact that it is encountered empirically in a given historical fragment. We must not transfer the picture of one particular present to another but must look at the sociological concepts in their functional aspect only, as indicating frameworks of occurrences. We should not look at them as material units. Sociological concepts fulfill a methodological function for historical investigation and nothing more, and should not be hypostatized. This is a restatement in this context of the criticism advanced before of historical materialism which projects our own present into every present and makes a prototype of every human reality in time. But if we follow this distinction between history and sociology by pointing out the mutual assistance they give each other, we can say that *sociology has to be more historical than history itself*. Historical research which tries to understand the process which is to explain the datum in the present takes into consideration all the causes effective in the process. An earthquake is a historical cause to the same extent that wars are. The historical process absorbs into itself various elements, even those which are nonhistorical in themselves but which play a historical role. Sociological research, in contrast, is not interested in the explanation of processes stretched between the present and the past. Instead it tries to conceive the whole of a present as a unit existing and acting in history. From this point of view it erects its building on top of the data which are already—or which are to be—explained historically. Therefore sociological investigation proper may not take into consideration the causes which affected the past process but must deal with the already existing situation. The already existing situation absorbed in itself all the genetic factors; sociologically we are not concerned with the genetic factors but with factors active within the situation itself. Sociology has a more historical character than history itself because sociology presumes history and adds to it the aspect of framework.

In other words, sociological investigation has to explore the situation as it is and not as it came into being historically. Historical investigation finds its data in documents or material remnants, the meaning of which is bestowed on them by the direction toward the past; a sociological datum is meaningful from the outset and its meaning is independent of the explanation furnished by the relation to the past, because this historical meaning is already taken for granted, that is to say provided by the logically prior historical explanation. The already meaningful datum retains its full meaning and acquires an additional one in sociology by being integrated into the frameworks of the social units or institutions. Sociological investigation deals with a *pure* historical datum, that is to say with human activity, and does not turn to factors that are nonhistorical. Let us describe the historical reality as one built upon geographical, biological, psychic, etc. realities. Sociological reality is built on top of all these, that is to say on top of the historical reality. All these realities are certainly encapsulated in the sociological reality, but for sociology an additional aspect arises, that of the totality of the given framework. Thus sociology ultimately presupposes history. From this point of view we may say that there is a historical nature to sociology but no intrinsic sociological nature to history.

Let us come back to the distinction between the three strata put forward in the first chapter on the two denotations of the term history. Let us apply the threefold distinction of datum, function, and meaning to this issue of the relationship between history and social science.

a. The sociological *datum* is a particular situation in the present, a situation which on its own part is a product of a historical occurrence.

b. The sociological *function* is a decision and a deed, forming the present and passing beyond it.

c. The sociological *meaning* is the totality of the situation as a framework of actual social existence. The empirical sociological investigation has to determine whether this framework is a single framework or a plurality of various frameworks, which of the frameworks is to be placed in the foreground of the explored present, and so forth.

Sociology and history meet each other in the first two strata.

a. The datum is one which came into being in history and is explainable genetically. Here sociology encounters *historical reflection*.

b. The sociological function qua decision and realization is common to history and sociology, and here sociology meets the *historical occurrence*. The difference between the two fields is determined by the direction of time. If this function of decision is understood as the cause of a given situation then it is stretched between the past and the present and belongs to history proper. If it is understood as an actual and changing activity it is directed toward the future and belongs to sociology proper. Thus the differences in dimensions of time imply differences in the systematic position of the functions in the two fields respectively. The function of the historical occurrence is to be understood in two different ways: by historical reflection and by sociological reflection. Thus the distinction between history and sociology is again one of *reflection* and not one of the *datum* in its ontological essence. This distinction is ultimately rooted in distinctions in meanings.

c. In the sphere of meanings the two ways of reflection differ. The meaning of the historical reflection is the involvement of the past within a present, while the meaning of the sociological reflection is the totality of the structures of a present and of institutions. Once sociological reflection advances the concept of institution and sums up the material nature of the various empirical institutions, the findings of sociology may be transplanted to the historical reflection. This is a post factum employment of sociological concepts by historical research.

There is thus an affinity and difference in the two branches of knowledge dealing with man's social reality.

Our discussion of the relationship between history and sociology centered around their respective relation to the problem of time. The elucidation of the sociological approach to the nature of historical time as an approach which encloses time puts a new stress on the essence of the historical approach to time, that of stretching the reflective bridge between the temporal dimensions of time.

This brings us to an examination of the conceptual tool for erecting the bridge, i.e. causality.

CHAPTER 5

CAUSALITY AND LAWS

A. *De Facto Application*

1. THE PROBLEM of causality in history has been frequently discussed and is still a controversial topic. It seems that its controversial character has had, to say the least, a negative impact on a thorough elucidation of the concept itself and on the delimitation of its position within the setting of historical knowledge.

In this situation only one way seems to be hopeful, namely a renewed consideration of the essence of the historical object. The historical object is the datum in the present to be explained by the events in the past. It is involved in a tension between the dimensions of time, and the knowledge of it is built by means of a bridge stretching across them. The question which must be asked is: How is this turn from the present to the past of historical knowledge brought about? The justification for this turn from the datum to the events can be based, in the last analysis, on the principle of causality alone. The past is the cause of the present—this is the very presupposition of historical knowledge. From this point of view historical knowledge is in its essence a causal knowledge, that is to say it is made possible only by being conditioned by the principles of causality. The "transcendental" basis of historical knowledge is to be found in the presupposition of

causality as a category of relationship in a single direction
—in our case the direction leading from the past to the
present. Historical knowledge as it manifests itself in historical research is just a concrete application of the category
of causality in regard to material time, or an application of
a transcendental principle to a meaningful sphere built up
on the relation existing between the past and the present.
All particular explanations concerning the specific features
of causality in history have a bearing only on the basis of
this transcendental presupposition. Let us now consider
some examples which are relevant to our main thesis.

2. If on July 14 a person goes out into the streets of
Paris he is very likely to come across a parade. He may get,
or at least guess at, different explanations for this event.
If he does not know the real nature of the parade he might
connect it with political or social problems of contemporary
France, that is to say he might create a causal chain between the parade and a particular present cause, such as
a military victory, a strike, etc. But if he knows the real
reason, that is to say the real meaning of this parade, he
will know that its object is to celebrate Bastille Day. He
will establish a causal chain between the actual parade and
the French Revolution. What is the nature of this kind
of connection which we encounter at every step both in
practical thinking and in the methodological thinking of
historical research? The parade in our example is clearly
an occurrence within the present. In the present as such,
in its limitations as a segment of time, we do not find the
reason for the parade. The cause of the actual present
cannot thus be the content of the parade, although
the parade takes place in the present. The present is what
it is because of the past, i.e. an event which took place
in the past produces an event which takes place in the
present. The parade in Paris is certainly not Bastille Day

itself, and the events in the parade do not repeat or
duplicate (fortunately) the events which occurred on the
original Bastille Day. The parade comés into being as a
product of Bastille Day although it differs from it not only
in its time position but also in its intrinsic content. The
reason for certain behavior in the present lies in the past,
although the occurrence in the present is different from
what produced it in the past. The past is involved in the
present not as its content but as a factor producing a
"field" of attachment, esteem, emotions, inspiration, ideas,
or behavior. Yet it is clear in the case under consideration
that there is a causal chain between Bastille Day and the
celebration taking place in the present.

Let us now consider another example: A Jew eats un-
leavened bread on Passover not only as a symbolic act
in remembrance of a historical event which took place
in the past, but also because he is observing a rite practiced
by his ancestors in the past and repeating it in the present.
Here too the reason for the behavior does not lie in the
present but in the past. Yet an identity of content, which
is not to be found in the symbolic celebration, is here
supposed to exist between the past and the present. The
present deed presumably has, in this case, its cause and
reason in the past, and hence its content is derived from
the past. The deed as such of course takes place in the
present, though in terms of content it reflects the past
because it repeats it. The relationship rooted in the identity
of content between past and present accounts for the fact
that past, though ontologically unrepeatable, continues to
exist in the deeds of the present, though the deeds as such
occur beyond the past as a dimension of time which has
already passed. A causal chain between the event in the
past and that in the present exists here, its particular

feature being the continuity in terms of content through time and in spite of the time interval.

From these two examples we learn that the historical datum can be understood only if we assume the involvement of the past in the present. This involvement may in turn be symbolic, as in the case of the parade in Paris commemorating Bastille Day. Here the value and standing of the past may stimulate the present to a specific action which is one of the present related to the past. Or the involvement may be real and in this sense a continuation of the past, as in the case of the Passover bread. Here the past still exists in the present as the content of deeds and ways of present behavior. This involvement is not causal and the involvement as such cannot be conceived of as an occurrence in time at all. It is a fact inherent in the deeds of the present and an explanation of them—a part of them but not an occurrence in itself. We do not encounter the past but only its involvement in the present. Only by means of historical reflection—the observer's reflection or the self-reflection of those participating in the occurrence —is this occurrence conceived of as having the content of the past because of its being causally related to the past.

The datum in the present is full of the content of the past since it came into being through the past, producing a similar content and a symbolic pattern of behavior. In both cases the causal relationship existing between the event or events in the past and the occurrence in the actual present explains the presence of the past in the present. Hence we realize how historical knowledge, being the investigation of the present produced by the past, is conditioned—indeed made possible—by the causal consideration of the relationship existing between the two dimensions of time. The phenomenon is a historical one since there exist in it traces of the content of the past. These traces exist since the phenomenon has been produced by the past. The *meaning* of the phenomenon depends upon its *real* relationship to the past as its *cause*.

3. In one of his last works Ernst Cassirer distinguished between three types of analysis of a cultural creation: *a*) the analysis of its coming into being, which employs the category of cause and effect as a means of explanation; *b*) the analysis of a work as it presents itself to an observer in terms of its being precisely a work of language, art, religion, etc.; *c*) the analysis of the form of the work.[1] Even if we accept this distinction and thus grant that cultural creations are not to be subsumed exhaustively under the category of causality (since one has to take into consideration the analysis of the structure of the work and its symbolic meaning as well), we still must assume that an explanation of genesis puts into relief all the more clearly the causal character of historical explanation. A Gothic cathedral may be investigated and understood from various points of view, but the historical investigation is always concerned with the question as to when the cathedral was built and with the spiritual and religious motives which expressed themselves in the Gothic structure against the background of time in which it was erected. The investigation of these motives is an investigation of a building existing in the present through what has been embodied in it in the past.

In this case we do not investigate a *dynamic* datum, like that present in the former examples of the symbolic celebration and the act of repeating a past deed. Here we investigate a *static* datum existing within time but yet not active in time. Here the religious, intellectual, social,

1. Ernst Cassirer, *Zur Logik der Kulturwissenschaften* (Göteborg, Elanders, 1942), p. 106.

architectonic, and other occurrences in the past are understood as being the reasons and causes for the existence of the datum in the present. The cathedral as a work of art certainly has additional reasons for its existence and appearance—morphological reasons, considerations of style and structure, etc. But from the historical point of view we meet here in addition to the two types of relations considered before (the symbolic and the real ones) a third type of involvement of the past in the present, i.e. involvement of *creation*. Something which was created in the past continues to exist in the present in spite of the fact that time has passed between the past and present. This continuity of existence as expressed in a creation which in a way defies the process of time is a characteristic feature of works of art. They are created in time and for certain reasons are active in time. The work emancipates itself from its total submergence in time. Yet in spite of this defiance of time, the relationship existing in this case too between the datum encountered in the present (the work of art) and its creation in the past is based on a causal relationship. The occurrence in the past is the historical reason for the existence of the work in the present since it is its cause. In history the cause located in the past is the reason for the meaning and the existence of the present phenomenon.

The essentially causal nature of historical knowledge can be advanced from a different angle as well. Kurt Lewin distinguished the investigation of *phenomenal features* from the *conditioning contexts* of coming into being. The phenomenal approach enables us to ask about the phenomenal features of psychic forms of occurrence—for instance, about the kinds of feeling which are qualitatively distinguished from the features of an experience of will. Apart from this distinction there are questions of why, questions about cause and effect, in brief about the condi-

tioning genetic context. What, for example, are the conditions in which a decision is taken and what particular
psychic effects does it entail? The determination of phenomenal features is usually called "description," while
the determination of the causal relation is called "explanation." [2] In line with this distinction we can say that historical knowledge is essentially *conditioning genetic*. If
we determine some features from a historical point of view,
for instance the nature of the parliamentary system of England or the party system of the United States, we are ipso
facto and immediately involved in a genetic explanation of
these features and hence attempt to point to the conditions
in which and because of which the investigated phenomena
came into being. There is no phenomenal historical
description which does not rest on and lead to a causal
explanation, that is to say to a genetic explanation through
a causal event of the past. The historical phenomenon
is essentially an effect of a cause.

4. Causality also applies beyond the relationship between
the datum in the present and its reasons, i.e. its causes in the
past. Historical knowledge starts with the datum in the
present, but it is to be applied to the past qua past as well.
It reaches the past by various ways. If we investigate, for
instance, the party system in the United States and explain
this system historically, that is to say by means of the involvement of the past in the present, we touch upon issues
like the Civil War. These issues are actual links in a particular historical causal chain.[3] We also explain causes in the
past as the effects of past events. Every historical datum
is an actual link in a causal chain, either directly in the
present or else indirectly in the past. There exist in the past

2. See Kurt Lewin's contribution, "Gesetz und Experiment in der
Psychologie," in *Symposion* (Berlin, Weltkreis Verlag, 1927), 1, 377.

3. Cf. Max Weber, *Gesammelte Aufsätze zur Wissenschaftslehre*, p. 241.

not only causes but effects as well. As soon as we reach the dimension of the past through our regression from the present the past appears as a plane, that is to say as having complexity and time dimensions of its own. Hence we may discern in it causes and effects, which distinction corresponds to the complexity inherent in the past itself. We may recall here the distinction put forward in connection with the analysis of historical time, where we introduced the term "the present of the past." Insofar as there is a present of the past we may ask again about the causes of that present, and hence employ the distinction between effect and cause beyond our own present.

The status of a past effect is not *necessarily* identical with that of a present. From the point of view of historical reflection, which is here naturally at variance with the historical acts and deeds, the datum in the present is always an effect. But the datum in the past is to be recognized as both cause and effect, and the determination of its position depends upon a causal chain established by the relationship between the past and the datum in the present. If we consider Abraham Lincoln's speeches, for instance, as our datum in the present—in this case a *documentary* datum—we conclude that the Civil War acts as the cause of these speeches, while from a different point of view the war is to be seen as an effect and not a cause. Lincoln's speeches also will be seen as the causes of various attempts to interpret and to implement them. What is decisive is not the position of the cause or the effect in isolation. The decisive factor is the causal *relationship* between the events in the past and those in the present and between the various events in the past itself. The presupposition of historical knowledge is that the present is not a cause of itself, and hence that the cause must be found in the past. This is why historical research investigates the causal relations within the past. We may find here a confirmation of Hermann Cohen's conception of the principles of causality, namely that its essence does not lie in the isolated cause but in *causation*. We encounter here a genuine *synthetic* composition of the present and the past, explained analytically as a composition of cause and effect, that is to say that within this genuine synthesis we distinguish between the position of the cause and that of the effect. The original synthesis which is grasped in and through the tools of historical knowledge is possible only on the basis of the principle of causality. This principle is actualized in the synthesis characteristic of the grasp of historical knowledge. Thus the principle of causality is both the starting point and the guiding line of the actual historical investigation. It is both its transcendental presupposition and its methodological-heuristic instrument. Historical knowledge is possible inasmuch as we know how to investigate the facts, i.e. to direct the investigation toward the past, even before we know the actual facts to be investigated and the specific past which will explain their meaning by explaining their existence as dependent on the causes in the past. We suppose the historical facts to exist as conditioned facts.

5. The causal essence of historical knowledge has been attacked from several angles. It will help our understanding of the notion of causality in history to discuss some of these criticisms. Let us deal first with the theory of "understanding" or "insight" (*Verstehen*) as outlined by some of the modern philosophic schools connected in one way or another with Wilhelm Dilthey.

The members of this school faced the question of the recognition of a genuine involvement of the past in the present. They answered that understanding or, rather, insight was the means by which we were able to distinguish between meaningful relations and sheer causal ones. We gain an insight into an action by grasping its motives: An explanation of a body movement tells you only the cause, e.g. that it was the result of an irritation of the nervous system. With insight it has been suggested that we have to distinguish between 1) a *static* insight with respect to a situation and 2) a *genetic* insight regarding a context: the emergence of one psychic act from another is understood in a genetic manner. The *evidence* of the genetic insight is something ultimate, which is a justification of itself and cannot be reduced to a more primary basis.[4] In a genetic insight we gain both the contact of relationship existing between events and the certainty that we *understand* this relationship as explaining the meaning of the events and their direction. Though the difference between an understanding of a situation and that of a genetic context has been advanced as relevant in the field of psychology, it seems that we have here a qualification which can be transferred to the field of history.

From the point of view of historical knowledge we are interested in the genetic insight, since the essence of historical knowledge lies in explaining situations by integrating them in genetic contexts. We have to clarify that epistemological reason underlying the attempt to elevate insight to the level of a self-contained and separate type of knowledge, different from that based on causality. It has been said above that insight is to be applied to the understanding of the emergence of one psychic act from another. The justification usually proposed for the special value and specific essence of insight is in the closeness between the

4. I refer here to Karl Jaspers' various papers, e.g., "Kausale und 'verständliche' Zusammenhänge zwischen Schicksal und Psychose bei der Dementia Praecox Schizophrenie," *Zeitschrift für die gesamte Neurologie und Psychiatrie*, Berlin and Leipzig, 1913.

knower and the known object. Insight is supposed to be that perception of the object—in this case the other person characterized by the equality of the selves. The theory of insight is thus built on the assumption of the particular ontological nature of the subject and the object under consideration. This particular nature presumably carries with it or requires a particular type of knowledge, i.e. insight rather than a causal explanation. This assumption calls for critical examination.

In dealing with a datum historically we try to understand it in its relationship to the past. The relationship to any *particular* past is not given. When we deal with a datum like World War I we do not start with any self-evident relationship of this datum to the historical process, such as the connections between Germany and the Austro-Hungarian monarchy, the Entente Cordiale, and the position of France in the European balance of power. All these relations must be specifically proved, that is to say discovered and justified by historical investigation itself. Within the general physical and the vague historical past we must search for the causal links connected with our particular datum. And furthermore the particular datum obtains its meaning only through this discovery of the links in the causal chain. The understanding of the datum as a historical occurrence is clearly an understanding of its position within the causal synthesis. Insight, that is to say the "immediate" realization of the content of the phenomenon and its meaning, is possible only through the application of the principle of historical causality. In other words, insight must be guided by historical knowledge as causal knowledge. Insight as such does not intrinsically possess this particular kind of guidance which directs it to look at the past as involved in the present of which it is the cause.

Hence insight does not dispose of causal knowledge but precisely presupposes it. Insight is at the most an interpretation of what is established through causality, but it cannot pretend to have an independent let alone parallel status with regard to a causal explanation.

Dilthey's doctrine could not emancipate itself from the use of the principle of causality, but this use is confused by the attitude and the vocabulary of the "philosophy of life." This theory claims that it is insufficient to determine the position of an event in a setting of historical occurrences. It takes the historical event to be an expression of the comprehensive sphere of "life." This theory aims at understanding an event not from its relationship to other events but by treating it as an expression of a sphere which is behind the events. Life is the background, events are its expressions, and insight is the instrument for the explanation of the events by relating them to the comprehensive sphere of life. This trinity is the guiding principle of Dilthey's doctrine. The theory does not lay down the background of life as an assumption disconnected from the actual historical datum. The background, it asserts, is set by the observation of our actual experiences. Just as experiences are expressions or manifestations of the living subject, so the given historical facts are supposed to be expressions of a background which is richer than the manifest event. The starting point of the humanities (*Geisteswissenschaften*) lies therefore in life, and the humanities maintain a permanent relationship with life. We must therefore understand a historical phenomenon not in its connection with the chain of events but in its isolation. The center of a spiritual phenomenon lies in the *phenomenon itself*. One may say that the assumption as to the center of the phenomenon is due to a prior assumption, that is to say that the phenomenon manifests a metaphysical source qua life. The phenomenon is isolated in terms of other phenomena but is interpreted in terms of what is common to all phenomena.[5]

The key to criticism of the theory of insight is this stress laid on the solitariness of the phenomenon on the one hand and its integration into the comprehensive, neutral background which lies behind the phenomena on the other. To restate it, historical knowledge recognizes and conceives of a phenomenon not by *isolating* it from the system and setting it over against the comprehensive, non-differentiated background of life but by investigating its *connections* with other events and in general with manifold other phenomena. Any insight is always accomplished by knowledge, that is to say by an act which sets up a network of relations. Historical knowledge guided by the compass of methods and based on the principle of causality does not need the ontological or quasi-ontological compass of the concept of life. Historical knowledge is essentially neutral with respect to the question of the ontological background from which historical occurrences as occurrences emerge. All metaphysics, both the metaphysics of nature, which looks at historical occurrences as a function of nature or a pathway in life, and the metaphysics of spirit, which considers historical occurrences as instruments and expressions of a hidden creative spirit—all metaphysics may or may not have the same justification within the domain of historical knowledge. This knowledge qua knowledge is immanent because it refers to facts in time and not to their supposed background. In other words, the immanence of knowledge connotes here that knowledge is concerned with relations and not with their ultimate and hidden ontological source. As long as we remain in the

5. See W. Dilthey, *Gesammelte Schriften* (Leipzig, 1921), 7, 85, 86, 118, 137, 157; 5, 265.

domain of immanence we have no means for investigating relations, save *methods* and above all the use of the principle of causality as the category of relations. Thus in this case the theory of insight suggests an understanding of the sources of the phenomena. Insight is here tied up with a jump from the understanding of relations to the understanding of sources. The suggested need for an insight lies in a blurring of the nature of historical knowledge.

Historical knowledge is able to conceive of an event by connecting it not with the general and vague background of life but with other *events*, even in the case where it is interested in the characterological or physiological background of a historical personality. The personality as it appears for investigation is always split up into settings of functions and relations, that is to say into settings of psychic or historical occurrences. "The emergence of the psychic from the psychic" is an emergence of an occurrence from an occurrence and as such cannot evade the searching after causal relations which make this emergence understandable. We may point here to what has been said in the preceding chapter about the concept of subject. Insofar as there is a subject in history it is presupposed by it and not discerned in it, as in the case of Napoleon or Alexander. Again the theory of insight as based on a *Lebensphilosophie* confuses the boundaries here. It pretends to be a phenomenology of history but actually goes beyond it by the very connection with life.

This criticism of the doctrine of insight is directed against its underlying principles. It also excludes any attempt to show that the system of concepts as employed in the humanities is based on the principle of substance and not on the principle of causality, as has been suggested in some modern schools. The idea is that while causality relates exterior events, the principle of substance can account for the relationship existing between the active agent considered to be a substance and his particular acts considered to be his attributes or accidents. Yet this attempt to bring into prominence the concept of substance and to confine the principle of causality to exterior, natural phenomena seems to rest on one main fallacious assumption: In the explanation of our own experience we may distinguish between meaningful elements rooted in the self and the objective elements determining the self from the outside, like stimuli, physiological reactions, etc. The latter, coming from the outside, are conditioned by causal impulses, while the meaningful elements appear as manifestations of the inner forces of the self and are a result of them. These elements are explained from within, as elements hidden in the inner structure of "the possibilities of experience" of the self. Therefore the understanding of the self from the inside, the theory argues, can never be a causal one. It conceives the self as a bearer of expressions and thus presupposes the category of substance qua substratum of appearances. The principle of causality is in this view a principle which establishes the objectivity of the external datum and is therefore a mechanical one, depriving the phenomenon of its intrinsic psychic character; the principle of substance is allegedly an anthropomorphic principle of our thinking instilling psyche into the phenomenon.

With reference to historical knowledge and its alleged relation to the category of substance as against the category of cause it is safe to make the following assertions.

Historical insight is not self-insight since it is an insight into something given in the external world, an understanding of something which is, from the beginning, outside the understanding subject. Hence it is sufficient to stress the fundamental fallacy of this conception which identifies the *introspective* cognition of the self with an *intersubjective* cognition as it is exhibited in historical knowledge. Historical knowledge is not concerned with the self; it is concerned with the objective data existing in trans-subjective historical time. Even in the case where historical knowledge explains a datum through its relation to a historical personality, the "I" of the personality is at most a "thou" or, rather, a historical agent and hence *has* to be looked at in its connection with a datum. In other words, the agent can be approached only as belonging to a setting. Historical knowledge is unable to understand the possibilities of experience of Alexander the Great or of Napoleon without an analysis of documentary data, political facts, ways of behavior, wars and strategic decisions, etc. Even if we conceive of these data as manifestations of a personality or, let us say, as accidents of a substance, we are able to conceive of them only by employing the principle of causality as the principle of explanation. Historical knowledge cannot be a monadological knowledge,[6] a knowledge of a self from within, since it is to be applied to data in an objective sphere, i.e. that of transsubjective material time, and not to data in the subjective sphere of immanent psychic time. We need the principle of causality since we move in an objective sphere and have to establish relations between events in .this plane. From this point of view there cannot be any justification for an exclusive distinction between the humanities (allegedly employing the principle of substance as the main principle of explanation) and the natural sciences (employing the principle of causality).

6. A similar objection against the application of causality in history, although not an objection pretending to put forward a methodological approach opposite to that of

6. Cf. H. Wildon Carr's contribution in *Proceedings of the Aristotelian Society*, Vol. 25.

causality, is implied in the conception which stresses the fact that historical knowledge examines and explains the phenomena while integrating them into a system. A revolution, for instance, is explained and understood as a political or social event by being put into a system of a state or society within which the event obtains its meaning and explanation. The historical event is grasped as meaningful because the single event ceases to be isolated and becomes integrated in a meaningful whole.

But if we examine this conception closely we find that the relationship between the particular events and the meaning bestowed on them does not preclude a causal relationship within the set of historical events. On the contrary, it makes the causal nature of the historical setting even more manifest. The objective of the integration of a single event in a system is to detect its meaning. This can be done only by detecting its causal position within the reality of historical time. Thus we are entitled and even compelled to carry out the act of integration of, say, a revolution into the domain of the state or of social and political actions, since we are engaged in an analysis of a datum and want to know its meaning. The detection of the causal relationship between events is a means for detecting their meanings. The level of meanings cannot be independent of the level of causal relations; it presupposes the level of causal relations. Hence the only way to encounter meanings in history is to study causal relations and to grasp the meaningfulness embedded in them. Here a structure similar to that advanced with regard to historical insight comes to the fore. The understanding of the meaning of an event through its integration into a setting presupposes causal knowledge just as is the case with insight.

In analyzing the essence of historical knowledge we also see that our device of connecting a single event with a

meaningful whole does not take our investigation out of
the domain of time. "Since history deals with occurrences
in time, the elements of temporal sequence must enter
into causality and distinguish it from the relations between
whole and part, form and content or any other abstract,
purely logical or mathematical, condition." [7] In connecting
the phenomenon of a revolution with a meaningful
whole of a state we actually connect a temporal phenomenon (i.e. the concrete acts comprised under the head-
ing "revolution") with the state as a meaning which exists
within time and through it and manifests itself in events.
The connection of a single fact with a whole is not a connection of an atemporal datum with a timelesss whole. The
connection brings together temporal phenomena. Therefore
the temporal relationship between successive phenomena
remains in force, and their connection—for instance with
a state as a whole—does not place the connected links
beyond the realm of temporal succession, precisely because it places them in it. The state does not exist as
an absolute meaning above succession, nor is the particular event a datum outside its position in the sequence of
time. But succession, if considered historically and not
only as the essential feature of time as form, is by no means
given; nor is the sequence of the events self-evident. Both
the historical succession and the meaningful sequence between the events are constructed, and their construction is
accomplished by means of causal relations.

7. Both in the theory of insight and in the attitude
which stresses the integration of a single fact into a whole
we encounter a composition of a particular historical
method and the essentials of the *object* dealt with by historical knowledge. Let us now consider two further attempts

7. Morris Raphael Cohen, "Causation and Its Application to History,"
Journal of the History of Ideas, 3, 14.

which undertake to shake the position of the principle of causality in historical knowledge. These two attempts are concerned only with the nature of the historical *object*, both in its material aspect as acts of *will* and in its formal nature as *individual objects*; the problem of method is a secondary one.

By bringing into prominence the factor of will as active in history the theory tries to undermine the validity of causality, arguing that the factor of will is essentially irrational and therefore cannot be contained in a causal setting which serves to establish rational, i.e. understandable, relations between historical events. The task of the principle of causality is to establish relations which explain the phenomena. But the very fact of the dependence— at least of some historical phenomena—upon human wills breaks the network of relations established by and in accordance with the rational principle of causality. In this view the attempt to explain events causally breaks down once we are aware that actions rooted in will or wills are ultimately inexplainable because of the fundamental fact that will is an irrational source of activity.

This argument, whether based on a methodological consideration or expressed in the name of common sense, is additional evidence of the prevailing confusion of concepts still existing in the field of the theory of historical knowledge. Does this argument suggest that the factor of will does not create data to be explained as historical phenomena, that is to say as effects of a cause, the cause being in this case the act of a will? Does the fact that the cause is a will of a historical personality and that the effect of this cause is a historical phenomenon mean that the connection between them is not contained in and mastered by the principle of causality? Or is it suggested that the very fact that the cause is a will prevents us from constructing a single set of relations, only one chain in which all the historical data would be included? If this is the case there would be no objection against the causal nature of the process conceived by historical knowledge. It is only the *continuity* and the *unity* of the process dependent upon many wills in originating processes which is doubted, since each will is supposed to create a causal chain of its own, disconnected from the chain created by a different will. The rationality of historical knowledge is shaken not by the abolition of this *principle* of causality but precisely by the application of this principle to various coexistent spheres, which are not united in their sources and which will not establish an all-comprehensive sphere of historical occurrences. The attack is directed chiefly against the view that there is one single historical process in which all the events are embraced and thus related one to another. By stressing the dependence upon a multitude of wills the unity of the historical process is shaken but not the application of the principle of causality to the process. What this argument actually amounts to is that there is no total *material* causality in history and not that the principle of causality does not hold good for history. But even stated in mitigated form in terms of application only, this argument cannot hold its own against two main difficulties which it fails to face.

a. It assumes that the will as a historical factor lies beyond the actual process as its transcendent cause. In this view will is therefore only and always a cause and never an effect. Being exclusively a cause it does not tend to be included in a setting but creates different and isolated settings time and again. As against this it is only justified to say that from the point of view of history the will is not a datum encountered immediately but is constructed or, rather, laid down in the course of the search for the reason of a given phenomenon. The will of Alexander the Great, for instance, is not given to us in the same way as our own in introspection. The will of a historical personality is *assumed* by a methodological device of a historical regression, starting, for instance, from the fact of the imperial expansion of the Macedonian state. Thus the fact that the will is not given but constructed is merely the other side of the shield of the essence of historical investigation which localizes causes in the past. Since the will too is in the past and not in the present (for this is the dimension of what is actually given) there is no other way of knowing it short of a construction based on a methodical analysis. We touch here on the problem discussed by Planck in the modern theory of physics in connection with the question of free will, but here in the context of historical knowledge the situation is even clearer than in physics. The will dealt with in history is what Planck called a "remembered will," though not one literally remembered by the self but rather constructed by the historical outside observer as a will of somebody in the past. For the sake of historical investigation it is necessary to make a clear distinction between an act of will as subjective, occurring as a decision in a monadological realm, and the will as a meaningful event in the intersubjective realm (e.g. the will to expansion, the strife for personal domination, etc.). As an event filled with content, i.e. one which has bearing upon history, the will ceases to be an absolute, irreducible, and irrational impulse.

Historical investigation may sometimes assume as plausible that acts of will are indispensable conditions for certain occasions, but that the vital occurrence of acts of will is essentially a pre- or antehistorical condition of historical occurrences proper. With reference to this precondition we may paraphrase the old saying, "Primum vivere, deinde historiam facere." But historical explanation proper does not explain its data in this way; it explains them by historical factors. The decisive feature is not the ontological nature of these historical factors, whether they are wills and ambitions or events in nature like the Russian winter or a volcanic eruption. The events of nature enter into the historical network insofar as they leave historical traces, that is to say insofar as they shape a human situation and leave traces in the present. The reasons for those traces are always in the past. The same procedure and deliberation hold good with regard to acts of will. They are introduced into historical settings insofar as we assume them through a regression from the traces in the present to causes in the past. Historical investigation does not consider events of nature which have no historical traces even if they are contemporaneous with historical events, nor does it consider any acts of will which did not objectify themselves in the historical intersubjective realm. Thus the will as a pre- or antehistorical act is no more historical than the movement of Mars, unless we discover some causal connection between it and any actual event in the present, which would make it imperative to consider it historically. Even in regard to acts of will we then remain within the scope of historical knowledge proper. We are therefore not only justified but even compelled to search for the cause of the will, although there is no sense in searching for the cause of the fact that the will wills. The search for the cause of the will amounts to placing the will into historical settings which are not entirely wills. The placement of the will in a setting brings about the understanding that will is not an ultimate factor on the one hand and outside the causal chain on the other.

b. The second difficulty confronting this conception lies in the fallacy described in the social and historical context by Max Weber, namely the mistaken assumption that the freedom of will is identical with the irrationality of an act, or that an irrational act is conditioned by a free will or identical with it. Weber has shown that irrational and incalculable behavior can be motivated only by blind instincts or blind natural forces and is the "privilege" of the insane. In contrast, the will as a historical factor is a will with a historical-meaningful determination. Being not an irrational act in the personal sphere but an occurrence of an intersubjective meaning, such a will is necessarily a cause and at the same time an effect. It is not an original cause arising from itself. The spontaneity of the will as will belongs to the conditions or to the boundaries of any historical investigation dealing with the activities of human beings. Yet the meaning and the status of a will as a causal factor in history is subordinated to the principles of historical knowledge in general and especially to the principle of causality which is its main transcendental presupposition.

We may go even further. There are irrational acts in history as there are irrational personalities active in it. An inquiry into the irrational sphere of a historical personality, like the various inquiries into Hitler's character, still employs the regression from historical effects in historical time to their causes in the supposed irrational nature of the historical personality. We come to be interested in the pre- or antehistorical nature of the historical agent precisely because he is a *historical* agent. The psychopathologist encounters the irrationality of a personality face to face in the realm of the personality, while the historian encounters this irrationality by taking advantage of psychopathological data for a historical, or causal, explanation of historical events. To be sure, even the psychopathologist does not work without a methodical guide, since there is an etiological procedure in this field as well. Yet in history there is not only an etiological procedure but also a regression from the present to the past. The irrational nature of the behavior is placed as a past cause for certain events and their traces in the present. The irrational nature is not immediately given but methodically introduced, and deliberately so, for the sake of a causal explanation. Again there may be here an argument as to the unity or disintegration of the historical process insofar as it is related to neurotic personalities behaving by definition in an autistic way. Yet this argument is confined—as in the case of the problem of will in general—to the practical application of the principle of causality, but does not involve this very principle.

8. In modern philosophy the criticism of the application of the principle of causality to history centers also around the concept of individuality. There is no need to discuss in this place the individual nature of historical objects. We are interested in determining whether or not the validity of the principle of causality can be impaired by the fact that historical objects are essentially individual— granted that this is the case. It seems that there is too much confusion here regarding the meaning of the problem. In some points this confusion has already been dealt with by Ernst Cassirer and Richard Hoenigswald, and in recent years by Maurice Mandelbaum. But the issue must be formulated again in order that systematic conclusions may be drawn.

Historical data are individual in their features and appear once only if we consider them from the point of view of their position within irreversible time. Precisely because the time position is part of the meaning of the historical event —as elucidated in the discussion of historical time—the time factor cannot be omitted. The individual nature of the historical object due to its position in time is essential. Yet one cannot help asking whether this fact in any way affects the genetic-causal relationship between historical data. The criticism of the principle of causality in history based on the individual nature of the object assumes, without putting forward any sound reason for this assumption, that the principle of causality affirms that *every* A implies B, that is to say that the principle of causality is but a statement of a factual relationship between a general A and a general B. But in fact the principle of causality in the case before us assumes that B, i.e. the historical datum, is an effect of an A, that is to say that through the principle of causality we discover a genetic relationship between events. This relationship and not the generic A and the generic B is of interest to us in this case. If we want to formulate the principle of causality in general and are not to be satisfied with the actual genetic relationship discovered or constructed through the application of the principle to a specific case before us, we may state it in a hypothetical form: if A then B, without assuming from the outset that A appears more than once in concreto, that is to say within the setting of historical time. Both the formulation of the actual relationship and the formulation of the principle serving as a guide in the discovery or in the constitution of the actual relationship do not diminish, let alone annihilate, the individual objects embraced in the actual causal chain as events in time. The individual nature of the object tied up with its position in time does not undermine the causal position of the object. The individual essence points to the *position* in time while the causal status points to the *relations* within time. Hence the two aspects are compatible.

We deal here with the application of the principle of causality (as the principle of the relations between events) to the events under consideration. We do not deal here with the deduction of the relations and the related terms from a law, the number of whose designata is indefinite. This observation leads us to a further elucidation of the essence of the causal relations. In this context it is essential to draw a distinction between the principle of causality as such and the particular laws resting on it, such as the law of gravitation in physics. Let us examine now whether the assumption of both the validity and factual application of the principle of causality within the domain of historical knowledge involves the validity and the necessity of any particular material laws and the formulation of their concrete content as in physics. Can we in history descend as it were from the top level of principle to the lower level of concrete, specific laws? This is the question we have to consider next.

B. *The Principle de Iure*

1. In order to be able to describe the essential features of causality in history, once we have assumed and shown its actual application there, we must first make some observations regarding the nature of the causal relationship in general. It has been indicated in the preceding analysis that the principle of causality is a principle of material relations. The distinctive feature of causal relations points to the structure of relations of dependence, that is to say every occurrence and every situation must be derived from or connected with an occurrence or a situation preceding it. This dependence in terms of derivation is the basis of the usual description of causality as pointing to the *growth* of something out of something else. The relationship of dependence between cause and effect is usually explained as the coming into being of an effect because of the cause. Indeed, it must be emphasized that in such a description of the nature of the causal dependence a definitely partial meaning has been given to the causal relations. The principle of causal relations as such implies only dependence or involvement, while in this case the dependence is interpreted as a real coming into being. This interpretation has been criticized in various ways, for instance by Bertrand

Russell. We may rightly assume that the principle of causality stresses only the dependence upon and involvement in. But in the various material spheres, for instance in biology or history, it is possible to understand the causal relationship as a coming into being according to the specific nature of the particular sphere under consideration. Yet there is no need and no justification for identifying this process of coming into being with the intrinsic meaning of the principle of causality as such. Here again we have to distinguish between the minimum meaning of causality common to all the spheres of experience and its more specific meaning which in turn depends upon the spheres themselves.

Once it has been assumed that the principle of causality is a principle of relations there is no warrant for setting a cause beyond the relations. The cause cannot be separated from the effect. It cannot be a self-sustained substance but must be a change in itself. It is a determination, one of the determinations, within a chain.[1] The cause itself is a change and therefore the notion of *causa prima* is meaningless within the scope of empirical relations. The very idea of a cause points to a position the cause occupies in the context of experience. It is a composition of elements and factors to which a concrete situation is related. The particular nature of the cause as against the effect does not have a special power for producing the effect; the cause is a position. To be sure, the anthropomorphic trend characteristic of our habits of thinking is likely to confuse the boundaries between the cause as indicating a position and the cause as connoting a creative power. Yet it is possible to show that even a naïve application of the causal conception does not attribute to the cause a reservoir of absolute pro-

1. S. Stebbing, *Modern Introduction to Logic* (London, 1950), p. 267.

ductivity but looks at it as a link within time, having the special feature of precedence in time.

2. This particularity in terms of position leads us now to a further elucidation of the connection between the principle of causality and time, namely the function of this principle with regard to time. Why is the principle of causality connected with time, or why is it employed and validly so with regard to time? What makes this principle not a purely logical-formal one but a principle to be applied to data? We may answer that the connection with time is a result of the very definition of causality as the principle of material relations, since time is the medium of the material data between which the relations are assumed to exist. But this connection with time gives rise to the problem of the connection between the position of cause and effect in time and the singly directed continuity and succession of time in terms of its irreversibility. The question before us is whether the difference of position between the causes and the effects defines the temporal relationship as one of precedence and sequence or the other way around, whether the relationship of precedence and sequence determines the respective positions of cause and effect. In other words, there is an immanent connection between causality and succession, but the question still remains open as to the direction of this connection—whether causality determines the order of elements in terms of succession, or whether once we know which is the preceding element we consequently attribute to it the status of a cause.

This problem has so far been discussed in philosophy mainly from the point of view of causality as it applies in physics. Since physical time does not contain a distinction between the past, present, and future, we cannot assume that the order in terms of succession is the starting

point. Hence it is assumed that the distinction between
and the positions of the cause and effect are not derived
from the given order of succession. In terms of causality
in physics the distinction between the cause and the effect
is presupposed as being the logical antecedent. Not that
what is precedent in time is the cause and what is subsequent in time is the effect, but rather the cause is that which
must precede and the effect is that which must follow. The
relationship in this case is also a material one and as such
it is connected with time as the medium of material data.
It is not time as such which determines the causal relationship, however; it is this relationship which determines
time. Thus one of the main functions of the principle
of causality is to determine the temporal relationship existing between the events.[2]

This function of determining the temporal relationship between events must be referred to natural science,
since the concept of time employed there is objective and
still nonmaterial. That is to say, natural time too is related
to the form of succession, but we do not find in the form
as such any indication as to the dimensions of this succession. In the domain of physical knowledge as a knowledge
concerned with a material experience we face this immanent difficulty: Materiality is given in time, but time
itself is nonmaterial. Therefore physical knowledge must
construct the material distinctions within time on a basis
different from time itself, that is to say on the basis
of the positions of cause and effect respectively. The position of cause and effect is, as it were, a topological equivalent for the lack of a material ground for distinctions within
the flow of time. But this is not the case in the domain of
historical knowledge, since this knowledge is to be applied

2. Hugo Bergmann, *Der Kampf um das Kausalgesetz in der jüngsten
Physik* (Braunschweig, 1929), p. 11.

from the outset to a material time constructed on the basis
of the delimitation of the dimensions of the past and the
present. Here we cannot assume that the distinction in
the position of the cause and the effect defines the difference
between the present and the past. Obviously the very
distinction between the past and the present is given from
the outset, although it may not be defined in an absolute,
rigid way, since the present is a moving dimension. But
even this changing character of the present brings into
prominence and maintains the basic distinction between
the past and the present, because the present moves toward
the past, that is to say into a dimension of time which is
already defined. For historical knowledge the distinction between the past and the present remains always in force,
although it is never definitely laid down just what the
content of the present and the past is and where the concrete line of demarcation between the two dimensions
is. At any rate it is clear that in history we cannot assign
to the principle of causality the function which physics
assigns to it, i.e. as constituting the very time dimensions
and the distinction between them. On the contrary, historical knowledge, being originally connected with the
distinction between the dimensions of time, constructs
causal relations according to the line already prescribed
by these dimensions, that is to say it searches for the cause
of the present in the past, knowing from the outset the
distinction between the past and the present. In historical
knowledge succession in time is the basis, and the respective positions in terms of causality are constructed according to it. From this point of view, paradoxical as this assumption may sound, historical knowledge is more rational
than physical knowledge, if we take into account the fact
that the material dealt with by historical knowledge, by
employing the principle of causality, is ordered before-

hand, even before the transcendental principle of causality is applied to it in a constructive, methodical way. Hence the rationality of history is to be found in the fact that the material itself guides knowledge not only in terms of detecting and understanding its meaning but also in terms of the structure of the data.

To put it differently, in historical knowledge the material as such, the data in time, does have a definite structure in terms of the position it occupies in time. Having a structure of its own the material guides knowledge and the search for knowledge; it tells where and how to apply the principle of causality to the data. Hence, as constructed according to the given divisions of time, the material is both *material* and *guide* for the establishment of the network of historical relations. The present is always after and thus must always be the effect of the past; it cannot be its cause. The immanent and inherent rationality of historical knowledge comes to the fore in this feature of the historical material existing and given in a structure of time. The material itself is thus transparent and lends itself to be interpreted in terms of a further or higher structure manifested in the structure of causal relations. Historical data, involved as they are from the outset in the texture of time, guide the historical apparatus itself.

3. In spite of the fact that it is the order of succession in history which prescribes the position of the related events in terms of causality, the principle of causality still determines succession. But this determination has a meaning in historical knowledge different from that in physics because it has a different function. The point of departure of historical knowledge is always the distinction between the present and the past. Therefore this knowledge searches the past for the cause of the present. We might assume *prima facie* that the entire past is the cause of the entire

present. But it is clear that historical knowledge is not concerned with the entire present. It is a knowledge concerned with a specific datum in the present, and in order to determine its meaning historical knowledge goes back from the present toward the past. Historical knowledge, when trying to explain the Jews' return to Israel or World War II does not search for an explanation in the past as such; it certainly does not go back to the past of China, for instance, for the explanation of these events. It tries to understand the particular data through a particular past, even when it expands the field of its investigation and deals with the past in terms of "universal history." Even in the case of a legitimate expansion of the explanation proposed for a historical occurrence—for instance an explanation of the internal occurrences of Jewish or European history, which takes account of the rise of nationalism in general or the development of Europe in the 19th century—even in such cases the field of discussion is not determined by the fact that the past in its totality is included in it. What really matters is the fact that the past, that is to say some specific events in it, holds a causal position which can be well defined with reference to the present. Morris R. Cohen has rightly observed in his criticism of Teggart [3] that the pointing out of a *correlation* between various historical events—for instance the wars in China and some particular occurrences within the Roman Empire—is not yet historical knowledge but only a point of departure for it, since the real objective is the establishment of meaningful relations through the principle of causality.

What is the purpose of selecting events from the "entire" past according to their causal position in regard to the present, if this selection is to be guided and justified through

3. See his above-mentioned article, "Causation and Its Application to History."

the principle of causality? We may answer that the distinction between the dimensions of the past and the present precedes the principle of causality and its application. But which particular past out of the whole of it is *the* past of the particular present—this is determinable only through the application of the principle of causality. We may introduce here a fundamental distinction: Historical investigation finds the ontological distinction between the past and the present as given and established and takes it for granted in its actual procedure. Hence this ontological distinction itself is independent of the principle of causality. Yet on the basis of this given ontological distinction another, i.e. a methodological and functional distinction, is made between a particular *present* and a particular *past*. This distinction depends upon the principle of causality and is made effective through it. Thus within the wide realm of the *entire* past a *particular* fragment of it is distinctly determined, since this specific past is the cause of the particular present under consideration. The methodological procedure is conditioned by the ontological distinction, since the functional or causal past must be a past in terms of its ontological status as well and hence contained in that past. Still the ontological past is introduced into the scope of the actual historical investigation only through the filter of the principle of causality. This sums up the outline of the first function of the principle of causality in history, in contradistinction to the application of this principle in physics, where time as such is not a guiding principle at all and hence does not allow for a distinction between its ontological and functional aspects.

4. The second function of the principle of causality is that "of directing the scientific treatment of perception in such a way that the *prediction of the future* is made pos-

sible." [4] The question which has to be posed in this context is whether this should be assumed to be the function of the principle of causality in history as well. Let us first clarify the status of prediction in general. The idea of prediction assumes from the outset the continuance of time beyond the time position in which the predictor is placed. If there were no time to come there would be no room for prediction, because there would be no need for it. Therefore prediction presupposes that time does not come to an end in the present. The time beyond the predictor is future for him. Thus the concept of prediction, even in the domain of physics, assumes that time is divided into two parts—the past and the future. To be sure, time is not divided into three parts as in history; but this difference does not affect the fact that even in physics the *dimension* of future is implied, though only indirectly through prediction. Hence prediction even in physics presupposes the distinction between what *has been* until now and what is *due to be* from now on. Beyond the temporal position of the now in which the predictor is placed, time exists in its completeness, to use here the term used before in connection with the dimensions of historical time. This attitude exhibited in the prediction of the future is simply an attitude of knowledge and consciousness, because no actual interference in the course of the events is involved on the part of the predictor. The predictor knows the movement to come as an observer but not as a participant.

Furthermore, prediction is possible only on the basis of a full knowledge of the past and the present, or else it is possible in regard to that fragment of future time which is included in a set of features and events now already completely known. The prediction of a solar eclipse, on the

4. H. Bergmann, p. 11.

second view, need not take into consideration a war in the Far East. It is limited to the knowledge of astronomical data and their already available laws. But in this limited field it presupposes the knowledge of all the relevant elements, and it is up to any branch of knowledge to determine what its relevant elements are. Indeed, there will always be the question of which data are to be considered relevant for prediction of a phenomenon about to occur in the future. We need not know the course of a military action in order to predict the eclipse of the sun, and our decision as to the relevant data is related to the nature of the domain of events or to the nature of the relationship between the various domains, as for instance the domain of astronomical events and that of the military.

This determination of the necessity for taking account of various domains and strata of events in predicting a course of events touches in a way on a problem of the structure of the universe; the astronomical events have a position in the universe which the historical or military events do not have. Or else it is a methodological problem for each branch of science to determine the minimum of indispensable knowledge needed for any prediction. At any rate a full knowledge of the basic facts—no matter why they are basic—is a *conditio sine qua non* for any prediction. Hence in prediction we know everything, or at least everything which it is *essential* to know, for this particular and confined prediction. An extensive or an intensive completeness of knowledge is indispensable.

Let us now consider the particular situation of historical knowledge as far as the two aspects of prediction—the nature of the future and the full knowledge of the data —are concerned. As to the nature of the future we must repeat, with a renewed emphasis, what has been expounded before regarding the future as a dimension of historical time. The future is not a dimension of historical *knowledge*, at least not directly. The future is a dimension of historical life or historical occurrences. Indeed, historical knowledge proper does not pretend to forecast the future as long as it remains within its legitimate limits as knowledge, being a knowledge of the span between past and present.

Sometimes we find criticisms made of an overemphasis on prediction in physics, since prediction is said to be a practical, technical device stemming from a practical, technical desire to master what is about to occur. Such criticism has certainly more ground in regard to history. Historical knowledge, being dependent upon the division of time into dimensions, is a knowledge not of the future but of the present and the past. Yet physical knowledge cannot easily free itself from its task of predicting the future, since it is empirical knowledge concerned with occurrences in time in general without being committed to a consideration of any particular dimension of time. Or, to put it differently, as a knowledge indifferent to the time dimensions it may not a priori dismiss any portion of time from its interests, including the future. Since physical knowledge refers to phenomena which do not have any particular relation to any particular "here and now" it cannot dismiss knowledge of events which have not yet occurred. The fact that they have not yet actually occurred is not an essential feature of their nature as physical phenomena, because their status in time is not considered to be essential to their nature as physical phenomena. It does not matter at all, from the physical point of view, whether a stone fell yesterday or is due to fall two thousand years from now. But historical knowledge is by definition related to time in its material-dimensional differentiation. Its subject matter is the time segment stretched from the past to the present. Historical knowledge as *knowledge* does not deal with future events since the dimension of the future is entirely beyond the reach of a knowledge of data, for the data are in the present and are to be understood through their relation to the past. Historical knowledge in its purity and by definition has therefore no relation to prediction. Prediction enters the horizon of historical discussion when we cease to be concerned with historical knowledge proper or else when historical knowledge makes itself instrumental for historical life. The very turn toward the future is not inherent in historical knowledge proper. The driving force for this turn originates in historical reality and decisions taken in it. Even the turning of knowledge into an instrument of reality is an outcome of a decision or a need in the reality. Knowledge is power not per se but because of the knower who is aware of power and turns knowledge into an extension of his lust for power or into an instrument for the achievement of the satisfaction of this lust. This is the case in natural science where knowledge faces a given reality and even more so in history where prediction is directed toward a reality which does not yet exist. The urge to master historical reality interferes with the attitude of knowing reality, i.e. the past and the present introduce the task of prediction into the realm of history.

To this we can add that in case of an eschatological expectation we do not strive for historical power but are concerned with historical redemption. In this case we do not master the future but expect it as the outcome of history. But the eschatological aspect as that of mastering is not an aspect of knowledge proper. Knowledge may be instrumental for it but not identical with it.

When we shift from knowledge to the domain of historical occurrences the future does not appear before us as a simple continuation of the time which has elapsed until now. It appears as a dimension of a different kind, being the sphere of what is not yet given. In this sphere, provided that we make the reservations considered before in the chapter on historical time, historical existence appears as the domain of decisions and formations and not merely as one of cognitive preparedness and knowing. In other words, the conceptual analysis concerning historical existence is bound to take into account and acknowledge the phenomenological structure of this existence as one of shaping and formation, as one of an activity directed toward the future. For historical investigation only two ways are open: either to keep strictly within its own limits—and in this case as knowledge proper it is indifferent to prediction—or to go out into the domain of historical existence and hence to be free to look at itself as connected with the attitude of decision, shaping and projecting the future. But the relation to the future of an attitude based on decision and shaping is not one of a prediction put forth by a passive observer standing outside the occurrences. It is one of active shaping by participation in the course of occurrences. Here again we encounter the point observed by Planck in connection with the problem of free will: The actual will does not recognize itself as being integrated in a determinate chain; only a later reflection on the will sees it this way. Similarly historical life does not primarily predict the future. The moment knowledge proper is present—and prediction is of course an attitude rooted in consciousness and is an act of knowledge—we find ourselves not in the stretch between the present and the future but in the span between the present and the past. Yet once we are placed between the present and the past we are again concerned with historical knowledge. In this case the perspective of the future disappears at least as a primary concern, and along with this disappearance the attitude of prediction disappears as well, becoming altogether pointless. Once there is no object to be predicted, there is no point in prediction as such. In sum, though historical knowledge is causal knowledge, prediction is not distinctive of it. Either there is historical knowledge proper and hence no room for a prediction of the future, since historical knowledge is not concerned with future, or there is an active attitude toward the future and no room for prediction, since prediction is a function of knowledge and not an activity of shaping what is to occur.

Furthermore, prediction is possible only through the assumption of a complete knowledge of conditions and data considered to be its starting points. As far as historical knowledge is concerned complete knowledge is out of the question, and this not for technical reasons only. Historical knowledge does not and cannot know the present fully, for the present is both the dimension of data and the dimension of ongoing occurrences, the meaning of which can only be understood in the future.

It is for reasons of principle therefore that historical knowledge does not possess the full data from which it would be in a position to predict the future. The historical datum is meaningful. Yet its meaning becomes manifest not in the temporal dimension of its occurrence but in the forthcoming reflection on it. In order to predict the future historically one must first live in the future, since only in the future can we be in a position to grasp the meaning of the event in the present. Yet to live both in the present and in the future is beyond the capacities even of an "opposite number" of Laplace's Mind, once we keep to the distinction between present and future, that is to say once we stick to the definition of the historical realm. To abolish this distinction would from this point of view tend to merge the realms of history and physics. Yet this is precluded as long as human nature is as it is—a thinking backward and a living forward. In other words, physical prediction is a prediction of events which are due to occur in the future. The pretended historical prediction is one about events due to occur in the future where the meaning of present events will become manifest. What happens in the present, for instance the foreign policy of the United States, conditions what will be meaningful for future man, that is to say for men to whom our future will be their own actual present. Because in the domain of history a perpetual transition from occurrences to meanings takes place, and because this transition presupposes actual, i.e. experiencing, human beings, that is to say human beings dwelling in a certain present of their own as prisms of this transition—because of all this, historical prediction is excluded by reason of principle. This is so even though one is tempted every once in a while to predict and to try to fulfill one's predictions.

Historical prediction must inevitably assume the structure of history in general, that is to say of a transition from the sphere of occurrences to the sphere of meanings. This transition is made by the man of the future as a being making decisions, i.e. living his own life and being determined by the occurrences which took place up to his time but which continue to live through his acts or decisions. Historical prediction—if we are to talk about it at all—must be different from physical prediction. The latter is arrived at through a linear time, without dialectical turning points. Historical prediction can foretell only the rhythm which is characteristic of the historical realm as such; it cannot predict the actual content embedded in this rhythm. The only justifiable attempt—and this in terms of common sense not precise epistemological deliberation—is that of a short-run prediction. A man in the present might

try to look forward to see the meaning of an occurrence for
himself for a short period while he as an agent is or can be
supposed to be a reflecting mirror of the events. In this
case prediction still remains in the domain in which the
present man is the prism of the transition from the sphere
of occurrences to the sphere of meanings. But we cannot
safeguard success for such a prediction, since the present
from which one proceeds in such a prediction is not clearly
defined and hence many futures will come to be for many
different men, as there may be many presents for many
different men. The predicted short-run future can turn out
not to be a continuation of the present we started with and
thus upset the prediction which did not take into account
the interference of a fragment of future not belonging to
the line of the present we started with.

Actually this kind of prediction can be discerned in a political decision. Political predictions are related to decisions
of acting men; they are not acts of knowledge. The "time
horizon" of a political decision involves a two-fold prediction: what is due to occur in case the decided act is not performed and the counterbalancing prediction of what will
occur if the act is performed. In any case this is a prediction
where facts and the short-term consequences of them are
envisaged. The main thing in a historical prediction is not
sheer fact but the meaning that facts will have for human
beings. Yet it is safe to say that political predictions sometimes pretend to know meanings but they actually can know
only some facts. This holds good for economic predictions
as well. Suppose an economist predicts a recession. He cannot predict the meaning, i.e. the human reaction to the
brute fact of recession, he cannot predict that it will cause
a revolution or apathy, that it will lead to a reshaping of
economic life or to more spending by the government, and
so on. The factor of meaning which is there—because we

dwell in the realm of history—appears, in terms of an act of prediction, as an ingredient of the predicted situation. But the actual shape of the meaning is outside the scope of prediction carried out by a knower in the present.

This suggestion can be put differently: Even a short-run prediction is concerned with the future. When men predicting the future will arrive at this future, which will become a present, they will be different men changed by the process they underwent and facing a situation which will become a reality. The actual meeting between the reality and the men facing it creates an experience in the proper sense of the word. Experience is an act encountering a content; it is a whole comprising the two factors. Prediction foretelling the events cannot foretell the meaning of them, because the meaning is part of the experience which is an act in the present. Prediction is unable to predict the present of the future and the future of the future. In historical reality there are turning points where the future becomes a present and a new present immediately faces a future, and precisely because of this a historical prediction falls short of the reality predicted.

More light may be thrown on this idea from another point of view as well. The occurrence in the present is influenced to some extent by the prediction of the future. From the point of view of the actual occurrence it is by no means decisive whether or not there is an epistemological justification for prediction in the precise sense of the term. The actual deed in the present takes into consideration the future and the possibilities hidden in it. The consideration of the future and its hypothetical anticipation involved in any conscious or planned action affects the action in the present and thus alters the future which is to be predicted. If the activity in the present is adequate to the actuality of the future then it changes it by bringing the future into the horizon of the present. For example, if there is a continuous or gradual process leading toward the future, those engaged in the process are not surprised by the events encountered by them in the future. In the first place they have already made the future part of their present—as in the case of a death occurring as the result of a prolonged disease. Part of the sorrow and the preparations to face the new situation connected with the death is already in the experience of those witnessing the process leading to death. Future, in this case, though a new reality, is not something entirely new in its meaning, because at least its partial meaning has been grasped before. Or if prediction is inadequate to the future then the very anticipation of what did not occur according to this anticipation creates a new "misanticipated" future and thus changes the actual course of affairs. This can be easily shown when it is necessary to change a situation created by misprediction, e.g. in a diplomatic development or in a military action. The situation which must be changed in order to reach the intended and predicted result affects the entire course of the action. It certainly makes a difference if the course of the action is "smooth" according to the prediction or if it must first overcome the difficulties created by the misconception of what the future holds for us. In any case the historical future is affected by the anticipation of it. When we predict a forthcoming war, for example, we behave according to our prediction by arming, making political alliances, etc. But this behavior in the present creates a reality. Thus the emerging future ceases to be just a predicted future. It is also a consequence of our deeds and not one anticipated in our knowledge of what is not yet present. This cannot be the case in physics or in chemistry because the course of the physical or chemical events is by definition beyond the scope of human intervention. In an experiment conducted in natural science we at most cause the events to occur according to their laws and particular nature. In an experiment we do not change future events but only allow them to take place.

Here again we come across the essential feature of the domain of history: the identity of subject and object. The subject interferes with the process of the object, that is to say man living in the present interferes with the objective course of the historical flow. But there is also a distance between the subject and the object, since the reflecting subject does not dwell in the sphere of the object. The sphere of historical reflection is opposed to the sphere of the object, as it is opposed to the sphere of the historical datum. When the subject maintains an ontological identity with his predicted object, prediction is impossible and precluded. Prediction is a reflective activity and hence presupposes the detachment of the subject from the object with which it is ontologically identical. In terms of the relationship of identity between the two poles, the subject must be said to exist in the historical occurrence and to be part of it.

Thus the subject is partially and yet cannot be fully identical with the knower in terms of historical reflections. When the subject dwells in the sphere of reflection he does not resort to prediction since reflection refers to the past and not to the future. Hence there is no room for prediction, which is an act of intentionality toward and a projection of the future.

Either the subject is submerged in the process and has not a reflective attitude toward it but only an active-formative one, striving for but not predicting the future in terms of a cognitive attitude, or the subject does have a reflective attitude toward the object as existing not in the future but in the past. The future, in order to be predicted, is actually outside his reflective horizon. The problem of prediction arises at the meeting point between the two kinds of relationship, where the *knowing* subject wants to know not only the past, which is the object of knowledge, but also the future, which is the realm to be formed by deeds. Here at this crucial meeting point we are confronted with all the difficulties and the dialectics of history in its two meanings and in the relation between these two meanings. Since the problem of prediction arises at this meeting point and since the meeting point is a legitimate part of the realm of history, this problem arises legitimately, although a closer epistemological investigation does show that prediction is excluded. The *genesis* of the pretense to prediction is legitimate, since it is based in the essential oscillation of history in its two aspects, although the pretense *as such* is illegitimate. In paraphrasing Kant we may say that prediction in history is an illusion but an understandable illusion.

5. The practical manifestation of this absence of prediction in historical knowledge is to be found in the essential feature of historical knowledge as recognizing the causes of the effects which are given and not of deriving effects from causes. Let us recall here John Stuart Mill's distinction between two ways of causal investigation: Knowing the cause that leads to effects enables us to make *experiments*; knowing the given effects of a cause allows us to rest with *observation*.[5] The deduction of effects from a cause is the foundation of prediction; the determination of the cause or causes of effects is the foundation of observation. In the absence of experiments the experimenter is unable to create the conditions which are the part of the occurrence under his control. Here again we find the paradoxical feature in history: In spite of the ontological identity between the reflective subject and his datum, the subject has only one way of

5. See John Stuart Mill, *System of Logic* (London, 1941), bk. 3, ch. 7, p. 247.

knowing his datum—that of observation. The sovereignty of an experiment is beyond his capacity.

In contrast to the situation in physics we find in history that the *ontological identity* and the *methodological chasm* are interrelated. Although in physics there is no ontological identity between the experimenter and the material he masters, he maintains a methodological sovereignty with regard to it and hence creates the conditions for his experiment. This difference between history and physics is conditioned by the difference in structure concentrated in the difference of the concepts of time in the two branches respectively. The existence of prediction in physics and the absence of it in history reflect this essential difference between the two branches of knowledge.

Indeed, the regression from effects to their causes is always uncertain. Historical knowledge possesses in this respect only one certainty resulting from its very essence, namely the certainty that the cause is always in the past. But on the basis of this fundamental certainty in terms of direction everything else is only guesswork, conjectures as to the past in which the cause is to be located. The past which serves as the cause of the datum (recognized from the outset as an effect of *some* cause) is open to guesses, hypothetical statements, which are always open to question. Yet it is clear that historical knowledge or, rather, practical historical investigation does not continue this regression from effects to causes ad infinitum. This discontinuance of the search for the causes is in fact a product of a certain methodological decision, of common sense and some heuristic rules of investigation set by the investigation itself. From the point of view of principles the regressive series is open. Its openness manifests the reflective or regressive character of the principle of causality in history. One may find in this discontinuance of the search for the causes—a discontinuance which is not justified in terms of principles—a characteristic feature of historical knowledge in practice. There is a difference between the concrete technique of investigation and the epistemological background for it. Just as the historian sometimes goes toward the future without a sound reason and predicts its course, so he stops his search for the cause of given effects, yet in the light of its presuppositions he should continue that search. In all these instances practical deliberations are decisive, that is to say that here we encounter the interference of historical life and the participation in it in historical reflection proper, or else we find a consideration based on material arguments if we are "convinced" practically that the events are explained by the causes laid down through the historical procedure.

One might argue that for this reason philosophic analysis of historical knowledge is pointless once it is shown to be inadequate to the actual procedure employed in historical investigation. Yet the philosophical analysis is by no means and in no sphere—certainly not in the sphere of physics—an interrogation of an actual investigator. It is a critical evaluation of an anonymous scientific procedure as a "pure sample" of scientific approach. It is hence an analysis of *necessary* presuppositions and not a description of the actual procedures of a historian. In the light of these presuppositions we may try to draw a line between the principle of any particular domain of knowledge and the actual techniques pursued in this domain. The analysis of the presuppositions should help us point to the deviations, if any, of the practical technique from the legitimate principles, and this more for the sake of an elucidation of the principles than for the sake of correction or prevention of the deviations.

6. A further aspect of causality in history is brought to the fore by the problem of spatial and temporal contiguity

between the cause and its effect. Even where, as in physics, we assume that the causal relationship serves to connect an earlier and a later time, we must observe that historical causality involves a connection of temporal distance between events as well. Indeed, the meaning of distance is not simple in this case. It does not connote that an event or an occurrence in the remote past affects the present without the mediation of time and the occurrences which took place between it and the present. Each effect in the temporal distance takes place within the concrete medium of the historical reality in between. Nevertheless this medium is invaded in such a way that the occurrence in the present is determined not by the immediately preceding occurrence but by a distant one.

All revival movements and trends in their various forms are illustrations of this character of historical causality, if we consider these movements from the point of view of the relationship between the present and the past manifested in them. In these movements it is the aim of the present to be influenced by an occurrence, for instance an idea or a historical period, which is not a contiguous precedent. In these movements an attempt can be clearly discerned to jump over the immediate predecessor of the historical era and to establish over the distance in time a contact with the earlier era of intellectual trend. The revival movement is very strongly aware of the fact of its contiguity in time to the preceding era, and even considers this era as a burden. This awareness of the relationship to the preceding era activates the reaction against it and gives momentum to the revival movement. Yet in spite of being affected by distant causes these movements also prove the other side of causation from a distance: The close reality cannot be turned away altogether. The distant cause acts through the real historical medium, and therefore the actual historical real-

ity "as it really was" is not identical with its status as the
cause of a present event. Greek philosophy which influenced
the Italian Renaissance was not the philosophy contained
in the dialogues of Plato and recovered through a precise
philological effort. This philosophy was a cause of a new
intellectual movement since a new meaning was bestowed
on it by the new present—a present which for its own part
had been shaped historically by the distant philosophy. In
other words, the influence of the distant event is a cause of
the present which has already been shaped by a causal chain
and yet tries to break, as it were, its immediate chain of
causes. This shaped present tries to find another cause to
shape it, and for this purpose it goes to a distant content.
The present must activate the distant content by turning it
from the position of an existing content to the cause of a
historical development. As a matter of fact we find here
again both distance and proximity between the historical
eras and the movements in them.

To put it another way, because the present has consciously to overcome its immediate predecessors—which in
terms of history are predecessors in both meaning and time
—its approach to the distant time is not *immediate*, neither
in time nor meaning. The present actively finds its own past,
and this activity on its part makes the past distant and yet
close, distant because it *has* to be reached and close because
it *is* reached.

We must reject in this context the theory of those who
follow the Italian idealistic school in our time and argue
that there is no historical action at a distance. Distance
may be historically possible only through the medium of a
close historical environment; still it is something *distant* in
time and meaning which the present enacts. Through this
tension between distance and proximity we are in a position
to understand various historical phenomena from different

points of view. We may look at Plato's philosophy as a link in the chain of occidental philosophy and also as one of the causes of its progress. In this case we are interested in an immediate influence, for instance in the relation of Aristotle to Plato. But we may look at this philosophy as a factor in the revival of ideas and science in the 16th century, and in that case place it as the cause of an effect distant in time.

This idea can also be put as follows: Historical events and institutions do not exhibit their causal influence in a void, merely by leaping over what occurred between the past and the present. The past event and the past institution are active through what happened in the meantime. But the fact that their influence works through time does not imply that there is actually no distance and that we have to consider only proximate occurrences. The time distance is there and is not just a neutral external framework for the real proximity. In the notion of historical causation across time and the notion of proximity between distant occurrences there is again apparent the characteristic tension between the aspect of time proper and that of meaning proper. Each of the two aspects has its own status and nature; time in this case connotes the aspect of distance while meaning points to the aspect of proximity. Both aspects are essential. Hence there is no justification for making history simpler than it really is.

Now that we have put forward the various reservations regarding the nature and meaning of the principle of causality in history we may go back to where we started and re-emphasize its central position and validity for historical knowledge. Let us say first that the principle of causality constitutes historical continuity. Continuity is not the basis for the assumption of causality; on the contrary, without the causal relation there would be no logical place for continuity. This can be explained in two ways.

The events which historical investigation deals with are

not continuous. To be sure, the historical occurrences and the historical reality are continuous, but historical reflection breaks the continuity of reality since it starts from the datum and regresses to its reasons. This regression creates a series of events which is initially not continuous in itself. This distinctive trait of historical investigation finds its expression in the event described by the investigation, for instance a military operation involving the shifting of forces from one front to another. In this case its object is not to describe all the details involved in this operation and thus conform to the continuity of the action in all particulars. It is sufficient from the point of view of the historical investigation—let alone from the point of view of the communication of its findings—to point out the main stages of this operation, insofar as these stages themselves not only are parts of a total operation but also have historical relevance of their own, that is to say insofar as they affect the matter under consideration. Historical investigation thus creates a discontinuous series in place of or superimposed on the continuity of reality. Therefore the question arises as to the basis and the reasons for this building up of the discontinuous series of events and as to the nature of the connections creating the new superimposed series.

The discontinuous series is built up according to the principle of causality through a conscious abandonment of several, and even many, links within the process of the actual occurrence. To consider one example, between the shots fired at Sarajevo and the declaration of World War I various events occurred. In spite of this, historical investigation —insofar as it proceeds along this line of explanation—usually connects the declaration of the war with the shots at Sarajevo. Yet there was a clear temporal distance between the two events, and many events occurred between them. The continuity in terms of time was broken in this case. In spite of this, historical investigation creates a continuity of its own. Instead of the continuity in terms of the sequence in time, a continuity in terms of meanings is constructed, i.e. a series of events between which a direct causal relationship exists. Maurice Mandelbaum [6] rightly connected causal investigation with the discovery of the relevance of one event to another. The principle of causality through its methodological capacity creates a continuity of its own even where there is no given continuity in terms of time.

This function of the principle of causality can be made apparent from another point of view as well. Through the principle of causality we can refer to events contiguous in time and yet not related to each other from the point of view of causality. Historical investigation proceeds here along the lines also found in psychological investigation. As Kurt Lewin observed, the transition between events different from one another in their structure can from the "phenotypical" point of view be contiguous. The transition from one game of a child to another, for instance, may occur gradually and even continuously, although genetically the two are different events. [7] This is the case in history too. Events subsequent in time are not necessarily events connected with each other in the same causal chain. It may be that they are causally connected, but it may also be that they are disconnected. Temporal contiguity as such cannot be decisive and cannot be the guiding principle. The investigation guided by the principle of causality is decisive here, since this investigation tries to overcome the sheer givenness

6. See *The Problem of Historical Knowledge* (New York, 1938), pp. 203 ff.

7. K. Lewin in his article "Gesetz und Experiment in der Psychologie" published in *Symposion*, 1, 404. See the treatise on the problem in Lewin's article included in David Rappaport's *Organization and Pathology of Thought* (New York, 1951), p. 91.

in terms of time relations and goes into real relations based
on meanings. Hence the principle of causality, creating a
continuity of its own, enables us to distinguish between
temporal and meaningful continuity. We realize again that
the synthesis between the aspect of meaning and that of
time remains in force. The causal-meaningful relationship
is not placed beyond time or outside it. On the contrary,
according to the very essence of historical knowledge the
causal relationship is constituted along the direction of time
from the past to the present. It is not just a *copy* of time,
however, but a *construction* in it. The composition of time
and meaning characteristic of the principle of historical
causality expresses the essential composition of historical
knowledge in general and the essence of historical time in
particular.

We may now extend the epistemological function of the
principle of causality. There is no doubt that this principle
creates a system of physical knowledge. The procedure
adopted according to this principle imposes the task of investigating meaningful connections between events placed
in time. An impulse is given to such an investigation when
these connections have not been discovered. The principle
of causality applied to history implies that the process lends
itself to understanding, that is to say that we will be in a
position to discover meaningful connections within time.
This assumption is certainly most significant for historical
knowledge in view of the optical illusion which still persists
in discussions of the philosophy of history, to the effect that
the understanding of the object might evade the conceptual
investigation by a kind of "direct knowledge" or insight into
the essence of the historical object. It has been attempted in
this analysis of ours to point to the dialectic characteristic of
the relation between the subject and the object in history.

Identity is only one side of the shield; the existing gulf is the other side of it. Identity between subject and object is characteristic of historical knowledge and provides for the possibility of deciphering the meaning of the object. Yet it is an impediment as well, because due to this identity there is in history a perpetual shift back and forth from the occurrences conceived in reflection to the reflection submerged in the sphere of the occurrences.

The principle of causality as the principle of historical knowledge tries to bridge the transition from one road to the other. Yet it is a bridge built by *reflection* in order to reach *reality*. Reflection breaks the continuity of the occurrence, but it builds up a new continuity instead. Historical reflection diverts the direction of the historical process proceeding toward the future, while the direction of the reflection is turned toward the past. This alteration of direction is but a manifestation of an alienation between the subject and the object in history. The method and its functional instruments try to overcome this alienation in the field of methods itself. Knowledge does not restore the "lost" identity but constitutes relations instead. Thus historical knowledge exhibits the essence of knowledge in general, i.e. the establishing of relations. These relations may be established against the ontological background of the gap between the knowing subject and the object; this is the case in the domain of physics and against the background of identity between the knowing subject and his object; this is the case in the domains of psychology and history. Yet in spite of this difference between the various domains of knowledge, most relevant in itself, the trend of knowledge is the same in all domains: the establishing of relations, no more and no less. It is within this context that the position of causality reveals itself.

C. *From the Principle of Causality to the Laws*

1. The emphasis placed on the position of the principle of causality in historical knowledge can be looked at only as laying down the fundamentals for a further elucidation of the problem before us. In the last analysis scientific investigation rests on the transcendental presuppositions called "principles" by Kant. But in concreto this scientific investigation is connected with material laws and takes advantage of them. These material laws in turn, when looked at from the point of view of the problem of causality, are related to the principle of causality as material differentiations of it. The differentiation of the principle takes place according to the various fields of experience and investigation. These fields are material ones and as such they break the unity of the principle into laws which are relevant to the various fields. We can watch causality when differentiated according to the various material fields, as exemplified in the law of gravitation, the law of the expansion of gases, the laws of thermodynamics, etc. The material law mastering a specific material field of occurrences may thus be considered as a third stage in the scale of empirical knowledge, the highest stage being that of the principle of unity in general, Kant's "transcendental unity of apperception." The next stage below this is the set of various categories or principles (causality, substance, etc.). The third and lowest rung in his ladder is that occupied by the various laws which are compositions of the various categories or principles in their application to an empirical datum. Thus the rung of the law is actually the concrete embodiment of the transcendental principles in their application to a datum. These various laws are dependent on the single principle, but there is still a plurality of laws since the very rung or stage of the law is determined by a particular relation of the principle to a

datum given in a defined field: motion, gases, organism, etc. Thus in spite of the fact that historical knowledge is essentially connected with the principle of causality there is no necessity that the material laws of history be the material laws of physics, biology, or psychology, because the unity of the principle does not necessarily lead to the conclusion that there is a unity in the stage of laws.

It is the characteristic trait of the stage of the material laws in general that they are originally differentiated. What is common to all the laws, in spite of their differentiation, is their position in terms of their logical function within a comprehensive system of knowledge. Every law determines the nature of an object by determining its behavior, i.e. its relation to another object. Every law puts forth the concept of the object to which it is applied, since the qualities of an object which appear in the description are but relations to other objects. The possibility of knowledge which every material law is to serve depends in the final analysis on the substitution of the dynamic behavior for the static features. The law defines the relational nature of the object subjected to it; the object is defined by the law to which it is subjected, as in the case of motion which is defined or described through the laws of motion. Thus when we spoke before about the hypothetical character of causality we meant to stress the hypothetical character of material laws as well, because these laws are constituted on the basis of the principle and according to the form of reasoning: *if—then*. It is clear that through the medium of hypothetical statements we free our determinations from their dependence upon singular instances experienced by us or observed in our experiments. We make these statements apply to many instances and not only to those already encountered in experience.

Hence the problem that historical knowledge is bound to

face: Is it possible to lay down material laws for historical knowledge which are parallel to the laws in science, or do reasons of principle implied in the very nature of historical knowledge prevent us from descending legitimately from the principle of causality to the material laws? This problem naturally precedes the determination and the formulation of any concrete material laws. If the answer to the main question is affirmative the way becomes clear for a formulation of material laws. Such a formulation in terms of the specific meaning of the material laws would of course be the task of the science of history itself and not of the theory of knowledge, just as the laws of thermodynamics are not formulated by the theory of knowledge but by physics. If a theory of knowledge or philosophy in general would pretend to formulate them it would cease to be what it is and would become *Naturphilosophie* in the romantic sense. But if the solution of the main problem as to the possibility of material laws in history is negative we may legitimately criticize the various concrete attempts at formulating historical laws. Thus the solution of the main problem is the task of a philosophic consideration. If there is a possibility of such laws, history as a branch of science can possibly proceed to formulate them. If there is no such possibility history cannot use the concept of law or quasi laws, as it does in some modern conceptions where the borderline between theory of knowledge or philosophy and historical investigation is confused. It is common for "philosophers of history" to pretend to know more in terms of material knowledge than historians do and to advance "historical laws," or to pretend to know more than they can know and formulate laws without asking the question as to the legitimacy of their procedure altogether.

2. The principle of causality in its transcendental meaning is to be applied to time and to the data in it. Each datum

holds a particular situation in time and space. The function of material laws—such laws as are formulated, for instance, in physics—is to mediate between the universality of the principle and the particularity of the datum. The law is not applied to the datum qua datum in the way the principle of causality or substance is applied. The law is applied to a *specific* datum while abstracting it from its particular and singular position in *this* time and *this* space. This essential feature of the nature of law is put forth in Maxwell's well-known maxim: "The difference between one event and another does not depend upon the mere difference of the places at which they occur, but only on differences in the nature, configuration, or motion of the bodies concerned." [1] As a rule this maxim of Maxwell's is understood in connection with the principle of causality as if the maxim exhausted the meaning of this principle. But this is not correct. This maxim does not add anything at all to the meaning of the principle of causality in its pure transcendental formulation, since the principle of causality as such does not deal with any *particular* bodies, with any *particular* moments, or any *particular* places. This principle deals with time in general and therefore with succession in general and hence with data in terms of their position in time and succession in general. Yet Maxwell's maxim is a real innovation with reference to the material laws of physics, since the maxim states that, although when applying laws we deal with particular bodies, we may nevertheless abstract them from their temporal-spatial particularity. This particularity in terms of time and space is not a part or a feature of the particularity of the phenomena as conceived of in science and therefore does not form their content. The generality of empirical laws is guaranteed by this abstraction from their temporal-spatial particularity. The concept of the

1. J. Clerk Maxwell, *Matter and Motion* (New York, 1892), p. 31.

law is bound up only with "the nature, configuration, or motion," that is to say with the material elements of the phenomenon and not with its temporal-spatial coordinates.

Cassirer summed up the tendency of this maxim of Maxwell by saying that each moment in time, chosen by us arbitrarily (other conditions being equal), is conceived to be *equivalent* with the given moment, so that the present moment contains the decision regarding the past and the future.[2] The importance of this comment of Cassirer lies in the fact that it puts into clear relief the connection between Maxwell's maxim and the justification of prediction implied in scientific findings based on material laws. Prediction is valid and altogether possible from the point of view of laws only because we are permitted to disregard—when dealing with the various phenomena—the temporal differences between them, that is to say to disregard the question whether they are placed now, before, or after. Hence we may consider the various phenomena, in spite of their factual differences in terms of the moments of time, as equivalent with one another. Maxwell's maxim expresses this distinctive trait of physical thinking and makes the way clear for the assumption of the real epistemological position of the laws qua general assertions applied to material instances in general and not to those "here and now."

Indeed, this precondition for the validity of laws and their application is not to be found in history. Historical knowledge by definition cannot abstract from the temporal position of the phenomenon (nor in a way from the spatial position either, but it is not necessary for our discussion to enlarge the field and discuss this matter) and deal with "the nature, configuration, or motion" since at least the

2. Ernst Cassirer, *Substanzbegriff und Funktionsbegriff* (Berlin, B. Cassirer, 1923), p. 331; English trans., *Substance and Function*, pp. 249–50.

temporal position of the phenomenon is an integral part of "the nature, configuration, or motion." In other words, the distinction between the nature of an event and its position in terms of time and space cannot be made in history. From the point of view of history it makes a great deal of difference whether the agrarian reform was carried out in the period of Gracchian Rome or in 19th century Russia, since time and the position in it are part of the very content of a historical event. Time and the position in it provide not only a chronological-passive background but also a manifestation, a medium, and a content of the "configuration" itself, to use Maxwell's terms here. Since the historical phenomenon is assumed by way of a synthesis of meaning and time, that is to say by meaning determining time and time determining meaning, there is no possibility of an abstraction from time. Such an abstraction at once annihilates the historical object altogether, or at least changes its intrinsic nature. There is no point in an abstraction from time in history if history is taken seriously. The zeal for a foundation of historical laws pretending to be a zeal for scientific status of historical research amounts actually to sacrificing history for laws, that is to say for uprooting the very *raison d'être* of historical laws.

Thus we must conclude that historical knowledge does not provide room for general laws, if we wish to keep strictly to the essence of this knowledge on the one hand and to the essence of the laws and their epistemological possibility on the other. Here we encounter another paradox implicit in historical knowledge: This knowledge is always *causal*, yet it is not based on material *laws*. In historical knowledge we do not find and are not permitted to establish a logical-functional mediation between the two poles of the principle of causality and of the data to which the principle of causality in its application refers. Historical knowledge puts the principle of causality into effect immediately, without the mediating link of the material laws. Hence the principle itself is as it were the law of historical knowledge, since this knowledge does not possess laws subordinated to the principle. It is therefore compelled to use the principle itself. Actually both the strength and the weakness of historical knowledge is that it is a knowledge arrived at by means of a transcendental principle, i.e. causality. Hence it may be regarded as being more immunized in terms of a possible rejection or replacement of the principle than the knowledge based on laws which are at least more hypothetical and provisional than the fundamental principle. But, being more immunized against a skeptical attack on the principle of causality, historical knowledge must give up the possibility and the pretension of using concepts which comprise in their functional networks an indefinite number of data, i.e. laws. In other words, the principle is applied to a single datum and each time to a new single datum, and not, as in the case of the material law in physics, for instance, to a set of an indefinite number of data. Historical knowledge starts every time at the very beginning, having only the single certainty that it must essentially be causal knowledge, and in this capacity it faces the datum in its meaning and position in time. Precisely because the time factor is essential historical knowledge always begins at the beginning and cannot take anything for granted except its own essence qua causal knowledge.

Here I have to add an observation in order to be more precise: Not only is historical knowledge unable to predict what will occur in the future, but it is also unable to formulate laws in order to determine general relations between events, even those in the past. It can always reach and assume as matters of *fact* the various existing relations, presupposing that they are causal. But it is not in a position to presuppose that from a universal law it will be able to determine relations between the events in the past. There is no possibility of *prediction* in history from reasons clarified before. Nor is there any possibility of a *deduction* of actual causal relations between events from a universal formula, because there is altogether no validity in the universal formula. The problem here is the relationship between a *material*-hypothetical law and a *particular* event where the time position of the event is a part of its very particularity. The impossibility of the deduction of data from laws lies not in the fact that the historical statement is categorical (as suggested, for instance, by Collingwood) but in the fact that this statement necessarily places the content in time and in a particular position in time. Hence the datum cannot be deduced from a formula without altogether abolishing its very particularity. What really matters here is not the fact that *categoricity* (the statement concerning the datum) is not to be derived from hypotheticity (law) but that specific *temporality* is not to be deduced from a relation in time in general. Since such a deduction is excluded we may say that a historical law, if it is to make sense, must be a punctual one, that is to say that it must state the relations of this particular configuration here and now. But in such a case the law ceases to be a law as something distinct from the configuration to which it is applied and with respect to which it is universal. In other words, each historical configuration is both factual and prototypical. Therefore there is no room for an epistemological basis of laws, since a law is by definition both a bond between facts and their pattern and at the same time a line of demarcation between them. Once there is no difference between the sample and the pattern there is no ground for the very idea of a law.

This argument to show the intrinsic impossibility of laws

in history is by no means identical with the usual argument stating that since historical events do not recur we cannot deduce them from general laws. Both Ernst Cassirer and Kurt Lewin showed that a law is not a device for reducing many instances to a common denominator, and that it is sufficient to employ one instance only in order to lay down a law. What is essential is not the expansion of the empirical basis on which the law rests but the possibility of passing from the basic case to other cases. Therefore the problem of law is not to be solved by determining whether events do or do not recur. It relates to the question of the nature and the meaning of the qualitative nonrecurrence of events. In the nature of a historical event we emphasize not its *single* appearance from the *chronological* point of view but the *qualitative situation* emerging from time and materialized in it. The impossibility of formulating a law does not lie in the absence of a multitude of instances as a basis for this law. It is due to the fact that we may not derive conclusions from one single event through a construction of "pure" events, i.e. events not embedded in a specific moment of time. Historical events are not "pure," that is to say they are not homogeneous, and thus it is impossible to subordinate them to a comprehensive material law. Once the time factor is decisive, as it is in history, homogeneity is excluded.

3. This conception can be formulated in another way by taking into consideration the problem of induction and its place in historical knowledge. If we are to adhere to the strict meaning of induction we should look at it not as though it were an inference from some cases to *many* cases and from many cases to *all* cases. "In a scientific experiment we do not infer from what is given now to what is not given now, but we consciously transcend the *point of*

view of here and now toward a new dimension." [3] This form of transcendence from one dimension to another, from that of here and now to that of general validity, is accomplished through induction. Actually this passage is carried out by means of material laws which are the concrete devices of induction. The particular case is severed from its particularity of here and now and made homogeneous with the other cases themselves severed from their particular here and now. Induction is thus made possible by the material law or induction gets materialized in material laws. As a matter of fact the law and the induction are but two sides of one and the same coin. The principle of induction calls for material laws and through them becomes a concrete scientific procedure. And material laws— looked at, as it were, teleologically—serve the main idea of induction in transcending the *given* framework of occurrences and facts and reaching the as yet nongiven occurrences and facts. Now, since there is no room for historical laws proper and since laws serve induction, we have to draw the conclusion that there is no historical induction proper. Historical knowledge is of course empirical knowledge, and yet not inductive, though usually empirical knowledge is considered to be inductive. It is necessary to make this distinction between empirical knowledge and the laws of induction because historical knowledge by nature of the empirical datum to which it is applied is unable to go beyond the datum it actually deals with and through this overstepping, i.e. inductive procedure, to reach a dimension of validity beyond the foundation. Historical knowledge is accumulative, that is to say it accumulates all

3. Ernst Cassirer, *Determinismus und Indeterminismus in der modernen Physik* (Göteborg, Elanders, 1937), pp. 52–3; Eng. trans., Yale University Press, 1956.

the statements made up to the present act of cognition. Induction by its very nature carries knowledge beyond the sphere of accumulated experience, while experience in history leaves us with what we have already accumulated.

4. In contrast, historical knowledge lays stress on invariant *elements* but not on invariant *relations* between the changing elements. The elements composing the historical process and revealed by historical knowledge are stable, but the situational contexts, that is to say the combinations of the various elements in particular situations, vary. Population, law, and the moral factor of the binding authority and the obedience to it, etc. may be found in the history of states, and it is sound to assume that those elements will be sought in any investigation applied to political data. Yet what distinguishes the various situations is their particular composition of the stable and hence recurring factors. In one situation the sociological element predominates, as for instance in a revolutionary situation where the decisive factor is the rise of the masses, while in another situation the factor of the binding authority of the government may be decisive. We still dwell in one and the same sphere of politics though the balance between the elements of the sphere changes historically. Historical reflection is aware—clearly or vaguely—of the elements composing situations insofar as these elements can be systematically described as they are in a study of politics, economics, etc. These stable elements manifest the nature of human activities and their inner structure. As such they are used either in the vague historical consciousness which is the starting point for the precise historical investigation, or they are deliberately borrowed by historical investigation from other forms of investigation like those of the social sciences proper. Hence historical reflection does not approach its data as a *tabula rasa*, without any precognition or precon-

ception as to what can be encountered in the facts themselves. It approaches its data with an assumption as to the nature of the elements and their presence in the situation. It tries to find out about the particularity of a situation as a configuration of the invariant elements. Indeed, historical knowledge must draw the conclusion that it is the combination which determines the meaning of the elements too, for instance that the elements of government in the total configuration of a state in modern society must be different from those in a feudal society. Yet the limited function of the precognition of the invariant elements remains in force, and it is therefore permitted and even necessary to employ the concepts indicating the stable elements in an investigation of a particular historical situation. Historical knowledge is bound to be of relations, with the related terms functioning as elements of meaning. The disclosure of a situation depends on the discovery of its invariant elements, since situations are determined by their invariant elements. As a matter of fact we encounter here again the function of the principle of causality which underlies historical knowledge. It is the function of knowledge to explain the distinction between one situation and another by explaining the distinctions between the various configurations of the elements.[4] The elements are invariant, but their activity, that is to say their causal power and position, is variant. The principle of causality enables us to detect the origin of the change and the distinction between particular situations by relating them to the past.

We have dealt before with the distinction between the various elements and consequently between the separate historical situations in the example of a state. This distinction exists in other domains of activity as well. When considering the dynamics of historical situations we are not

4. R. M. MacIver, *Social Causation* (Boston, 1942), p. 149.

concerned with dynamics within one domain only, such as that of the state. Historical situations are more than different combinations of elements in one and the same domain. They are combinations of elements stemming from and embedded in various different domains as well, as for instance the combination of politics and economics, politics and religion, or all these domains together. In a historical situation we therefore find a twofold combination from the point of view of the component elements: On the one hand there are various combinations of meaningful elements related to *one* domain (e.g. politics) and on the other hand there are different and changing combinations of meaningful elements related to *various* domains (e.g. politics and economics). Thus a concrete historical situation becomes a cross-section of different domains to be defined in terms of content. There may for instance be a combination of the political and religious domains in one situation and a combination of the social and religious domains in another. There is clearly no a priori and no empirical justification for historical knowledge to look at only one meaningful combination as constant, nor is there any a priori or empirical justification for considering a given or possible combination of elements belonging to different domains as an exclusive and prototypical combination characteristic of each historical situation. Invariant are only the various domains as such, but their existence in historical situations is a manifestation of meaningful human activity and is not identical with the changing situations.

In what has been said above there is implied a criticism of any attempt to put forth one domain of historical activity as having exclusively causative power, or at any rate causative power in the final analysis. Marxism is the best known example of such a doctrine. Marxism is a methodological attempt to determine the material essence of historical lawfulness, although one can hardly find in Marxist literature a clear statement of its epistemological position.[5] In any case economic activity or productive activity in general is considered the causal activity in the final analysis. Some observations on this attempt follow in the light of the foregoing analysis of the concept of law in history and the nature of a historical situation in general.

a. Actually this theory sees history as a hierarchical structure, that is to say it distinguishes between the basis of the historical process and what is erected upon it. This alleged hierarchical structure of history finds its expression in the well-known distinction between "structure" and "superstructure." Such an approach to the historical process results from the tendency characteristic of Marx to show that the *essence* of man as a being possessing the power of production is identical with the historical *cause* of the historical occurrences. The essential historical cause qua productivity is in his view the *differentia specifica* of man as such. The essential feature of man is praxis; hence praxis is the historical cause and as such makes itself apparent in economic activity. In other words, since anthropologically man is a *practical* being, historically he is an *economic* being. Since economic activity is essential, it therefore has to be considered *the* determining stratum of the process of history. The process of history in terms of its structure reflects the nature of man.

But it is precisely here that the main fallacy of the entire conception lies. From the outset this conception puts forward the essence of man in such a way as to make him exclusively a historical being. Man is assumed to possess praxis as his characteristic feature. Yet this very assumption is but a projection of the dynamic and practical character

5. See the analysis in H. B. Acton, *The Illusion of the Epoch*, London, 1955.

of historical life. The course of reasoning seems to be that history is the proper manifestation of the essence of man, history is practical, *ergo* man is bound to be a practical-economic being in his very essence. Hence historical materialism—called by Marx himself "practical materialism" —is connected with the criticism of religion as a domain of what is beyond history ("other worldliness"). Man cannot be considered to be a genuinely religious being since this would imply that man belongs or is related to a domain outside the domain of history, to be mastered by man's own deeds. According to this line of argument religion itself is an outcome of historical life. This whole concept is put forth in order to keep human existence contracted to the historical-social domain. Actually we can see here a leap being made from the historical to an anthropological reflection. Although the theory tries to put forth the historical conception as an outcome of the anthropological one, actually the anthropological conception is only a rationalization of the historical. The anthropological is constructed in order to provide a metaphysical presupposition or ground for confining man's existence to the historical setting. In order to safeguard the identity of the historical cause qua economic activity of man it is denied that economic activity is a mere historical phenomenon. It is turned into the "essence of man." This is a hypostasis of historical phenomena into metaphysical qualities in spite of Marx' own denunciation of any kind of hypostasis. But it seems that no other way was open for him to formulate *permanent* material-historical laws short of this way of elevating history from its proper realm into the realm of the essence of man. One might say that this elevation took history out of the realm of the study of relations into the realm of essences. One may wonder whether Marx would agree to being considered as an ontologist or even an essentialist, as he turns out to be in spite of himself.

b. This historical conception disregards the cumulative character of history. Even assuming that economic activity is actually the "first historical deed," as Marx puts it, that is to say that this is the deed which removes man from the biological domain of satisfaction of his needs to the historical domain of work, production, creation of new needs, etc.—assuming all this, it does not follow that because this was the *first* historical deed it is the *primary* or basic cause of the whole historical process. The presupposition behind this doctrine is that since economic productivity produced or brought history into effect, this activity produces, maintains, and guides history forever. We encounter here a historical induction from the origins of history in general to the actual course of historical events in particular. This induction must be objected to even more than the usual historical induction which only tries to go from one historical event to another. The usual induction is within the realm of history from events to events, from one economic crisis to another; the Marxian induction is from the biological to the historical realm proper, i.e. from the start of history to events and processes within the immanent historical realm itself. Furthermore, if economic activity is the cause of the historical processes in the final analysis, then it follows that every historical situation is arranged in such a way that the hierarchical structure, and *the same one*, is maintained forever and that the historical process itself is unable to change it. According to such a conception there is no room for historical cumulation; historical occurrences as a process cannot become causes on their own. To be sure, the materialistic conception of history is compelled to compromise on this question and assume the power of "secondary causes." But the assumption of secondary causes breaks the cumulative totality of the historical process in the horizontal line and builds up a hierarchical totality in the vertical line instead. This is an example of the illegitimate introduction of sociological concepts into historical investigations. Actually a hierarchic structure becomes a whole and ceases to be a process, that is is to say the notion of process is replaced by the notion of framework.

c. In this criticism we did not argue against historical materialism as *materialism* but against its presuppositions in terms of the hidden categories it is based on. This theory puts invariancy of *relations* where there is at most only a justification for invariancy of *elements* as elucidated before. It connects the definition of historical causes with a philosophical or anthropological doctrine, yet actually establishes the anthropological doctrine as auxiliary to the historical conception. It maintains a hierarchical structure of history instead of a cumulative one. It is therefore unable to explain the pluralism of historical occurrences and its differentiation into economics, government, law, social relations, ideologies, etc.

Materialism as a hierarchical conception tries to see various domains of history as causally connected with the single domain of economics and the structure of its process. Actually it is unable to explain how various "secondary" domains are related to the primary domain in different modes of causal dependence. In one case the relation between the effect and its cause is a relation between means and ends, as where the state and its legal system are supposed to exist in order to serve the economic interests of the dominant social-economic class. Yet in the case of the dependence of philosophy upon the economic structure, the causal relationship is allegedly one of reflection and transformation, that is to say the class interests are supposed to find their reflection in the ideology of the class. But here again the concept of the reflection and consequently the causal dependence of the superstructure on the basic structure is far from clear. For instance, religion is conceived of not as a prolonged social situation or a situation translated from the language of social existence to the language of concepts or belief. Religion is supposed to be an "opiate," that is to say not a mirror of a social situation or an expression of it in terms of concepts and articles of faith but an attempt to divert the attention of the people to a goal outside their real social situation and thus to motivate them not to change the social situation.

This is an indication of the real problem implied in the entire hierarchical conception of the nature of the historical process. The causal relationship between the various strata is not clear and cannot be clear because of the whole trend which denies the *genuine pluralism* of history and puts a hierarchical structure in its stead. The justification for this is supposed to be in an existent permanent and primary causal activity embodied in the economic activity. Here again the real difficulty does not lie in the fact that it is *economic* activity which is unable to explain the nature of all the domains and the nature of the relations between each domain and its historical basis on the one hand and the combination of the various domains themselves on the other. The difficulty results from the very tendency to explain the distinction between various domains by a single permanent causal factor. Hierarchy abolishes historical pluralism while cumulation preserves it. Cumulation connotes preservation of pluralism within time and in the course of the process.

5. There is a widespread use of the term "historical evolution" in both everyday and scholarly vocabularies.

Since the idea of evolution is laden with biological content we must reject its application to the historical domain. The term "evolution" as used in biology connotes the material content and organization of the biological process. Hence the assumption of evolution is connected with the assumption of certain material laws of the process, for example the laws of natural selection or the laws of mutation. It follows from what has been said up to this point that in history we cannot connect evolution with any kind of material laws.

The content of the concept of evolution cannot fit the presuppositions of the domain of history. We must distinguish between evolution proper and the genesis of a fact or its coming into being. Historical phenomena are events which come to be, but they do not *evolve* in the strict sense of the term, since the historical process does not manifest or reveal any latent seed and is not a "realization of possibilities." [6] Nor can the process be differentiated into stages of development as can for instance the growth process of an embryo. Furthermore, the concept of evolution presupposes the possibility of surveying the various stages of the process from a qualitative point of view, for instance from the point of view of the maturity of the organism or from the point of view of the existence of human beings. When we look at the prehuman stages of evolution either we compare the mature, "complete" entity with an embryo or we compare the entity better suited to the struggle for survival with an entity less suited or one suited to different ecological circumstances. Actually from the point of view of evolution one does not consider an entity or a stage in the process of growth for its own sake and on its own merits only. The consideration of any individual stage is *eo ipso*

6. Julian Huxley, *Evolution in Action* (London, Chatto and Windus, 1953), p. 81.

a consideration of its position in the entire setting. For this reason the concept of evolution can be, as it frequently has been, the basis for a consideration of the phenomenon from the teleological point of view. Since a phenomenon is considered from the point of view of, among other things, what will come into being in the later stage of the growth process, the point of view of what is later can very easily be understood as the point of view of finality. Now all these traits characteristic of the concept of evolution and its application to biology cannot be found in historical knowledge. For historical knowledge each phenomenon is a prototype in itself and must not be looked at as only a transitory phase. As Ranke remarked, each era stands in an immediate relation to God. In history we look at the phenomena from the angle of the present but not from the angle of an entity more complete than the entities preceding it. The present is a continuation of the past and emerges from it, but the present is not at a higher stage of development than the past. We remain within the scope of cumulation and may not identify accumulation with evolution.

As long as we use "evolution" in a vague sense there is nothing which militates against the introduction of the term into the scope of historical discussions. But once we pay attention to the strict sense of the term the incommensurability becomes clear. This can be shown by a brief consideration of some traits characteristic of the modern theory of evolution.

The problem is again connected with the concept of progress. Sometimes it is simply assumed that there is a progressive line in the road of evolution. The nature of the progress is stated as "improvement which permits or facilitates further improvement, or, if you prefer, a series of advances which do not stand in the way of further advances." [7]

7. *Ibid.*

George Gaylord Simpson is more cautious when he says
that "progress has occurred within it [i.e. evolution] but is
not of its essence." In any case, "To man, evolutionary
change in the direction of man *is* progress, of this particular sort." [8]

The concept of evolution is clearly put forth from the
point of view of the status of man; this is only plausible
since the concept is one formulated by human beings. We
have to see the difference between the status of man in evolution and the status of the present in history. To be sure,
man in evolution as representing the present, i.e. the ultimate or until now ultimate stage, is a being with a special
status, just as the present in history is also a dimension with
a special status. Yet the relationship between beings related
to each other in the line of evolution is different from the
relationship between various dimensions of time. Hence in
biological evolution the representatives of the prehuman
stages of evolution are, at least partially, contemporaries of
the human stage, though all are included in the present.
Past and present exist simultaneously, as it were, as do
changes and men. In history the past is not contemporaneous with the present but incapsulated in it, and hence the
past is not immediately a datum in the present but has to
be approached through the medium of historical regression.

In a way the point of view of the status of man in the
line of evolution is ultimate, whereas the status of any particular present in history is transitory. In evolution what
preceded man is so to speak transitory. Yet the status of
man, being the point of view which serves as the basis for
the formulation of the theory of evolution, is not transitory,
as is the present in history by its very definition. Put differently, there is a stable or semistable position from which

8. George Gaylord Simpson, *The Meaning of Evolution* (New Haven,
Yale University Press, 1950), pp. 261–2; Mentor ed., p. 123.

to look at the stages of evolution, i.e. the position of man within the whole development. Man is defined through some qualitative features which came into being within the process but now present a configuration defined not through the process but on man's own merits. Man in evolution is a qualitative reality. As against this the present in history is to be defined in terms of dimensions of time and not in terms of qualitative features—or in terms of position, as a locus of the historical datum or deed, and not in terms of a semicomplete stage of development. In terms of evolution we deal with time as a coordinate but not as an ingredient of the very content, and this again shows that the very notion of historical time excludes any fargoing analogy between the essence of history and that of biological evolution.

6. This analysis of the status of laws in history has to be completed by a brief outline of a further concept which might be called *principium* proper. Principia in this sense are different from both the particular material laws and the presuppositions of knowledge in general. I refer here to the distinction made by Cassirer, who observed that the principium employed in science is not to be identified with laws of nature. A principium is supposed to be the place of the origin of the material laws, their matrix but not a law in itself. As an example of this stage of knowledge Cassirer adduced the "principle of the least effect," which is neither a transcendental presupposition like the principle of causality or substance, nor a material law like the law of gravitation or the second law of thermodynamics.[9]

It is interesting to observe that in the theory of historical knowledge this intermediate stage of principles was indicated long before by Wilhelm Wundt. Indeed, Wundt did

9. Cassirer, *Determinismus und Indeterminismus in der modernen Phyisk*, p. 66.

not draw this sharp distinction between laws proper and a principium but used the two terms indiscriminately. But if we are to be strict and want to exhaust the meaning of the concept of principles as suggested by Wundt in relation to history we will find that his intention was to put forth some directing lines of historical knowledge different from laws proper. There is no need to dwell here on Wundt's special theory, which placed the justification of these principles to be used in history in psychology—a conception to be rejected because it blurs the boundaries between history and psychology. Hence we may consider the concepts themselves disconnected from their doubtful justification.

a. The first principium introduced is that of historical results. According to this principium all historical content is to be conceived of as a summarized result of many conditions. The historical content is in a sense independent of the factors which produced it. The effect is different from the cause which brought it into being. This rule, or rather maxim, was introduced in connection with the psychological law of the creative synthesis.[10]

b. The second rule is that of historical relations. This rule states that in the breaking up of complex historical combinations each content in the combination appears as a compound of factors and elements close to each other in spirit. Thus we may say that each part of a total culture is in some degree a mirror of the totality, and from each part we may infer something of the nature of this totality.

c. The third rule is that of historical contrast. It states that any particular historical trend on reaching a climax produces tendencies contradicting it.

Let us now examine these three rules:

a. There can be no doubt that the first rule expresses

10. See W. Wundt, *Logik* (Stuttgart, 1893), p. 428.

the cumulative essence of the historical process. Since the relationship between the cause and the effect is not continuous in terms of a time sequence, and since this relation is constructed according to the presupposition that the effect must be in a different dimension of time from that of the cause, the effect cannot be equal to the cause. The cause is a historical occurrence and the effect is equally an occurrence and therefore each of the two related parts of the chain is a configuration in itself. But since the effect occurs at a later moment and since each moment preserves the content of the preceding one, the effect is necessarily different from the cause and even richer than it, if we look at the factors forming its essence. Hence the first rule actually expresses the nature of the historical process as such. However, it expresses too little. The effect is not only richer than the cause but, as pointed out before, it lies in a different dimension if considered from the point of view of the two fundamental aspects of history. The effect is the process which has already objectified itself, while the cause in its relation to the effect has to be considered as an occurrence. The effect is an occurrence which is finished at least from the point of view of historical reflection and for all practical purposes of historical investigation. Historical reflection, because it deals with a datum, conceives of it as an effect and by reflection on it objectifies the process which brought the effect into being. Thus it brings the process—methodologically of course—to a standstill. This transition from the domain of process to the domain of established objectified facts does not get its due in the rule of the creative synthesis. This rule considers only the continuity in history but disregards the complementary aspect of discontinuity and the aspect of the perpetual shift from the domain of processes to that of knowledge referring to data.

b. The rule of relations expresses too much. It assumes

not only historical accumulation but also a *direction* of accumulation which makes any historical situation homogeneous in itself. Only through the assumption that historical situations are homogeneous is one in a position to state that every part or component of the life of a culture is representative of the totality of it. But from the point of view of historical cumulation it necessarily follows that a historical situation cannot be homogeneous, because it preserves the past in its various aspects and does not establish itself by selecting only some aspects of the past to keep them alive in the present. A historical situation is a fragment of time in which various configurations in terms of content exist side by side. To paraphrase an example which we find in Bronislaw Malinowski, an airplane and a camel exist side by side in a given historical situation, that is to say within one and the same temporal reality there exist means of communication which manifest different stages of the process of technical civilization. Historical reality as such preserves not only the influences of the past on the present but also material relics of the past such as the camel as a means of transport in the era of the airplane. The homogeneous cultural situation is at most a methodological construction set up for the sake of the investigation of an isolated fragment of a historical process. But as a matter of principle we must insist on the accumulation characteristic of the process; and accumulation is not identical with homogeneity. Historical time does not create cultural "organisms," if the term is used precisely. It creates situations where the various contents of the past and the present intermingle or at least exist side by side. This distinctive trait of historical reality in general becomes apparent in the meeting between the generations. Generations are sequential to one another and do not create for themselves monocultural environments. It is not that one climate of existence and of opinion simply replaces the other. Generations and their trends, biases, creations, etc. exist contemporaneously in spite of the temporal succession implied in the relation between them as a characteristic of the concept of generation as such. It is because of the nature of time that historical reality is one of both succession and duration and thus cannot be homogeneous on nature.[11] The interplay of the two aspects of historical time clearly seen in the "changing of the guard" of generations exhibits the intermixture of various trends existing simultaneously in a given fragment of time. The heterogeneity of the situation prevents one from treating it as a composition of ingredients, where each ingredient is supposed to fit into the totality in terms of its inner relationship and affinity to it.

c. Again the rule of contrast assumes too much, since it identifies *differences* between historical situations with *contrast* between them. It is clear that historical situations are different from one another, since they are formed by different compositions of elements and placed in different time positions. The task of causal investigation is to reveal these differences, but nobody can be justified in stating a priori that the differences in the composition of these elements, over against distinctions in terms of time positions, are bound to be *contrasts*. In the domain of the state, for instance, a shift is possible and conceivable from the moral to the legal aspect of government, and this cannot be considered as a shift in terms of a contrast. Even the shift from the legal aspect to the social aspect can hardly be understood as a contrast, if the concept of a contrast is to have a clear meaning, that is to say if it is not to be just a

11. ". . . no social system is really well integrated or fully integrated." See Talcott Parsons, "Personality and Social Structure," included in *Personality and Political Crisis*, ed. by Alfred H. Stanton and Stewart E. Perry (Chicago, Free Press, 1951), p. 65.

cover for any distinction or difference. Historical differences qua differences in the composition of elements can sometimes appear as contrasting differences, but a contrast is only *one* of the possibilities of a difference and is by no means identical with difference as such. As a rule for an approach to any historical situation we lay down the presupposition of the existing differences between the various situations but not the prenotion of contrasts between them.

This criticism of a theory which tries to put forward some rules of historical knowledge, if not exactly precise laws of historical process, brings us back to the main assumption laid down earlier: In the domain of history there is no justification for an assumption of material laws in the strict meaning of the term. In historical knowledge we encounter the paradoxical situation that the transcendental principle of causality itself is the law of the process and the rule of knowledge referring to it.

The exploration of the principle of causality in history and the status of laws there is but a mirror which reflects the essence of historical knowledge and its immanent problems. The nature of the historical object is connected with the nature of historical time. The nature of historical time in turn determines the causal character of this knowledge on the one hand and removes the possibility of establishing historical laws on the other.

In sum, the past is the cause of the present which, historically speaking, is always an effect. Yet we cannot go beyond the assumption of causality in general. Historical knowledge must henceforth be guided by itself, by the minute investigation of the particularities, and must not go astray after patterns which are only material laws in disguise.

Historical reality is given to, even imposed on, the knower. What the knower knows in the first place is that this reality is created by the past. Everything else the imposed reality compels him to learn through the "fertile depth" of historical experience.[12]

12. The reader is referred to Karl Popper, *The Open Society and Its Enemies* (2 vols. London, 1945), and to I. Berlin, *Historical Inevitability*, London, 1954. The problem of historical laws and of historical predictions is discussed there, though from a different point of view from that presented in the above discussion.

RESTATEMENT

Let us now, after the detailed analysis of some of the main problems related to history and historical knowledge, return to what seems to be the main characteristic features of history and the very problematic situation of history in general. The historical process is meaningful as a process because meanings are bestowed on it by human actions, either individual or collective. Its meanings are not of the process as such, nor of its cosmic position as a realm of existence different from and additional to the realm of nature. The very existence of the realm of history is due to human action and is not independent of it. Precisely because history is not given, i.e. is not nature, but is perpetually created, it presupposes the act of creation which is identical with the act of decision of human beings and their pursuit of the objectives toward which decision is directed.

Yet, because the process as a process borrows its meanings from the actions of men, there is no total meaning in history outside the plurality of meanings transfused into it by human actions. History grows with human actions, and in no place and at no time is it a totality closed in itself which can be looked at and discerned from above.

Moreover, history is not only meaningful but also rational insofar as the rational ingredient is part of human activity carried out in history. This is, as it were, a rationality from below, from the ingredients of history. But it is also rational, as it were, from above because history is in time and time has a structure, that of the difference, tension, and involvement of its dimensions. This structure of history providing the ground for its rationality is again not independent but an outcome of the specific combination of the facet of meaning stemming from action and the facet of time where action occurs. The structure of history is meditated, and the partial rationality of history is meditated through structure.

Because this structure exists history is capable of being known. The knowledge of history is guided by the principle of causality, which principle in turn is guided by the structure of time. There is the given structure of the process and the understood structure of causes dwelling in the past and of effects in the present.

The meaningfulness of history in its process find its crystallization not only in data to be known but also in institutions, the latter being the concern of the social sciences.

Yet there is another side of the medal of history—in spite of its being meaningful it does not guarantee the possibility of an adequate knowledge of it. The power and the shortcomings of history are to be found in the fundamental fact that knowing history becomes a part of history itself, and hence there is no definite position, no ultimate and irreducible status of the knower in history. The relationship between the subject and object, being a fundamental cognitive relationship, gets blurred, as it were, in history. Hence history is a fertile ground for pretenses to abolish the difference between subject and object to unify them. In spite of that we have seen that historical knowledge gets sunk in the historical process, yet reflection and knowledge are not exhausted by and in the historical process. There is the primacy of reflection due to its roots in the rationality of man, who is both in history and above it.

Moreover, the structure of history and the substratum of its rationality inherent in its temporal character and its causal nature do not provide for laws in history. This is an indication of the fact that history is rational but also less than rational. The advantage of rationality has its correlate in the disadvantage of the lack of transition from the principle of rationality, i.e. from causality, to concrete devices for the realization of this rationality in given events and fragments of time.

And ultimately, though there are crystallizations of the process in institutions, institutions are not placed beyond, above, or outside history but in the last analysis are aspects of the process and hence are not immune to its nature.

The oscillation between meaningfulness and the knowledge of it leads to an observation of the problem and pretense of historicism. Historicism assumes that history is the only or the ultimate realm of human existence. Hence whatever is human is historical and whatever is known of history is ultimately determined by history. The object to be known is regarded from a historicist view as the determining factor. It is one of the objectives of this analysis to show that history is a transcending of the given situation, and that in history there is not only a process but also a bridge over the process as well, a bridge erected by the reflection of the present. But reflection as such is not created by history, as historicism is ultimately compelled to assume in order to eradicate what is not historical only. Reflection is the metaphysical and cognitive presupposition of history. It is related to the essence of man and not to the nature of history. Reflection is always excessive and hence cannot be totally determined by what it is about to know. Hence the correlation of the subject and object is not destroyed for the sake of a kind of mystical union between the two. The relationship between subject and object is fundamentally not a historical relation and cannot be shaken by the nature of the historical process. To know is to be more than historical.

Or, to put it differently, man is a historical being because he is *homo sapiens,* but homo sapiens is not an essence created by history. Homo sapiens is the presupposition of history and not in himself an upshot of it. The emergence of homo sapiens may be considered as an event in the evolution of the cosmos but not as an event in the historical process itself. Man is historical precisely because he is more than historical.

INDEX

Achievement, 118
Acton, H. B., 180
Adequacy, 47; of knowledge and process, 19
Adler, Max, 136
Aesthetics, 22
Analysis, 11–12, 246
Application, 162–3
A priori, 135–7
Art, 200
Augustine, St., 109 ff., 112

Barth, Heinrich, 61
Bergmann, Hugo, 266, 271
Bergson, Henri, 55–6, 58, 60, 76, 96
Berlin, Isaiah, 319
Biology, 231
Boeckh, August, 10
Bradley, F. H., 12
Buber, Martin, 166
Burckhardt, Jacob, 154 ff., 158

Carr, H. Wildon, 253
Cassirer, Ernst, 51, 52, 61, 242, 261, 296, 300, 301, 313
Category, 32, 132
Causality, 33, 238 ff., 321; *causa prima*, 264; causative factor, 11; cause, 15, 235; cause, economic, 229
Change, 14, 200
Choosing (for explanation), 14, 15
Christianity, 205
Civilization, 157, 171
Cohen, Hermann, 246
Cohen, Morris Raphael, 255, 269
Cohn, Jonas, 61
Collingwood, R. G., 2, 3, 39, 47, 62, 109 ff., 112, 113, 115–16, 129, 299
Community (opposed to society), 208–9
Comte, August, 152, 180, 183

Concept, concepts, 26, 28, 30, 32, 34, 37, 39, 40, 66, 68, 149; individual, 2, 179; general, 74, 167, 169, 176, 184
Configuration, 295 ff., 303
Consciousness, 22, 23, 24, 25, 36, 37, 45, 46, 123, 127, 199
Construction, 10, 12, 101, 104, 106, 108, 130, 170, 172, 173, 175, 182, 257–8, 289, 290
Contiguity, 285 ff., 289
Continuity, 53, 73, 79, 84, 94, 96, 107, 108, 132, 257, 287 ff.; of the self, 83, 107
Correlation, 10, 11, 15, 22, 31, 34, 36, 39, 40, 75, 88, 269
Creation, 243
Croce, Benedetto, 3, 39, 49, 109 ff., 113
Culture, 156, 157, 161 ff.

Datum, data, 6, 7, 8, 9, 10, 11–12, 14, 15, 17, 18, 19, 20, 27, 30, 31, 35, 36, 49, 50, 66, 67, 94–5, 99, 102, 104, 105, 106, 108, 110, 117, 138, 139, 140, 145, 147, 159, 216, 234, 236 ff., 238, 242, 244, 248, 253, 281, 283, 288, 292, 293, 294–5, 315, 321
Decision, 103, 106, 128, 275, 277, 320
Decline, 120
Deduction, 299. *See also* Laws
Dependence, 262. *See also* Causality
Determinism, 123
Dialectic, 36, 71
Dilthey, Wilhelm, 246 ff.
Discontinuity, 53
Duration, 53, 90 ff., 92, 116, 317. *See also* Time
Durée, 55–6, 76, 96. *See also* Bergson

325

E4